PRAISE FOR
GOD'S PATIENT PURSUIT OF MY SOUL

THIS BOOK WILL HELP MANY TO INCREASE THEIR CONFIDENCE IN GOD'S GREAT LOVE FOR US.

—**Father Thomas Keating, OSB,** founding member of Contemplative Outreach LTD, author, and a central figure in the initiation of the Centering Prayer movement

A MAGNIFICENT FETE OF GRACE AND CREATIVITY. The Lord surely is enabled to manifest through this brilliant new author most of the time, as K. G. Durckheim would say.

—**Pascaline Coff, OSB,** co-founder of Osage Monastery in Sand Springs, Oklahoma, and former secretary for the Monastic Interreligious Dialogue

A LIGHT OUT OF THE WILDERNESS FROM THESE DIZZY TIMES OF SO MANY PATHS, SPIRITUALITIES, AND TEACHERS. This is an amazing story of a Catholic woman, who married, raised a family near Chicago, and excelled in the billion-dollar direct selling industry. I was looking for wisdom from lay Catholic women, and I found it in this intelligent book, *God's Patient Pursuit of My Soul*. She's not only found her voice, but her vocation as a writer.

—**Meg Funk,** Benedictine nun and author of the Matter series *(Tools Matter, Thoughts Matter, Humility Matters, Discernment Matters)*

A**N INCREDIBLE READ... A LYRICAL, INTELLIGENT, SELF-EFFACING GORGEOUS WRITER. I LOVED IT SO MUCH.** The pacing is fabulous. Her voice is engaging and inclusive … a truly talented writer with metaphoric aptitude … language is full of imagery, depth, and perception. The writing is measured, lush and extremely readable … A stand out in today's business memoirs … She has broken the mold by creating a confluence of not only business success and spiritual depth but also a grasp of the language that hails her as a literary talent. This book is cutting edge. It WILL change lives! The images have already changed mine!
—**Suzanne Kingsbury,** editor, author of award-winning *The Summer Fletcher Greel Loved Me* and *The Gospel According to Gracey*

I **WAS MESMERIZED BY THE TALE IN** *GOD'S PATIENT PURSUIT OF MY SOUL.* Manion weaves her spirituality through every facet of her life with an exquisite writing style. She brings spirituality alive in a way that is seldom done in "religious" books. Even though this is her first book, I am confident it won't be her last. More, please....
—**Jerilyn Dufresne,** author of the Sam Darling mystery series

I**N** *GOD'S PATIENT PURSUIT OF MY SOUL,* C**HRIS** M**ANION SHARES HER STRUGGLE TO GIVE HER FULL LOVE AND DEDICATION TO** G**OD, WHILE BEING A WIFE AND MOTHER, AND SUCCESSFUL ENTREPRENEUR.** It is an ambitious book of self-reflection and vigorous self-improvement. Manion has become an acclaimed leader and mentor in the direct selling field as well as a member of the Catholic laity, who practices contemplative and sometimes mystical prayer. Her vibrant personality and boundless energy come through on every page.
—**Elizabeth Jeep, Ph.D.,** teacher, speaker, catechist, and author of *Sweeter than Honey: Prayers for Catechists; Children's Daily Prayer;* and *Blessings and Prayers through the Year*

A BEAUTIFUL BOOK. THIS ELEGANT AND AUTHENTIC MEMOIR OF A FAITH-FILLED WOMAN shows how it is possible to be very successful and yet vulnerable enough to completely depend on the indwelling Spirit to enliven your soul day by day. Chris says, "Life is precious, and what we accomplish through our little successes adds little ripples that affect the rest of us. One ripple touches another, and soon clusters, families, whole communities are moved and touched and encouraged by our little successes." Chris's book is a ripple that encourages us to be committed and faithful to God, to be free and true, to be loved and to give love.
—**Gail Fitzpatrick-Hopler,** Executive Director of Contemplative Outreach, LTD

A HEART AND SOUL PAGE TURNER BAPTIZED IN BLOOD, SWEAT, AND TEARS. At the same time, she's funny! As I devoured this big, beautiful memoir, I was challenged, enlightened, transformed. Oh, and did I mention, she's funny?
—**Sarah Fishburn,** author and mixed media artist. www.sarahfishburn.com

VERY MOVING! AN OUTSTANDING BUSINESS MEMOIR FROM A LEADER IN THE DIRECT SELLING PROFESSION UNAFRAID TO ACKNOWLEDGE HER EVER-DEEPENING RELATIONSHIP WITH THE DIVINE AND THE SOURCE OF HER GIFTS AND TALENTS. Her sophisticated memoir walks us through her climb to the top of our industry's field leadership with humor, twists, and wise insights. I loved her role reversal of recruiter/recruited, what caused her to realign her priorities, and the cliff hanger. From entrepreneur to literary talent, Chris Manion resonates with the DSWA's mission of personal and professional development by pointing out that the more deeply you commit to serving the Lord and His purpose, the more you are called upon to develop yourself to the fullest. I recommend it to all direct sellers.

—**Nicki Keohohou,** CEO and co-founder of the Direct Selling World Alliance - DSWA.org

CHRIS MANION HAS CREATED A HANDBOOK, IN THE FORM OF A MEMOIR, ON HOW TO LET THE BEAUTY OF LIFE BE A FEAST FOR THE SOUL. Through trial and triumph, she carefully examines the potential in each moment, and each time breaks through to something significant, instructive, and graceful. It is a joy to behold. This may not be what we expect from a corporate superstar, but it is what we get from her generosity of spirit, the result of which is real insight into living life in the light.

—**Marion Roach Smith,** author of *The Memoir Project, A Thoroughly Non-Standardized Text for Writing & Life*

AN ARRESTING AND ABSORBING MEMOIR THAT TELLS THE DEEPLY PERSONAL STORY OF ONE WOMAN'S RELATIONSHIP WITH GOD. It's also a how-to-succeed-in-business story, with the emphasis on both spiritual and economic growth. Chris Manion sifts through her memories, tracing the intertwined nature of her spiritual life and her career. A touching and beautiful testimony.

—**William McKeen,** author of *Outlaw Journalist* and *Mile Marker Zero*

FILLED WITH WISDOM, INSIGHT ... Not everyone will relate to Chris' perspectives on life, but readers will be exposed to a person who is resilient and creative and humorous. She's original and spunky."
—**Dennis E. Hensley, Ph.D.**, author of *The Power of Positive Productivity*

I HAD NEVER HEARD OF THE SPIRITUAL GIFT OF TEARS; however, I have experienced this gift. Sometimes when I am worshipping God through music, the Spirit of God will rain down on me, and I will weep tender tears. It is an emotional experience that Manion describes very well in her chapter "The Gift of Tears."

I was encouraged by Manion's chapter about Centering Prayer. Recently, I was introduced to meditating for twenty-minute periods of time. I'd always meditated for five minutes after a Christian yoga class, but twenty was a great extension for my patience. However, when reading about the author's experience with spending the first twenty minutes of her day with the Lord, I was encouraged to do so, too. Like Manion says, "It is like giving God the first fruits of your day."
—**Susan Neal,** author of *Scripture Yoga: 21 Bible Lessons for Christian Yoga Classes* and *Yoga for Beginners: 60 Basic Yoga Poses for Flexibility, Stress Release, and Inner Peace*

GOD'S PATIENT
PURSUIT
OF MY SOUL

Lyn,
One of life's greatest treasures is
a true friend, which you are to me.
Your encouragement, love, and urging
sustained and buoyed me in the
rigors of the battle to get this book
published. I am forever grateful.
Love,
Chris Manion
March 16, 2017

CHRIS MANION

GOD'S PATIENT

PURSUIT

OF MY SOUL

REDEMPTION
PRESS

Published by Redemption Press, PO Box 427, Enumclaw, WA 98022. Toll free (844) 2REDEEM (273-3336)

Redemption Press is honored to present this title in partnership with the author. The views expressed or implied in this work are those of the author. Redemption Press provides our imprint seal representing design excellence, creative content, and high quality production.

www.chrismanion.com

ISBN 13: 978-1-68314-066-5 (Print)
        978-1-68314-068-9 (ePub)
        978-1-68314-069-6 (Mobi)

Library of Congress Catalog Card Number: 2016949473

Dedicated to my better half.
You live up to your name, Joe,
always protecting, forgiving, supporting,
providing, teaching by quiet example,
and loving us in amazing ways.

O God, you have taught me from my youth,
and I proclaim your wonders still.

—Psalm 71:17

CONTENTS

INTRODUCTION

SHAPING A LIFE, both the living of it and the telling of it, is an elusive creative process, somewhat like a pointillist painting. Up close, nothing seems clear. Only as one steps back enough from the painting does an image appear from the multitude of tiny brush strokes.

Once at the dinner table, my father asked my mother, who was an excellent cook, "Is this stuff supposed to have any flavor?" Being almost as obtuse as my beloved father, I didn't realize how much shaping God had to do as He drew me close. All along, I thought I was the one pursuing Him.

He began shaping me in the early sixties when I found myself accepting Dad's invitation to accompany him to daily Lenten Latin Masses in the wee hours before school. I was in third grade at St. Katherine of Siena School in Philadelphia. God pursued me through the hills of childhood in Pittsburgh, Pennsylvania, and through public high school in Bloomington, Indiana, where my search began for a personal relationship with Jesus. Having been reared Catholic, I didn't know such a relationship with the Founder of all intelligence[1] was possible. The idea that God lived way up in heaven and somehow inside us at the same time never connected with me. I chalked it up to "Mystery," the answer to many of my childhood questions. When I heard someone refer to Jesus as his best friend, I wondered, *How does that happen?*

God pursued me through college, several companies, marriage, and motherhood. I used to think I could get away with some behaviors, that God couldn't always see what I was doing, that He had to be busy with others some of the time. The tides turned when I realized He saw into every room and closet, as well as my every thought.

For years I read books on spirituality, mostly by saints or members of cloistered religious orders. My soul longed to connect with them. Their words seemed to separate my roles as a daughter of God, corporate executive, working mom, and wife like oil from vinegar.

I developed a multi-million dollar sales team in a home-based direct selling business. My flexible work schedule as an entrepreneur provided pockets of time to reduce the internal obstacles on my spiritual journey, just as my Irish ancestors cleared stones from their fields, piling them into uneven walls throughout their land.

Well into my thirties, I clung to the notion that God lived above us in His heaven listening to our prayers as they floated up to Him. It took a while to get Jesus' "as" concept into my heart: work *as* prayer, prayer *as* work. Love one another *as* I have loved you. Forgive us our trespasses *as* we forgive others.

In 1995, God guided me to a vibrant online contemplative lay community, perhaps the first of its kind affiliated with no one but Him. The founder of that community posed a question one day: "What does it mean for you to be a contemplative in contemporary society?" The question haunted me and planted the seed for this book. Until then, I'd been happily going along as a nice little Catholic girl active in her faith. The question made me think about how I lived out my faith, how intentionally my actions followed my beliefs, and if I was a contemplative, how I felt about that. Through this one question, God drew me into depths I knew nothing about. I still know nothing except the knowledge I receive from His grace. I often think I know stuff, but there's a chasm between what I think and what I know.

A year or two before his death in 2005, I spoke to author and abbot Dom Basil Pennington, OSCO, about how my work and spiritual journey felt like two separate paths. He helped me see that the tables where I worked were all places that share the bread of life. No division exists between them. All are one. My sense of separation was false. Why was this concept so hard to integrate? Because "Mystery cannot be penetrated from without,"[2] wrote Monsignor Romano Guardini, a little-known German philosopher-priest often cited by Pope Francis.

Dom Basil helped me realize that the private life of a working contemplative should not be secret. It takes courage to share, especially when the journey includes mystical experiences. I felt like Alice in Wonderland in a strange land experiencing mysterious occurrences, not knowing what to do or how to act. Out of place and uncomfortable at times, I also felt incredible peace and overwhelming love, none of which I could discuss. I pictured people rolling their eyes if I told them about God talking to me.

My experiences—God's startling appearance in response to my reaching out to Him—seemed like descriptions from books of saints, not a laywoman with a honky laugh raising a family and trying to make lots of money. Like others before me, I sensed Someone wanted me to write the experiences down. If I did, perhaps I could help others feel less alienated as they experienced similar God-moments. Perhaps I could find others who would talk as if this was something God does with all of us.

God firmly but subtly brought the Johannine passage before me: "Feed my sheep." Years earlier my spiritual director had asked me to ponder this passage. I decided I'd better follow the Boss's advice. As God told St. Maria Faustina shortly before her death, it is painful to Him when we reject sharing our bread. And so as you read this now, I know He is pleased since it is His fingers that have kneaded His yeast into me. I'm still a stubborn Irish loaf, but less resistant now that the yeast has done its work. When God blesses, breaks, and encourages us to share ourselves like the little boy's bread in the loaves and fishes Gospel story, is there not more at the end than there was at the beginning?

This is too personal, I often thought as I chose what to share of my journey thus far.

"Share it anyway," came the reply.

I trembled as I lived the words of the famous hymn "Trust and Obey" by John H. Sammis:

When we walk with the Lord in the light of His Word,
What a glory He sheds on our way!
While we do His good will, He abides with us still,
And with all who will trust and obey.

Refrain:
Trust and obey, for there's no other way
To be happy in Jesus, but to trust and obey.

CHAPTER 1

THE FOREST OF PEACE

The desire for God leads to the search for God
and hence to love of God.

—Ilia Delio

2004

HE KEPT BREAKING into my life. It's not that I didn't ask for it, I know. Every time it happened, I took days to recover. I didn't know how to integrate it. Too often, I did not even recognize it. He changed all that one mild, summer day.

"You should go to Osage and meet Sister Pascaline," my spiritual director urged me.

"Who is she?" I asked.

"She is an amma, one of the wise ones like the desert fathers, a holy woman whom I'd like you to meet. She can guide you, but go soon. She is already very old."

I Googled Sister Pascaline Coff and found her at Osage Monastery in Oklahoma. She had been the former Secretary of the international organization MID, Monastic Interreligious Dialog, preceding Sister Meg Funk, whom I'd meet later. Sister Pascaline had participated in the Gethsemane Encounter during the early, heady times with the Dalai Lama and Trappist monk Thomas Merton, both good friends who attended with other leaders of worldwide religious communities, including Buddhists, Sufis, and Cistercians. Sister Pascaline, the prioress of her community, lived with five other Benedictine nuns. She offered spiritual direction to individuals making retreats in her monastery.

"We need to be open and eager to encounter the Divine in everything, in everyone," she wrote. I couldn't agree more. As I read her bio online, I glossed over references to her studying at Father Bede Griffiths' ashram in India and being his close friend. She founded her monastery to implement Dom Bede's ashram life and interreligious dialogue. I didn't know anything about ashrams or Bede Griffiths, although I did begin reading one of his books to learn more about him. I went to meet Sister Pascaline solely on the counsel of my spiritual director, Mercedes Scopetta, an amma herself and recipient of an award from Rome for her work among Hispanics in her archdiocese.

I would soon discover Sister Pascaline's love for the prophet Isaiah. She wrote: "'Today if you hear the Voice, harden not your hearts,' but recognize, love, praise, and adore the divine Heart who calls to us through the prophet Isaiah."

You are my witnesses …
You are precious in my sight, and I love you,
My servants whom I have chosen
To know and believe in Me
And to understand that it is I.

—Isaiah 43:10

I booked a week's retreat and, in blind faith, found a flight to meet her. I was in my mid-forties, my husband worked from home then, and my children were in their teens. Leaving my family for a week would not be a hardship. Besides, I liked the example it set for taking the time to prioritize one's relationship with God.

"There's no need to rent a car, Chris," my spiritual director advised. "They have a hospitality ministry, the Benedictines. They'll meet you at the airport. Just tell them your flight number and arrival time."

Sure enough, when I walked out from baggage to the sidewalk outside the airport, an elderly nun in a modest habit without a headpiece stood near the door looking for me. She greeted me and walked me to a waiting car where another white-haired nun sat at the wheel. I stored my suitcase in the trunk.

"Welcome!" the driver said as I closed the car door.

"Thank you!" I smiled self-consciously, not knowing what to expect. I put on my seat belt.

"Tell us about yourself," said the driver as we drove back to their monastery. I gave a short answer and then shared how I looked forward to meeting Sister Pascaline.

"I'm Sister Pascaline," said the driver.

My eyebrows lifted. I blinked a few times. I hadn't paid much attention to this nun—barely tall enough to see over the steering wheel—but that was about to change. I looked at her more carefully. She appeared quiet and soft-spoken, revealing little energy. It never occurred to me the Prioress herself would be the one driving out to the airport to pick me up.

At that moment, in grace-filled insight, I realized it hadn't occurred to me that The Divine One had been the driver of my life either. I hadn't paid much attention to the Omniscient Driver up until that moment. I had been happy to move along in my life, never really noticing Who got me there, thinking I'd done most of the work myself. I'd been more interested in the journey itself until then, less aware of the One guiding my way.

As we left the paved road, a sign announced "The Forest of Peace." Dirt and gravel ricocheted off the undercarriage of the car. After parking beneath the canopy of aged trees, Sister Pascaline gave me a brief tour of the monastery, ending at my cabin in the woods. The little house consisted of a bedroom and bathroom. Two windows looked out into thick woods, and a wooden desk and chair waited timelessly beside the single bed tucked into the corner. Across from the desk stood a dresser bearing an icon of the Blessed Mother with Jesus encircled in light over her heart. The "closet" of three wall hooks quietly welcomed me to minimal simplicity. Cleaning supplies waited below the bathroom sink.

"Leave the bathroom wiped down upon departure, with the bed stripped," Sister Pascaline instructed. Compliance cemented itself when

I saw the tiniest of nuns and the oldest, probably in her late-eighties, heading with a bucket to clean one of the retreat homes.

An ascetic front porch with a chair facing the ranch style monastery completed the amenities. Similar houses for the nuns knelt behind the monastery. Silence descended from the thick trees shading this Forest of Peace. I let it touch me. My spirit slipped into it as one eases into a warm bath.

"Make yourself at home. Let us know if you need anything, anything at all," said Sister Pascaline as she turned and walked to the monastery.

> *The psalmist tells us to "Be still and know that I am God." This quieting down and being still is the role of meditation (what we call contemplation in the West). And this is where the Eastern religious traditions have so much to share with us.*
>
> —Pascaline Coff

The stillness settled around me like a cat snuggling in for a nap. I sat on the bed and studied the schedule for prayer times and meals. The structure of the day imitated that of other retreats I'd attended. I had a little more than an hour before 4:30-afternoon prayers, so I unpacked and walked along one of the paths. I allowed the decompression from the outside world to begin, consciously trying to slow my pace, although I knew it would occur naturally as I immersed myself in the gentle rhythm of the sisters' prayer life.

The five-minute warning bell, rung at each prayer time, invited me to join the community in the chapel. Crunching old leaves underfoot, I walked beneath outstretched branches to the monastery and entered the front door. To my immediate left a stationary bicycle sat tucked into a hallway. It would hum each morning as one of the sisters spun its wheels. In the kitchen, a long counter stretched around the sink and cabinets. An oversized dining table yawned at windows facing the forest. Picnic tables scattered themselves like tossed jacks beyond the window. The room for viewing the nightly news snuggled itself next to a small, cozy library where audio tapes and books nestled to the right of the chapel.

Abandoned shoes bowed before the chapel entrance, pointing to their owners' location. An involuntary gasp escaped during my tour when Sister Pascaline opened the chapel doors. The room's magnificence rooted itself in the imagery of nature. A floor-to-ceiling wall of windows welcomed light through the filter of the forest. My eyes followed the rays of sunshine into a sunken prayer circle in the center of the chapel. Full of colorful floor pillows, the pit reflected the Sundance Circle of American Indians. Above the pit, or Sundance Circle, was a large cosmic wheel with the eight-fold Buddhist noble paths in its wooden spokes: right view, right thought, right speech, right behavior, right livelihood, right effort, right mindfulness, and right concentration. I knew nothing at the time of these noble paths. What came to mind from the circle was Revelation 22:13: "*I am the Alpha and the Omega, the first and the last, the beginning and the end.*"

To the right stood a small organ and additional seating for those unable to sit on the floor. To the left, a lit candle—signifying Christ's presence in the tabernacle—hung from intricately woven tree branches suspended from the ceiling. The prayer circle reclaimed my attention. *What a welcome alternative to the traditional architecture of churches and cathedrals,* I thought.

The emphasis on the circle resonated within me, reminding me of unending love; of the world without end in the Glory Be to God prayer; of our all-knowing and all-abiding God Who loves all of His creation. The circle contained the symbol of the wedding ring bringing to mind how the nuns were brides of Christ. Some of my favorite words of Jesus arose: "May they be one, Father, just as You are in Me and I in You." The circle had two entrances. All could be seen from within and without. For liturgies, the priest descends into it, sits on a low twig stool, and uses a small wooden table for an altar.

The descent into the prayer circle felt like a lowering into the arms of my Lord, like walking into the ocean, into waters that refresh and invigorate, envelope and buoy. I nestled myself on a pillow much the way I'd done when, as an insecure teen, I had hidden away in the rafters above the theater at University High School in Bloomington, Indiana. Eager to open myself to the half hour of silent meditation, I watched the five nuns settle down, observing their rituals as the sun grew sleepy.

When the twenty minutes of silent prayer time ended, we quietly filed out of the chapel. A few of the nuns moved to the kitchen; the rest sat to watch the evening news. As soon as the news program took a commercial break, one sister lifted the remote control and immediately muted the television, a practice my husband and I have happily adopted ever since. I saw magazines or newspapers rise almost in unison from each of the nuns' laps. They either read or conversed about a news story, never looking at the television screen while the commercials played. When the news returned, they lowered their magazines and newspapers to their laps and looked back up. They turned the TV off when the news ended, and everyone immediately rose to their dinner duties. I appreciated the care they took to limit what entered their minds as well as their light touch on the world and local news. "Consider carefully what you hear," said Jesus (Mark 4:24). They certainly did.

At dinner someone introduced me and one other new retreatant. We each received a unique napkin ring to identify our dinner napkin for the rest of the week. After the meal all were expected to chip in cleaning up the kitchen and washing the dishes. While we waited for the water to turn hot, a nun placed empty, plastic milk cartons under the spigot to catch the cool water. They used it for watering house plants and herbs. Everything was conserved, respected, and recycled. Not long after dark, most retired early. The next prayer time was pre-dawn, the best time of the day for prayer, with its unique, pure energies.

Sister Pascaline set an appointment each day for a half hour of directed spiritual guidance. It was up to me to determine the rest of my schedule. The trails of the property beckoned. I looked forward to using the map from my room to explore them.

Let Thought Become Your Beautiful Lover[3]

Let thought become the beautiful Woman.
Cultivate your mind and heart to that depth
That it can give you everything
A warm body can.
Why just keep making love with God's child –
Form
When the Friend Himself is standing

Before us
So open-armed?
My dear,
Let prayer become your beautiful Lover
And become free,
Become free of this whole world
Like Hafiz.

—Hafiz

To follow the daily schedule of prayer and Eucharist each day meant rising in the pre-dawn dark to walk with my flashlight along the dirt path under the forest canopy to the little monastery. I removed my shoes outside the chapel door and added them to those huddled closely together like monks bent deep in prayer. Each prayer session began with the same chant.

Salutations to the Word
Present in the earth,
The heavens, and that which is beyond.
May I meditate on your glorious Wisdom
O Divine Giver of life.
May You illuminate our prayer
And give us peace.

In low, early-morning gravelly voices, the sisters chanted the beautiful Hindu Gayatri Mantra chant that Father Bede had given them, adapted from his ashram in India. Silence followed in the holy darkness, leading us gently into contemplative prayer and sometimes, for passing moments, into divine union with God.

Ding! A tiny resonating chime announced the end of prayer time as abruptly as a proud rooster in the barnyard calling all to a new day of work and activity. We moved our stiff limbs and unlocked our crossed legs. It took several moments to get ourselves into a standing position once again, and not just because we weren't thirty-year-olds anymore. Meditation draws the body's metabolism to a deeper, slower-paced level of activity. Slowly, very slowly, meta-spiritual awareness shifted to meta-cognitive awareness. A deep bow of reverence toward the tabernacle concluded our prayer time, and we silently padded out of the chapel in sock feet to our waiting shoes.

Breakfast was on our own and in silence. Each person moved mindfully toward coffee or hot water, cereal or fruit and chose a place apart to eat quietly and continue praying, reading, or gazing out through a window to dawn's awakening. I followed suit. Sister Pascaline moved to the audio listening room each day and sat with black headphones over her white hair as she ate her breakfast. And so each day began.

Most people experience the relaxing effects of a vacation by the third or fourth day as their bodies unwind, releasing the tight, bulldog grip on the tension necessary to manage the frenetic pace at which we live and move. So it is on a retreat as well, although I think the full immersion into the slow-paced quiet of most monasteries accelerates the decompression process. Following the structure of the monastery's day, I spent my afternoon divided between reading, journal writing, and walking different paths through the deep woods of the Forest of Peace. If one rose early enough on most mornings, a small number of deer could be observed peacefully grazing among the trees. They were deeper in the woods during my afternoon walks, but plenty of other creatures delighted my senses. When I fell asleep at night, the forest's animal sounds intrigued me. I pushed aside fear when an unusual sound occurred, wondering instead what animal had made it. I reassured myself I was as safe as the diminutive, yet sturdy nuns who lived there all year long.

> *Contemplative prayer is God's gift, wholly gratuitous.*
> *No one can earn it.*
> —The Cloud of Unknowing

Each day, I looked forward to my directed interview with Sister Pascaline, who inquired about my journey with God and shared her amma wisdom to guide me deeper into my relationship with Him. She asked me about my recent dreams. I had nothing to share with her.

"I rarely remember my dreams," I told her.

"Pay attention to them," she instructed me, "for God often speaks to us there, and see if you can remember them to tell me next time."

"Okay," I said, shrugging, none too certain about what occurs once I close my eyes at night but hoping not to displease her the next day if I had nothing to report.

You called, you shouted, you broke through my deafness, you flared, blazed, and banished my blindness, you lavished your fragrance, and I gasped.
—St. Augustine

The next morning, I was surprised to remember one of my dreams from the night before. I had dreamt that a tall man offered me a piggyback ride. We stood in a wide, grassy field. I remember trusting him easily, climbing on his back. He smelled wonderful and carried me effortlessly, so I never worried about being too heavy for him. A warm bubble of comforting protection seemed to surround us. An easy, natural air of acceptance and affection flowed back and forth between us, although I wasn't sure who he was.

In my dream he jostled me around the field on his back and made me laugh. I felt like a little kid having fun again. My husband and son appeared in the distance and, seeing them, he turned sideways slightly, as if to show them he had me on his back and everything was okay. He wanted them to see me happy and having fun. I remember having mixed emotions, for I loved my husband and son with all my heart, yet, I clung to this man's back with no desire to let go, enjoying the closeness of my face near his neck as he playfully bounced me in a light jog. He delighted in making me smile and giggle. I felt drawn to him in an extraordinary way and looked over my shoulder at my husband as we turned away, hoping he'd somehow understand and not feel jealous.

How could I be so attracted to this stranger when I loved my husband so deeply? I couldn't dwell on this perplexity long. The piggyback ride jostled me into physical awareness with new jiggles and bounces. I tightened my grip and buried my face in the crook of his neck, inhaling the scent of a primal connection. I closed my eyes. Breathing in his scent reminded me of opening the door after traveling and smelling the familiar fragrance that signaled: Home at last. You're safe. You can relax. Let down your guard. Rest.

I described my dream to Sister Pascaline at our meeting later that morning. She listened and asked a few clarifying questions. Although she seemed not to realize the identity of the tall stranger, in my awe at her wisdom, I assumed she knew. Upon awakening I had drawn my conclusion. "To know and believe in Me and to understand that it is I" Isaiah 43:10.

"He's Jesus," I told her. "I don't know how I know, I just do." I couldn't remember His face once I'd realized who He was, because, in most of the dream, my perspective viewed Him from His back. How handsome He had seemed!

"You must celebrate," Sister Pascaline suggested as she helped me understand this dream as a sign of a new depth in my relationship with Jesus, a new level of playful friendship and intimacy. Not fully grasping the dream's significance, I lit some incense and danced before the icon of Mary and Jesus on my dresser, feeling a little silly. Years later, Celtic poet, speaker, and priest John O'Donohue helped me understand this celebration directive from Sister Pascaline.

"There's something very holy about real celebration," said Fr. John O'Donohue. "I often think real celebration alters things at a profound level. Real celebration is not the banal, garish, self-gratifying shouting and self-congratulation that goes on. Real celebration is about the lyrical dance of joy at the center of the human heart. And when you celebrate in that way, then you are adding to the magical light of the universe."[4]

I allowed the happiness and joy from the piggyback ride to fall afresh upon me. I accepted Sister Pascaline's statement that this was an important moment in my relationship with Jesus, although it didn't feel all that special. It seemed natural. Stilling. Awe surrounded it like the hush of fog.

Where and when God finds you ready, he must act and overflow into you, just as when the air is clear and pure, the sun must overflow into it and cannot refrain from doing that.

—Meister Eckhart

Although I wanted it, it didn't seem possible that I could attain the inner peace of a still pond, an image I had held before me for years in haphazard attempts at serenity. It seemed unattainable for a drama queen, Type A personality full of vim and vigor and high levels of stress. An enthusiastic bundle of energy could not be melted into a pool of peaceful tranquility, at least not for very long, could she? I saw myself more like a Jack-in-the-Box, capable of making pretty music and luring others into thinking I was relaxed and then, Bang! Surprise! Ha! I'm baaa-ack! Wiggle-wiggle, goofy smile! Ga-boing! Ga-boing!

CHAPTER 2

THE PRESENCE

*What does it gain a man to win world
success if he loses his true self?*

—Luke 9:25

THIS NEW PLAYFUL aspect to my relationship with Jesus glistened within me like freshly fallen snow twinkling in the moonlight. The refreshing lightheartedness He introduced intrigued me. What a lovely change. After years of reading works by saints, mystics, and theologians, I understood the need for something less cerebral. All work and no play. My desire since adolescence to have a personal relationship with Jesus was coming true, and my heart beat hard with excitement.

Mondays were the nuns' day of silence. With no spiritual direction scheduled that day, I walked in wonder and gratitude through the woods in the Forest of Peace not knowing what to do with myself exactly. I felt open, as Christ's mother Mary had been, pondering all these things in my heart.

With more available time on my hands than usual, I went in search of a spot overlooking a lake that someone had mentioned. Water always attracts my spirit. After a half an hour's walk, a little off the path, up a slight hill, I found a bench on a high point. I sat and enjoyed peace whispered on a soft breeze and thanked God for all He was displaying before me. Through a narrow opening of trees, a lake glistened in the distance.

The afternoon barely moved, the way a child feels the slowness of time in summer. The leaves of the hundred-year-old trees above me kept the sun's heat in check. Insects hummed, and occasional calls from forest birds soon faded as I closed my eyes and sunk deeper into time with God.

Descending with my mind's eye into my heart, I opened to an awareness of God's presence all around me. It was a peaceful place to pray. The sounds of the forest drew me in, gentle and restful in the heat of the afternoon.

I don't know how long I sat in prayer. Softly, yet undeniably, I became aware of the energy of someone standing before me. All my senses heightened and went to full alert. I stopped breathing. My heart began to race as I felt a Presence, very tall and radiant, standing in front of my bench. I did not open my eyes. I didn't need to. The Presence stood full of energy and power. It rose above me like a long beam from space. I lifted my head, my eyes still closed, to sense its height.

"I didn't realize You were so tall!" I gasped with my inner voice. I tried to comprehend what was happening, but the purity of this Presence, the power I could feel radiating from It caused my breathing to quicken into fast, shallow breaths. I didn't know what to do. What was happening here? *This can't be Who I think it is.*

There was no mistaking it. A great Presence stood silently in front of me, without moving, bathing me in a radiant energy like someone turning a light on while I'm asleep. I can feel the light through my eyelids, but I choose not to open them.

The waiting seemed as though I was before an elevator door about to open. I knew something stood poised, ready to act. I tried to breathe normally. It was impossible. Such power pulsed there, such radiating energy so exquisitely pure that I was afraid I would melt like the wicked witch of the west in the *Wizard of Oz* if It touched me. It was not static. It felt like silent high-frequency vibrations. I had to keep remembering to breathe. Tense in anticipation, my body couldn't move. I did not know what to do.

It was an essence, not a physical form, which beamed in a column before me. I was pretty sure of that, although my eyes remained shut. *So tall,* I kept thinking, amazed at the height this Presence reached far above me. I could not sense how high it reached. It seemed to go on forever. Not knowing what to do, I sat overwhelmed by the radiance of love and purity and holiness before me. Right in front of me. Almost touching my knees and rising above me vibrantly.

Tears streamed down my face. My heart couldn't take in this pure loving holiness. It was too much. My heart was too little.

I kept taking tiny breaths. I couldn't stop the tears. They continued to fall from the love overflowing my heart. I sat very still and kept waiting for something to happen. Maybe this was an angel before me, about to tell me something. I couldn't bring myself to accept what my heart was telling me. Whoever beamed before me, Whoever it was, waited there, a heavenly presence, pure patience, and love. I considered the possibility I might die. I wanted to open my eyes to see this Presence, but I knew from scripture no one sees the face of God and lives. I didn't know what to do.

Another small breath. Silence. What was about to happen? It felt like something immanent poised patiently, waiting to do something. There was no movement. Nothing. The Presence hovered.

Waiting is not my strong suit. How is one supposed to act in this situation? What's the etiquette? What a goofy thought. In a moment like this my internal wiring was still trying to make a good impression? *What am I supposed to do?* Unable to move, I searched my mind in panic for some idea of what to do. I was sure I was supposed to do something. I didn't want to do the wrong thing. I didn't want to ruin this divine moment. I didn't want to make this Presence go away by some ignorant action. So I waited, still barely breathing.

Nothing changed. Nothing happened. The power of this Presence continued to take my breath away. It did not move.

What surrounded me? Radiant energy? Light? Grace? My eyes pressed firmly closed. But even with closed eyes, I knew someone was standing right next to me. I could *feel* it.

A second time, I pondered if this was an angel of the Lord. *This couldn't be Who I think it is,* I thought again. As I searched for a resonance of truth that the Presence might be angelic, I found none. Not that I've had any Presence before me like this to know one way or another.

As I struggled to accept Who hovered before me, I kept thinking: *How can this be happening to me? Odd things like this happen to saints. And I'm no saint.* I knew I was expected to do something. I could *feel* the silent One waiting patiently. There was no hurry, but I felt uncomfortable knowing I was supposed to act in some way yet not knowing the proper thing to do.

If I open my eyes, I just may die, I thought. I was so curious to see Who was standing there, though. Who *was* It?

My heart knew. It spoke to Him right away. My head struggled to accept it.

Bursting with an urgent need to do something, I squirmed internally. The pressure of waiting continued to build. I couldn't sit still with my eyes closed much longer. Waiting is excruciating for me. I couldn't take it. The energy from the Presence pulsed at me from all sides. I had to break the pent-up tension.

This is it. I'm going to die, I said to myself, *but what a way to go!* Not knowing what else to do, I steeled myself and opened my eyes.

CHAPTER 3

BEGINNINGS

*We must make the choices that enable us to fulfill
the deepest capacities of our real selves.*
—Thomas Merton

WHEN SACRED HEART High School in Shadyside measured me for my uniform in 1968, skirt lengths had to touch the floor upon kneeling. Then Westinghouse transferred my dad from Pittsburgh, Pennsylvania, to Bloomington, Indiana. The move saved me from that plaid delight.

At age fourteen, we moved—my folks, four brothers, and my sister—to a box of a house on a block of other boxes with a pasture of pallid cows chewing their cud on the other side of the road. A previous owner had added a family room big enough for a couch, a chair, a TV, and a five-foot yellow bookcase. We had eight such boxy rooms plus the breakfast room extension of the kitchen. It framed a long, rectangular dinner table and eight wooden chairs on a linoleum floor whose pattern helped hide the dirt. The white washer and dryer constantly rumbled behind louvered doors within five or six steps of the dishwasher and stove, the path Mom endlessly triangulated each day as she washed clothes and cooked for us. Four small, square bedrooms sat politely above the kitchen, dining room, living room, and front hallway.

The basement garage provided escape from box boredom. Alongside space for two cars, a cramped storage area housed a ping pong table between concrete block walls in front of the furnace. On one side of the table hovered brown moving boxes on gunmetal Home Depot utility shelves. The smell of gasoline and exhaust fumes didn't bother us much.

Outside the garage door, a basketball hoop stood as an open invitation for another escape of the oppressive box. Having honed moderate skills in the sport with neighborhood boys in Pittsburgh, I played with my dad and siblings. Few neighborhood children came over to play with us that I remember.

Developers spaced houses farther apart in Bloomington than in Pittsburgh. Each of us would bring a friend home from time to time, but a bunch of kids dropping by to play a friendly game of kick-the-can, basketball, or kickball never materialized. The neighborhood had a different feel from the Steel City. Lonelier.

No fences separated homesteads. The grass rolled from yard to yard with stark transformer-topped utility poles creating the only visual border. This move was our fifth relocation. Dad had come here as the new manager of the Westinghouse plant and Mom hated the house they bought. They had flown in for two quick weekend house searches but had found nothing big enough for a family of eight. She settled on the box, deciding she could tolerate it for the three years Dad would be there. She endured it for ten.

Without sidewalks, Third Street posed too much of a risk to ride bikes on its shoulder to the movie theater and mall a few miles away. We took bike rides and explored country roads by the cow pasture across the street just to get out of the house. Those roads seemed visually more appealing than the subdivision roads behind our house with their cookie cutter homes dotted with potted geraniums neatly popping red buds by front doors. The trees reminded me of the woods in Pittsburgh's Frick Park where Dad would take us on Sunday afternoon walks along woodsy paths to discover nature's secrets and beauty and solitude.

Although my relationship with God began in the Catholic church with my family's strong faith and commitment to the sacraments, the missions and volunteer work, the loneliness of adolescence moved my faith to a more personal level. I did not feel at home in Bloomington. I was a walnut in a pecan pie. Nobody seemed to mind me there, and a few other nuts even accepted me, but like Mom in her too-small house, I mostly bided my time. The loneliness of my social isolation gave birth to the search for a deeper, more meaningful friendship.

Public high school began in a new state without hills. I made a few friends. Sweet Gail Grimshaw died a few years later when she touched a live electrical wire in a limestone quarry while swimming. I still pray for her. My best friend, Sarah Fishburn, moved to the Southwest at the end of that year. A flower child of the sixties, Sarah's beautiful free spirit flutters today through her art.[5] One of my fondest memories is responding yes to her invitation to cut class senior year on a perfect summer day. We lay in a field of tall grasses beside the school and spoke our wild imaginings in butterfly words.

After Sarah left, I felt even more like an outsider. Music gave me solace. Occasionally, I played piano in a casual trio with violinist Steve Shipps (who later joined Mannheim Steamroller) and Adriana Contino (now a professor of cello in Indianapolis). Others kept me playing happily on tennis courts. One crush but no romances bloomed. No prom invitations materialized. I made fifty cents an hour babysitting most weekends. A typical Saturday night found me sitting on the couch watching TV, drinking a root beer float, eating M&M peanuts, and looking out the window wondering what everyone else was doing.

During my sixteenth year I had a pretty good pity party going for myself. My lack of friends had become painful. In desperation one day, I prayed a passionate prayer to God in my bedroom. It went something like this: "I know YOU love me, Lord. I turn my life over to You. I place myself in the palm of Your hand and trust You completely to lead me where You would have me go." Much later, I understood the full consequences of this prayer. At the time, it seemed like a spontaneous prayer from my heart. Nothing more. It was a baby version of Thomas Merton's prayer I would read years later.

MY LORD GOD, I have no idea where I am going.
I do not see the road ahead of me. I cannot know for certain where
it will end.
Nor do I really know myself, and the fact that I think that I am
following your will
does not mean that I am actually doing so.
But I believe that the desire to please you does, in fact, please you.
And I hope I have that desire in all that I am doing.
I hope that I will never do anything apart from that desire.
And I know that if I do this, you will lead me by the right road
though I may know nothing about it.
Therefore will I trust you always
though I may seem to be lost and in the shadow of death.
I will not fear, for you are ever with me,
and you will never leave me to face my perils alone.
—Thomas Merton, *Thoughts in Solitude*

Something shifted within me after that spontaneous prayer. It was a distinct sensation. Had I been in a movie, a music change would have been cued. I had no idea what the shift meant. I wondered what I had just done. Fear gripped me for a moment. Or was it grace? I reviewed my prayer in my mind. Did I say anything dangerous? It didn't seem so. I confirmed I had meant the prayer as if He had asked, "Are you sure?"

I suspect God intentionally steered young men away from me in high school so He could have me all to Himself. That would explain why no one asked me to a prom. "God feigns disinterest or worse for those He loves very much," said Dom Basil Pennington at a retreat in Conyers, Georgia.

Around this time I found myself drawn to a non-denominational Young Life group, partly as a result of a boring catechism class. No Catholic high schools existed in Bloomington then or now. God hounded me for more time with Him through a nuanced longing for something beyond Mass on Sunday. Maybe Young Life would be the answer. My parents always took their faith very seriously and asked me to bring the

Young Life minister/leader ("whatever he is") home to ask him a few questions before they would give me permission to attend the meetings.

How embarrassing! thought my seventeen-year-old self. *How can I ever ask him to do something like that?* But my desire to go to the meetings outweighed my embarrassment at asking him to "the interrogation." He came to my house one night after dinner and won my parents over.

His folksy guitar songs spoke to my heart as jam sweetens dry toast. Ron spoke of Jesus as his best friend. I had no idea how I could get Jesus to be my best friend, but I hoped by hanging out with Ron, I'd get a clue. I never heard Catholics talking about Jesus that way. Young Life was my first non-Catholic experience of Bible study and praise-and-worship singing. I experienced my first retreat with them. The deep well of longing began to fill up. A little.

Throughout my life, my father gave me many gifts—the good kind, the kind you can't wrap—including how to make big, life-changing decisions. At the beginning of my senior year, he sat me down and asked me fundamental questions about what I wanted from college, including the ratio of boys to girls, trees or city campus, small or large student body, and distance from home. He helped me narrow down the choices with a strong recommendation to choose a Catholic college to increase my chances of marrying someone with the same spiritual values. He and Mom didn't have a problem with me marrying someone outside my faith. They warned that marriage provided many challenges throughout the years and to add another one—such as a different faith or tradition, requiring long discussions about critical values or rituals—just made life more difficult.

We decided on the University of Dayton in Ohio, a leading Marianist college that suited five of the six of us kids. I considered a drama scholarship offer from St. Mary of the Woods in Indiana, extended for my rendition of Anastasia in a small play at church, but I turned it down. I wanted young men on the campus of my choice. Good decision. I might never have met the love of my life otherwise.

Freshman year at Dayton went smoothly. Assigned to Marycrest, the women's dorm, Pam Langdon had to endure me as a randomly chosen roommate—until she didn't return the second semester. Again, I was alone.

Before freshman year ended, my luck changed. Blond, easygoing Michael welcomed me into a romantic interlude, a perfect first movement to my studious college opus. An out-of-the-blue invitation created my new tribe when five freshman women asked me to join them in an off-campus apartment at Campus South. We spent the rest of our college years happily experiencing the ups and downs of romances and friendships.

After sophomore year I participated in University of Dayton's extraordinary 1974 Summer Abroad program: three tantalizing months in Italy, Greece, and England. A remarkable way to learn art, world culture, and history.

My poorly developed social skills did not help in my travels. I befriended few of the thirty or so fellow-traveling students. By month three in London the lack of friends grew old (social media didn't exist then). After finding a piano in one of the university buildings, I walked to a music shop, purchased several books of classical music, and played some of the world's great piano compositions to soothe my soul.

Dorothy Day came to mind.

We have all known the long loneliness, and we have learned that the only solution is love and that love comes with community.
—Dorothy Day, *The Long Loneliness*

Upon my return to the states for my third year of college, my dean informed me that I had senior status.

"No, I don't."

"Yes, you do."

"No, I'm a junior. All my friends are juniors."

"No, you're now a senior," he said. "You have senior status with your Summer Abroad credits, fully loaded previous semesters, and Spanish credits from Indiana University."

He smiled at my sputtering protest. My Irish or German heritage must have a proclivity to arguing wired into it. I can't seem to help myself. My first reaction to something is often to find an argument against it. After a while I adjusted to the fact that I would enter the workforce a year sooner than I'd planned. My roommates took it in stride.

With mild frustration mixed with curiosity at never attending a prom, I agreed to join my housemates for the last Turnabout Dance before I graduated. Sadie Hawkins, or Turnabout, is where the girls ask the guys to the dance. My date had the voice of Richard Burton: an English tour guide I'd met in London the previous summer. We'd dated for three weeks and kept in touch through airmail. He would arrive stateside before the dance to acquire new business for the summer tour season. Dropping the news that my date was a Brit made my day.

Michael (yes, another Michael) arrived in January and invited me to join him for a weekend drive to Canada to visit a friend and sign up tour groups. We drove for six hours and stayed near Toronto. Except for the awkwardness of not knowing a soul besides Michael, whose social skills seemed to match mine, Saturday came and went without a hitch. Without warning, Michael proposed marriage that night. He never mentioned love.

"Of course, you'd have to live in the U.K.," he added, "since my family and I couldn't possibly live in the U.S." I blinked a few times as my teeth clamped tight. My heart seemed to press on my throat. I looked hard into his eyes. They looked back blandly as if we were discussing a dinner menu.

"I don't know who you think I am, Michael, but you have the wrong American girl," I finally managed, blinking, frowning, and backpedaling all at once. "Look," I said as I took a deep, steadying breath to stammer out a response. "This is how it's supposed to work. First, you tell me you love me. Then, you tell me you can't live without me. Then, you ask me to marry you. Your idea of marriage is ..."

I shook my head. "I have nothing more to say to you." The ride home to Dayton the next day was long and silent. I replayed his lamentable proposal, searching for anything redeeming about this man. I reviewed my memories of our dates in London to see if I had missed any clues about how emotionless he seemed to be. Finding nothing, I slumped into a blue funk as I let the air out of my beautiful British dream. For seven years of teenage life, I'd imagined finding a man who'd love me and want to marry me. I felt disappointed in the reality, and a little depressed. And that is how I found myself suddenly without a date two weeks before the dance.

My social status, what little I had, vanished like his car after he dropped me at home. I had pumped myself up for months bragging about my romantic Englishman. Attending the dance now was out of the question. Sitting in my room reading a book and feeling sorry for myself became the new plan. My roommates threatened to get me a blind date if I didn't find someone else. That had no appeal whatsoever. Knowing their determination, I decided to start shopping.

I thought of two guys capable of making me laugh despite my pity party and decided upon Joe Manion, who seemed the better choice and less likely to grope me after a few beers. He'd dated Linda Neal, one of my roommates, for a while. I called and invited him to a champagne cocktail party we had planned. He easily agreed after I answered his question: "Who is this again?" I casually mentioned we'd be going to Sadie Hawkins afterward. That little detail caught him off guard. He tried a stalling tactic, saying he would get back to me after the weekend. I found out later he secretly hoped another girl would ask him instead, but when she didn't, he finally agreed to be my date. He turned up in a sling.

I was late, as usual, in getting ready for the dance. I descended the stairs in an elegant, olive green evening gown that my roommate, Becky O'Connell, had loaned me. It had a smooth, floor-length flow and fit me like a dream. I had Joe's full attention. He stood in the living room eyeing me appreciatively in a dark suit coat, navy blue turtleneck, and white medical sling over his left arm. He had played basketball the night before, went up for a rebound, and someone knocked his legs out from under him. He landed hard, dislocating his shoulder.

Joe's natural charm and good nature made the evening much more pleasant than I expected. True to his nature, Joe checked on me throughout the evening, as often as every twenty minutes. "Are you having a good time? How are you doing?"

"I'm fine. Thanks."

"Can I get you anything?"

"No, thanks. Not right now."

I'd look at him, see the white sling, and feel mortified I never once thought to ask him how *he* was feeling. My embarrassment snuffed the question. His apparent selflessness pricked my self-centeredness and taught me a new lesson in serving others. I'd done a few service projects at Dayton, but here stood a man dedicated to helping others in the same humble manner of Jesus' earthly father with the same name. I could do wonderful things for total strangers; the ones closest to me seemed not to count.

By the time we got home that night, Joe's day had caught up with him. I didn't know the emergency room staff had given him a prescription for Darvon. Champagne at our house, a few beers at the dance, and the muscle relaxant could knock anyone out. I offered to let him sleep at our house for the night. He gladly accepted. I took off his suit coat. He fell asleep the moment he lay on the living room couch. I went upstairs, hung up Becky's dress, and changed into my nightgown, a K-Mart special that had a goofy-looking owl embroidered above a long leg slit on one side. A wave of emotion swept over me as I thought of Joe sleeping downstairs. I decided to go down and check on him the way a mother checks her child.

As I quietly descended the stairs for the second time that night, I became self-conscious of the design of my nightgown. It had never bothered me before. I glanced at Joe on the sofa. His eyes were closed. Admiring this suddenly handsome man, I tiptoed to the arm of the couch near his head, so if he awoke, he couldn't see my nightgown. Looking at him upside down, I bent over to kiss his forehead. He stretched his head back at that moment and kissed me on the lips. His right arm reached over his head and touched my side.

"Hmmm." He stroked the soft material of my gown. I stepped back quickly. He seemed to be in no discomfort.

"Good night, Joe," I said as I turned and hurried back up the stairs. I slept with a smile that night. Cupid's arrow had met its mark. God began reeling us in.

CHAPTER 4

ASK THE RIGHT QUESTION

Nothing we do, however virtuous, can be accomplished alone;
therefore, we are saved by love.

—Reinhold Niebuhr

1975

JOE AND I had something special between us, and we knew it from that first date. As smoothly as a hand slides into a fine leather glove, we fitted together effortlessly, vocalizing thoughts simultaneously, finishing each other's sentences, and laughing delightedly at our shared view on the world. Despite having absolutely no interest in each before the dance—he wasn't my type, nor I, his—we clearly had Michael's impetuous proposal to thank for the feeling between us now. It would be another decade or two before I'd begin to recognize how God used negative experiences to direct me closer.

We didn't use the word—*love*—for months. We sensed the sacredness of what moved between us. Using the word *love* too easily felt wrong. Despite being in love, however, I knew long distance relationships rarely succeeded, so letting my head rule over my heart, I assumed my relationship with Joe Manion would end when I graduated. He thought otherwise and would have nothing of the goodbye speech I had written, practiced, and tried to deliver during my last day on campus.

My degree in communication arts with a specialty in TV broadcasting got me a few on-air interviews at local TV stations for anchor positions, but no job offers. The effort to send two hundred résumés across the country should have generated *something* in the television industry. My real world education had begun.

Two days after returning from college, my dad was his usual direct self.

"It's time to leave the nest," he said. "What job interviews have you got set up?"

I admitted I had none. I got to work analyzing my rejection letters, grouped them geographically, and sorted them by cities: Chicago, Indianapolis, and Columbus, Ohio. Choosing the biggest pile first, I called each of the Chicago companies. I told them I'd be in town for a few days and wanted to stop by to introduce myself. I understood they had no openings. Visiting these companies generated two job offers. I took the most lucrative and settled into the Three Arts Club, a private home and club for women in the three arts of music, painting, and drama on Chicago's near north side arranged by my boss, Jan Mons Britt, until I could find an apartment. I made enough that first year to get by with much frugality.

A Greek restaurateur noticed my pattern of sitting by myself at lunch and asked permission to seat me with "some friends" one day. They turned out to be undercover detectives who taught me the difference between Chicago's Blue Island and uptown as I searched for an apartment in the classifieds. I settled near Loyola on the north side and joined St. Gertrude's church choir. I knew no one else in the city.

A few weeks later I had lunch with an associate who asked me what I *really* wanted to do, since he could see I exceeded the qualifications for the typing job. He put me in touch with Mike Gilroy at Vista Communications, who hired me to be his executive assistant. I loved the work. We met some of his clients—Seven-Up was the first—scripted their marketing plans, hired a freelance film crew and voice-over talent, shot the scenes, laid down the audio at Universal Recording Studios, rolled the film onto two-inch videotape, and began editing. For an entire week, we took shots of foamy Root Beer and spliced scenes at Telemation from dawn to dark. We emerged with a finished video product like bears from hibernation, blinking at world events flashing on our TV screens as we unpacked and caught up with the world.

Gilroy gave me a spiral notebook full of commentary and advice on how to comport myself and fulfill my duties to him as a newbie to the industry. I read it regularly, ever the student ready to learn and improve. I wish I could say the same for my Bible then.

After starting my new job, Joe and I began meeting at my parents' home in Bloomington. By the fourth of July weekend, after five months of dating, he popped a question. It was another "you've got to be kidding" moment.

We were watching a drive-in movie in his car. Social outlets were fairly limited in Bloomington. As the movie played, we talked. "So what do you think about marriage?" he asked.

The question hung in the air. The movie played on. I had a funny feeling about the question. "If you're asking what I think you're asking, I think you better rephrase the question." I looked at him sideways. He did it right after that.

Our relationship strengthened during our thirteen-month engagement while he finished his degree in psychology. My job limited us to seeing each other for thirty-six hours a weekend every two to three weeks. I drove six hours from my one-bedroom north-Chicago apartment to his Dayton off-campus apartment. With the exorbitant cost of long-distance phone calls and the nascent state of email, we wrote letters (saved in a shoebox to this day) and anticipated the daily mail.

Joe visited a few more times that summer. We felt it prudent to get my parents used to him before he asked my dad's permission to marry me. They'd only met him at my graduation. He test drove brake lining for Bendix in Detroit that summer, driving for eight hours each day. On a few Fridays he'd grab some sandwiches in a brown paper sack his mother had prepared for him and drive another six hours to Bloomington, Indiana, arriving shortly after midnight.

When he finally felt comfortable about approaching my father, they spoke for about forty-five minutes, after which Dad suggested they talk to Kathryn, my mother, and me. Being the first to marry among the six of us kids and poor Joe being without a job or degree begged a few questions. Mom, the holdout on approving our plans, grilled him for several hours sitting in a chair across from him with her arms folded firmly like a security guard. She eventually gave Joe her approval after he passed her killer question, "How do you know this love you have for our daughter will last?" *Whoa*, I thought, as he digested that one. We'd anticipated every other question and planned our answers together. I held my breath as he spoke honestly about not knowing the future, but knowing his feelings for me were strong and true.

We decided to get married in Bloomington, Indiana. My mother handled most of the details. One day I received a printed invitation in the mail. She'd ordered the wedding invitations, chose the font, wording, and paper all on her own. I'm sure it had more to do with my location than anything else. Long distance phone calls were expensive. We didn't have the Internet. I knew nothing about wedding details and had little interest in anything but the marriage ceremony itself. Still, I would have chosen a different font.

A post-wedding luncheon would take place at the Student Union of the University of Indiana. The budget could not include a big band and dinner party afterward. Five siblings had yet to finish college, which my parents fully financed.

August 14, 1976, arrived hot and humid. The sleeves on my wedding gown were sheer but long. We had no air conditioning in the church or car. I knew nothing about the hair salon/makeup artist tradition that brides do today. I washed and brushed my waist-length hair, wore it down in a simple fashion, and applied minimal makeup as usual. We weren't a fancy family, and I liked it that way.

The Gospel reading Joe and I chose for our wedding has become a core value:

> ... *that all of them may be one, Father, just as you are in me and I am in you. May they also be in us so that the world may believe that you have sent me. I have given them the glory that you gave me, that they may be one as we are one—I in them and you in*

*me—so that they may be brought to complete unity. Then the
world will know that you sent me and have loved them even as
you have loved me.*

—John 17:21-23

We saw ourselves as one with all His creation. We also saw ourselves
as part of a three-threaded cord with God, Who'd give us strength beyond
measure through life's trials and human weaknesses.

My father walked me down the aisle, shook Joe's hand with a big,
happy smile, and handed me over. Joe turned to me full of joy and
offered me his arm.

"Relax," he whispered with a smile. "This is our time now. Let's
enjoy it."

I drew my next breath and hooked my arm under his. All that self-
consciousness from walking down the aisle with my dad in my flowing
wedding dress trying to remember every moment of this long-awaited
day disappeared. I exhaled and knew beyond a shadow of a doubt that
this man was my soul mate, my best friend, my true love. To this day,
there's no place I'd rather be than in his arms.

We loved the symbol of lighting the wedding candle: a sign of
the two becoming one, of dying to self. Two small candles lit by our
mothers before Mass symbolized our former lives and the love of our
parents who had brought us to that moment; taking their flames and
joining them on our larger wedding candle represented the two of us
becoming one. We blew out the small candles our mothers had lit, and
we continue to light that same wedding candle to this day as part of
each year's anniversary celebration.

We took a short trip to Mary's altar after our vows to acknowledge
her "Yes" to God's request to bear His Son—her own dying to self—for
surely she thought that becoming pregnant would be the end of her
betrothal to her Joseph. Joe and I had written individual prayers that
we read near the end of the Mass, professing the childlike faith we had
in God and one another, asking Him to grow our faith into a steady
flame, a sure sign to others of the strong "I am" love we felt between us.

A day later, we settled into my apartment one block from Lake
Michigan. I'd changed jobs to Jovan Inc. two weeks before the wedding.
Although they graciously gave me Friday off to drive to Bloomington

for the wedding rehearsal, Monday was a work day. I had no earned vacation time to tap as their new Associate Creative Services Manager. For the next three years, I honed my sarcasm under the influence of double-entendre-genius Dick Meyers, the company President. Joe began work on his master's degree. We were both twenty-two years old.

One of God's greatest gifts to me is my soul mate and husband. We complete each other; at least, he completes me. Our love grows deeper every year. I've been able to accept God's overwhelming love because I experienced unconditional love from both my parents and Joe. His excellent sense of humor has seeped into my bones, coloring my thoughts like Easter egg dye. As a Type A high achiever, I need humor to balance my innate intensity. It has helped to have a goofy Irishman counterbalance the unique "engineer" humor of my father. If you know an engineer, you may know what I mean.

> *I think the chief reason why we have so little joy*
> *is that we take ourselves too seriously.*[6]
> —Thomas Merton

Until Joe and I started dating, I never knew I was incomplete. He smoothed my rough spots with his complementary qualities. His spirituality was quiet and stable. More times than he will ever know, he represented Christ to me, acting just as I imagined Jesus would act or speak or look at me. His parents named him aptly—he completely dedicates himself to his family and his work. To be loved by him is an exquisite experience.

One day when I was marveling at Joe's love, God planted this thought in my heart: *If you think you're loved by Joe so well, you can't begin to imagine what I have in store for you if you'll just let Me love you, too.*

In one of my favorite books, *He and I*, God spoke to French actress Gabrielle Bossis in a similar way: "Open to Me. Fling the doors of your heart wide open, dear little one."[7]

We didn't do too well socially in the city. Two guys from my freelance film crew showed up at a party we threw one weekend. They were our only guests. They sat in politeness eating chips and dip for an hour before leaving.

In 1978, we bought a condo at 444 West Washington Avenue in Oak Park, Illinois, nine miles west of Chicago. Oak Park was a contemporary, diverse community of young professional families enhanced by the architecture Frank Lloyd Wright left there. The move coincided with a job change from the wild world of the fourth largest fragrance company in the U.S. to the conservative, staid corporation of Helene Curtis Industries, Inc. on North Avenue, where I was now Senior Product Manager in charge of a retail line of hair care products sold in beauty salons. In anticipation of starting a family, I wanted a less exciting job than the rapid-fire pace of Jovan.

To discover our new neighborhood, we rode our bikes from Oak Park into the tree colonnaded streets of River Forest. Meticulously manicured lawns moated the northern village mansions, shaded by century-old oaks and elms. It seemed like a magic land to us. On each ride, I'd wonder what kind of people lived there.

Our condo nestled us in a quiet corner one block away from Dominican Fenwick High School. My boss at Helene Curtis Industries, Jim Marino, would tell stories of his high school days there. Swim class took place in the nude when it was an all-boys school, he said. I'm not sure what he said after that. My imagination kicked into full gear and to this day still delights in the image created by that one piece of data.

In the decade after college, I'd set a career goal to achieve midlevel management so I could take off a few years to rear our family. After our littlest one started school, I planned to re-enter the workforce without having to re-climb the corporate ladder. However, when I left Helene Curtis in 1983 after three years of working there to begin life as a stay-at-home mother, I didn't realize I would never return to corporate life. I never missed it.

What a dream to be the co-creator of a beautiful child! Bryan had such deep eyes at birth that they made me uncomfortable. It almost seemed that God was looking through them, looking right into my soul with the purest look of unconditional love I'd ever experienced. The look was as if his eyes had no back to them. (I would see this look only one other time, in the eyes of Father Theophane,[8] a happy Trappist monk from St. Benedict's Monastery in Snowmass, Colorado.) The purity of Bryan's eyes was too intense for me. I had to look away, almost ashamed that I couldn't meet the look. It was a God moment, for God is love, and I saw unadulterated, unconditional, I'll-never-stop-loving-you love in Bryan's baby eyes fresh from heaven. It quickened my heart and awakened within me the covenant I'd made with God when I was sixteen and placed my life in His hands. My heart ached that my husband didn't get as many love-drenched moments alone with our little angel from heaven as I did.

My heart went to a place it had never been before when Bryan was born. It was pierced and vulnerable and protective. I felt grateful for this sweet tiny gift from God and afraid of the exposed opening in my heart that would never close. I thanked God for the precious gift of life. The vulnerability of love throbbed in my heart as I held that beautiful little boy. I knew my heart would break if anything happened to him, so I handed him back to God, acknowledging Bryan was His, and promised to love him and care for him all the days of my life, however long or short either of us would live. Like a feather falling from the sky, peace landed on my heart and covered it protectively. Joe and I took him home, laid him on the couch and just stared at him. We had become parents and a little baby boy now totally depended upon us. We were thunderstruck with the reality.

Months flew by. As a young mom, I didn't know how to meet other moms or get involved in the community. When Bryan drove me crazy with his pounding on the front door to "go out, go out," I'd take him on stroller rides and find no one playing outside in those early morning hours. Everyone had gone off to work, it seemed. Despite my lack of new friends, I enjoyed the solitude of those walks, seeing squirrels running up trees again, daffodils proudly trumpeting the spring, and tulips promising to show their beauty soon. I had missed seeing the changes of seasons in the city due to the busyness of my sixty-hour work week. It was good to rest my body, mind, and soul and to bask in the love of my sensitive, blue-eyed son.

At eighteen months Bryan chafed at being cooped up in the condo with little room to roam, looking down at Washington Boulevard from the couch. He would occasionally yelp "truck, truck" in his beautiful little boy voice, pointing through the leaves of the maple tree outside our fourth-floor window. We wanted to give him a backyard to play in, a swing to swing in, and neighborhood children to grow up with.

After months of searching for a starter home in contemporary, integrated Oak Park and conservative River Forest, we fell in love with one located two blocks south of St. Luke Church. We sang in the contemporary choir at that church. Our children could walk to St. Luke School from this house. We were delighted to see redheaded children like Bryan in an old-fashioned neighborhood that seemed ideal. Unfortunately, the price far exceeded our meager budget, so much so that Joe asked me why we were even going to the Open House. But after tense negotiations and a pledge to eat hot dogs and baked beans for a year, we finalized the purchase. Friends, including Tom and Mary Bromann, fellow choir members who had sung for our son's baptism, helped us move eight years' worth of accumulated garage sale possessions.

The neighborhood replicated the old TV show, *Ozzie and Harriet*. Sixty-five children lived on our block alone. Friendly neighbors with strong family values welcomed us with open door policies whenever we needed anything. We went to church with many of them: twenty children between the McCahills and Reardons; the Keltys added a trinity of red-headed boys (Carolyn bounced in later). The Keuers, Boyers, Pantos, and Petersons contributed four children each; the Sheehans' twins, Margaret and Tim, became our babysitters; a half-dozen more families completed the pack. We frolicked in carefree summers, shoveled snow for each other in harsh winters, and watched over one another in times of need and new babies. In January 1986, little Tess was born, a fiery, strong-willed go-getter who added a whole new dimension to our lives and those around us.

Old-fashioned social gatherings abounded, cinching the bonds of friendship among neighbors like a tight corset. We tossed eggs and water balloons during annual block parties, splashed in our pool at monthly summer potlucks, and enjoyed "Hallo-weenies" grilled in the Krusinskis' or Silhas' yard each Halloween.

This lovely neighborhood became our sheltering "tribe," supporting and nurturing us for more than twenty years. We couldn't have asked for a better place to raise our children.

I didn't keep detailed records of those years, but my lovely Irish mother documented selective memories of her years as a "stay-at-home" mom. Her reflections remind me of my own such days. Mom reared us with the patience of a saint, seemingly tireless in her love for us. After she died, I retrieved copies of her correspondence and found the following diary of one of her days with her first four children, similar in age to mine at the time. In her journal entry, I was the four-year-old, Michael was thirty months, Jean-Marie, eighteen months, and David was the baby.

1958

5:30 a.m. Get milk for the baby. Find older two with six boxes of cereals, bowls, etc. in the living room watching the TEST PATTERN on TV! They don't go back to bed. I go back to bed after feeding the baby.

6:45 Vacuum the cereal in the living room. Jeannie gets up. Dress Jeannie. Then get Mike out of baby's crib.

7:00-9:00 Eat breakfast. Settle two fights. Wash dishes. Make beds. Wash out Bon Ami from Jeannie's mouth. Wonder how much she ate. Remake my bed (jam and peanut butter over pillowcases and sheet). Remove Mike from cookie jar on counter and Jeannie from on top of the dryer. Re-sweep kitchen floor of All and Ivory Snow. Put baby to sleep.

9:00-11:00 Remove smashed crayons from the rug, crayons from Jeannie's mouth, also modeling clay. Sweep up broken glass (Jeannie threw two pop bottles down cellar stairs). Bring Jeannie in twice from front lawn with only socks on. Temperature 27 degrees. Their beds are now all undone. Bring Jeannie uncounted number of times to potty. Always wet. Remove wet corduroys and replace – at least four pairs. Start on third wash of the morning. Remove Christine from plastic clothes bag in the cellar.

11:00 Baby wakes up. Everyone is in his crib. While I change him, the others get to work in either the bathroom or kitchen. Get Mike and Jeannie out of bathroom tub, washing toys. Both wet. Change them. Give juice to baby. Mop up half a quart of juice someone spilled on kitchen floor. Baby wet again. Everyone jumps on my bed while changing him. Park baby and lift box spring up again on supports (the bed was almost flat on the floor). Get Jeannie out of cookie jar. Lock three older ones down in cellar while preparing lunch. Answer two phone calls, one door call.

12:00 Lunch

1:00 Naps for Jeannie (after getting out of crib three times) and baby. Wash dishes, fold diapers while trying to keep two older ones quiet. Useless. Read them a story. Take down coloring paints and crayons. Wash coloring out of Mike's hair. Mop up color from kitchen floor.

2:30 Baby wakes up. Others wake Jeannie. Everyone is unhappy for some reason. Too early for cartoons. Now, what? More paperwork. Get out old Christmas cards for them. Rescue David (they had him wrapped a la barber style with a blanket and were starting to work on his hair with dull scissors). Soothe David. Juice for everyone. Try to remove button from ear of Mike – he says Jeannie put it in. Look up Spock for advice. Aspirin. For me. Put door back on furnace – someone removed it. Remove Mike from plaster in garage. Several fights and some cartoons later, dinner is ready. Bedlam. More spilled milk. Refuse to mop the floor again. Just going to let the puddle evaporate!

7-7:30 Get everyone dressed for bed. Too tired to wash them. Look over newspaper.

8:00 Dishes. Three loads of clothes to fold. Nuts. More diapers to go in washer. To bed.

What a woman! Whereas I didn't experience the exhaustion of rearing six children, in typical overachiever fashion, I became involved in a few parish ministries: CCD, choir, lector, Eucharistic minister, sacristan, and altar server at daily Mass. The Renew program taught me valuable lessons about small group facilitating. I chaired or served on liturgy planning, spiritual life, bereavement, peace and justice, and welcoming committees. Our sister parish, Blessed Sacrament in Lawndale, needed ESL tutors (English as a Second Language), so I became one. A few community service projects got my commitment as well, my favorite being local CROP Walks.

Joe and I worked actively to make friends in our neighborhood and parish. It may have been slow going finding new friends, however, God was about to make a bold move for which I was not well prepared.

CHAPTER 5

THE MUSIC

Through all the tumult and the strife, I hear that music ringing.
It sounds and echoes in my soul. How can I keep from singing?
—Text attributed to Pauline T., originally titled
"Always Rejoicing"

I WHISKED PAST God in books, in volunteer work, in the faces of babies and children, in my husband's tender actions, and in the eyes of certain elders. These God-moments had a dream-like quality to them. I couldn't quite recognize what they meant or Who was tapping my shoulder for attention. They faded quickly whenever something else distracted my attention. They reminded me of bumping into an old acquaintance from time to time. "Oh, funny I should meet you here, Lord...." These moments happened too fast and irregularly. I never connected them in the same way a child never seems to pay attention to what her mother says. It's funny how children can go next door, listen to the same words from a neighbor's lips, and finally "hear" them.

Music made that connection for me through hymns and psalms. They found their way through a crack in my heart to drip God's Word in ever so slowly throughout decades of volunteering for church choirs. The lyrics lingered in my mind, often replaying themselves like a repetitive audio loop, growing in substance and girth like a stalactite.

Catholic understanding of the third commandment does not allow for optional attendance at Sunday liturgies, which always made sense to me. The least I can give God is an hour a week of my time for all the many gifts and blessings He's given me.

As choir members we rarely sat during Mass. Homilies were one such resting moment. Some Sunday homilies haunted me. The prickly ones pointed out that true believers are called to the Gospel words every day, not just on Sunday. I wouldn't think about the Gospel message except at Mass when it was preached. Then I found myself feeling guilty for my lack of conscious awareness of the Gospel message throughout the week.

After years of watching me sing in the choirs of St. Gertrude in Chicago and St. Luke in River Forest, Joe joined St. Luke's contemporary choir as a tenor in 1980. After Tess's birth, he stepped away for a while, taking over bedtime responsibilities so I could rehearse on Tuesday nights. No other church in the area allowed guitar music in the church proper. We preferred contemporary music over the more traditional organ music, which we felt moved too slowly and heavily for us. Other local Catholic churches relegated guitar Masses to the church basement or a social hall with metal folding chairs that squeaked a shock of tinny music of their own.

Music resonates in all of us. I remember twirling around as fast as I could as a young teen to the sounds of the "Flight of the Bumble Bee" played on a 33 rpm record in my parents' living room until I fell dizzied to the floor. Piano lessons lasted until my final year in high school. When Fr. Tom Bromann, the lead guitarist of St. Luke's Contemporary Choir, neared the end of his six-year assignment, I decided to see if I could play a stringed instrument to carry on after his departure. The chances of the next priest playing guitar seemed slim. I bought a guitar for ten dollars at a garage sale, not realizing it had a broken neck. It didn't matter. I wasn't sure I would succeed. Playing a stringed instrument felt odd. I followed pictures of chords in a beginner book and placed my fingers on the strings awkwardly. With practice, I learned to play adequately.

In my early thirties I studied the violin as a stress management tool under the patient tutelage of Kristen Capelli in her home on Park Avenue. After a few years of practice, Dr. Paul Urbanek invited me to play in his adult Chamber Orchestra in downtown Chicago. I had begun playing with the Oak Park-River Forest Symphony Orchestra when I learned of my father's diagnosis of lung cancer in 1999. I couldn't play the violin after that. It made the same sound as my breaking heart.

In the same way that we love God with the love He's given us, I played music back to the author of music itself. I'm not sure when it became a form of prayer. What I do know is that spending four to five hours a week praying to God through song and music for choir had a cumulative effect. The songs acted as a precursor to contemplative prayer. With the words already written, my voice just opened and lifted itself, and my soul, encouraged by the music, turned its face to our Lord. Once I learned the words and music through repetition and rehearsal, I could pray the songs purely with no distracting thoughts. My heart opened wide. My mind and soul joined as one in adoration and praise of God.

Some people use the Jesus Prayer—*Lord Jesus Christ, Son of the Living God, have mercy on me, a sinner*—as their active prayer through their days and nights. The choir hymns became my active prayers throughout the day, rising unbidden within my soul, floating along a river of subconscious praise much like a mother snuggles a loved child on her hip and carries him during her daily tasks, putting him down and picking him up as she goes along. These active prayer songs carried my soul across a bridge toward the greatest commandment: Love the Lord your God with all your heart, with all your mind, with all your soul, and with all your strength. The prayer songs helped soften my rough edges and Irish temper. A little.

CHAPTER 6

A PARKING LOT REVELATION

*The Spirit suggests what is to be done at each moment
in our relationship to God, ourselves, others and the cosmos.*
—Thomas Keating

IN THE EARLY 1980s, St. Luke parish often held healing services with Fr. Dennis Kelleher, a Redemptorist, who received the gift of healing reluctantly. He literally ran away from it at first. The contemporary choir sang for these three-hour services. That meant four hours of playing and singing, including the hour of rehearsal beforehand. The slow-paced songs for these services, often charismatic in nature, moved me deeply.

Curiosity and a little skepticism stirred in my soul about the many people "slain in the Spirit." People who sought healing stood in front of the altar steps, much like they used to kneel for communion in pre-Vatican II days. Fr. Kelleher would move from one to another, placing his hands on their head or shoulder, silently praying over them, sometimes speaking briefly to them. Some turned and walked back to their seats after he moved to the next person. Some would slowly fall backward into the arms of the usher, "catcher" or Deacon, who would ease them to the floor to rest.

This falling to the floor is called "slain in the Spirit," often associated with the practice of laying on of hands. Also called "resting in the Spirit," author Thomas Csordas says it "can serve the purposes of exhibiting the faith of those who are 'open' to such power; of preparing a person to receive and exercise a spiritual gift; or of healing."[9] Fr. Kelleher emphasized that if any healing occurred, Jesus was the One doing it. He also taught us that although we may be attending the service for physical healing, we may receive spiritual healing instead.

I had no education about this sort of thing from any previous parishes I attended. Because it looked a bit like tele-evangelist healer mumbo jumbo, I did not fully understand it or believe it. After the service, Fr. Kelleher would offer to pray over us choir members if we desired it. Despite my skepticism, I decided to experience this praying and laying on of hands. I wanted to assure myself that it was different from the few televangelists I'd watched who did not seem to speak in the Spirit, but leaned on drama and theatrics to generate "good television." At least that's how it seemed to me.

When Father Dennis softly placed his hands on my head, I felt the "fire" or energy or power of the Holy Spirit, but not knowing or understanding the sensation at the time, I interpreted it as him pushing me to fall to the floor. I resisted and pushed back, remaining upright. My legs felt weak, but I made sure I stayed standing. Walking back to my guitar, I packed it up and left the church with the other choir members, pondering the experience. About half an hour later, as I got out of my car in the parking lot of my Oak Park apartment building, still trying to figure out what I had experienced, an unmistakable revelation opened within me informing me it was God, not the priest, Whom I had experienced. It caused me to want to go deeper in my understanding of the spiritual nature of things.

We moved to River Forest in 1984. A few years later, I began a Bible study course at Calvary Memorial Church on Lake Street in Oak Park at the invitation of my Protestant friend, Chris Keuer, who lived a block away on Ashland Avenue. Bible Study Fellowship (BSF) is an interdenominational, neo-evangelical approach to several books of the Bible through lecture, group sharing, and daily homework assignments. My parish offered nothing like this at the time.[10] To answer the BSF Bible study homework questions, I repeatedly had to cross-reference the Old and New Testaments, which showed how Christ was the fulfillment of the promised Messiah. Through this question-and-answer process, I fulfilled one of my goals in this Bible study: to become more familiar with all the books of the Bible. Often, I found myself stopping and letting God's Word seep deeply into my heart. My studying transitioned into lectio divina[11] in those years, though I knew nothing of the practice at the time.

When calls went out for new BSF leaders, I was ineligible as a Catholic. BSF held to the belief "if a teaching isn't explicit in the Bible, then we don't accept it as doctrine," commonly known as "sola scriptura." Many Protestants point to 2 Timothy 3:16-17 to validate this belief, however, that passage only states Scripture is inspired, not the sole source of all one needs to determine truth. (See End Notes for further Catholic answers to this discussion.[12])

Apostolic succession makes the Catholic faith unique according to the Catechism of the Catholic Church (hereafter cited as CCC). In keeping with the Lord's command, the Gospel was handed on in two ways:

—orally "by the apostles who handed on, by the spoken word of their preaching, by the example they gave ... what they themselves had received—whether from the lips of Christ, from His way of life and His works, or whether ... at the prompting of the Holy Spirit;"

—in writing "by those apostles and other men ... who, under the inspiration of the same Holy Spirit, committed the message of salvation to writing.

"The apostolic preaching ... was to be preserved in a continuous line of succession until the end of time. This living transmission, accomplished in the Holy Spirit, is called Tradition.... Sacred Tradition and Sacred Scriptures are bound closely together and communicate

one with the other … flowing out from the same divine well-spring."
(CCC76-78,80)

In an odd kind of way, I learned to appreciate my Catholic faith
more because it excluded me from BSF leadership. It made me learn and
realize the limitations that other denominations experience by cutting
themselves off from the tradition of the apostles' rich life in the Holy
Spirit. Catholics accept and honor both Scripture and Holy Tradition
with equal reverence (CCC82). I can deny neither the apostles' tradition
passed along from their knowledge of Christ's words nor what the Holy
Spirit placed deep in my heart on occasion. The Holy Spirit remains
present and active in the Church today in the living Tradition (CCC79).
The New Testament itself demonstrates the process of living Tradition
(CCC83).

After BSF had ended one year, my friend Chris invited me to do
homiletics with her (the study of composing and delivering a sermon).
I liked the idea of it, welcoming any opportunity to read Scripture on a
regular basis. My friend had only one time available: 5:30 a.m.

"You've got to be kidding!"

I struggled when my children woke me at the crack of dawn. She
suggested pre-dawn here. And I had one long *no* for an answer.

"I'll make us fresh ground coffee, and we can sit out in the back
yard. It'll be quiet and lovely."

"I don't think so, Chris. I love you and all, but that means I'd have
to get up at 5 a.m."

With sweet persistence, Chris tried to make this early morning hour
sound as enticing as she could. I tried several alternatives, but she held
firm. I sighed. My love for her and my hunger for deeper drinks from
the cup of God's Word eked out a reluctant "Oh, all right."

We worked through First Corinthians that summer, rewriting small
sections of chapters, one week at a time until we'd reduced the essence
of the chapter to a ten-word sentence. "A" and "the" counted as words.
Homiletics proved a challenge, but one I appreciated for the discipline
and the knowledge I gained from it.

One day Chris extended an invitation to a one-day retreat at her
church given by author Karen Mains on the subject of prayer journals.
From this firsthand experience, I learned the effectiveness of prayer. If

you don't think God answers your prayers, I dare you to keep a prayer journal. Begin by telling God what you're feeling that day or what is on your mind, Mains taught. Then praise God in your journal for something that day. Make a list of situations or people you want our Lord to take special care of (petitions or intercessory prayer). End with thanksgiving.

I liked the formula. Simple, straightforward, and efficient: greeting, praise, petition, and thanksgiving. It's amazing when you re-read your entries and mark when God answered your requests. This seeing with my own eyes through the lens of time created a trust in God from the pure evidence that He does answer prayer. It became a foundation stone to increase my prayer time with Him.

One of my favorite books, entitled *He and I,* contains the words of Our Lord to French actress Gabrielle de Bossis. She heard a mysterious inner voice in her early life. At age sixty-two, their dialog began in earnest. One day He asked her: "Aren't you beginning to understand that the words of your prayers have been shaped like arrows, not to beat the air, but to go straight to the heart of the Father who receives them with love? Every prayer has its arrow. Be certain of receiving an answer ... If He doesn't give you the answer you were hoping to get, it will be another—a better one.... But you are heard by the One who is enthroned in your very center."[13] His words confirmed what my prayer journal showed me.

One of my business associates, Stephanie, shared the following story with me about how she learned God answered prayers. "When my dad died, I complained to my mother that I had prayed and prayed for him to get better and God had shunned me. She told me a story of a little boy. His parents were very poor, and he decided one Christmas that he would really like a red bicycle. He prayed every night for that bike, and his mom watched knowing she didn't have the money for it. On Christmas morning when the boy opened his meager gifts, his mother told him she was sorry God hadn't answered his prayers for a bicycle. He told her, 'But mommy, He did answer my prayers - He just said no' and went on to play with a smile."

I understood further the preciousness of this prayer time with God when Sister Briege McKenna explained in her book, *Miracles Do Happen,* that God highly valued the three hours she spent with Him each day when she sat before His Presence in the sanctuary. As she became more sought after for her priest retreats, the only way she figured she could see more people for spiritual direction would be to cut back on her three hours before God. When she cut back to two hours at the next retreat and scheduled additional appointments, one priest couldn't sleep. He tossed and turned the whole night. In the morning, he approached Sister Briege and told her he had a message for her. "I want my three hours back." He had no idea what it meant but he said he sure hoped she did, because he wanted a good night's sleep that night.

A breakthrough occurred one morning while I prayed in bed. I'd spent an inordinate amount of time praying to God for a particular person, explaining my request, and positioning the supplication in different lights so God could see the purity of what I was asking. I struggled to find just the right words so He would understand the nature and motive of my request. It suddenly dawned on me that I was an idiot. "What a goose," Pascaline Coff whispered to me when I told this story to her fellow Benedictine sisters. God already knew my heart. He knew everything about me. He knew why I prayed for this person and the exact nature of my request. Duh! I shut up after that.

Thus began my centering prayer, although I didn't understand it as such at the time. I decided to focus on His Presence while sitting still.

> *Do not hurry to speak or be in a hurry as you think what to tell God.*
> *For God is in heaven and you are on the earth.*
> *So let your words be few.*
> —Ecclesiastes 5:2

I figured God knows what I'm thinking and feeling, and what's best in each situation, so I just lift up people or requests to Him and release them to His good care. Mostly I sit in silence and let God hug me, love me, transform me, do whatever He wants with me. And I listen. This is the essence of meditation or centering prayer: alertly paying attention to God in silence, stilling ourselves, consenting to be in His presence, giving Him a little of our time. He so cherishes this time, like a grandparent who gets a visit from a grandchild.

"I got her all to myself this morning!" I often hear from a grandpar-ent. God is the same when we turn our gaze inward toward His presence deep within us. How happy that makes Him.

Parents of teenagers have similar experiences. They long to spend time with their teens. They're growing up so quickly, zooming in and out of the house, cell phones or iPods to their ears. "Gotta go, Mom!" they toss over their shoulder. And before you can ask where they're going, or even if you do, they shout something, and they're off. Again. The lament of every parent of a teenager is, I'm guessing, the same as God's: "I never get to see them anymore! I want to sit with them and see what they're thinking. I want to spend a little time with them ... I have so much I want to share with them."

Years later, when I read "About Contemplation" on Prodigy, I met this God there. I learned the prayer I fell into had a name and a method with hundreds of years of history in the Catholic Church behind it. Who knew? Centering prayer is enjoying a global renewal. See www.contemplativeoutreach.org for more on this prayer form. Like snorkeling, it requires practice at calming your breathing and relaxing. When we snorkel, we trust the snorkel will bring air to our lungs with the water supporting us. When we center, we trust the method of centering prayer will open our hearts to the mystery of God within us Who protects and supports us, filling our hearts with pure love, ever more important than air filling our lungs.

I have called you to union. My invitation is for every man, woman, and child. Yet few have listened. Very few have responded to the call. Consent to this oneness. There is still time.
—Jesus to Gabrielle Bossis in *He and I*[14]

CHAPTER 7

THE CUSTOMER
FROM HELL

Man's main task in life is to give birth to himself.
—Erich Fromm

AN INVITATION TO "one of those home demonstrations" arrived at my house one day in September 1987 sent by a woman who'd recently moved into our neighborhood. Her husband and mine had become friends and started golfing together. I decided I'd stop by her house beforehand to get to know her a little. I did not intend to stay for her party.

Years earlier, I had attended my first Tupperware show as a favor to help a friend's daughter. It was pretty awful. Her presentation looked stiff and bland. Having no desire for any of the overpriced products in the catalog, I hated the trapped feeling of being unable to leave without buying something. Since our young family lived on one small but sufficient income, I shopped K-Mart and Target. Back and forth I went through the catalog looking for the least expensive item I'd use. After the third dismal pass-through, I finally settled on a set of four square plates that cost seven to eight dollars at the time, an atrocious price to pay for poly-plastic. Back then, that was a lot of money to me. I vowed never to get caught in a home demonstration like that again.

I concocted an exit line in advance because I had no intention of staying there long. Start time was 7:30 p.m. At 7:25, I planned to deliver my line and leave.

Donna Olewinski turned out to be a lovely new neighbor, tall and attractive with a friendly smile. She was athletic like her husband and a gracious host. As my departure time neared, I couldn't help but notice the demonstrator doing something clever. *How did she do that?* Donna's doorbell started ringing with arriving guests. I kept watching the demonstrator get ready and found myself mesmerized. When I next looked down at my watch, it showed 7:24. I needed to get Donna's attention to depart quickly according to plan.

Then in walked Chris Keuer, one of my dearest friends. *Oh, shoot! How can I leave now? I rarely get to spend time with Chris.* I greeted her with a big hug, and we sat together. In a flash, I decided to stay. Besides wanting to spend time with Chris, I'd contracted FOMO ("fear of missing out"). If I left, I realized, all my neighbors would be "in" on how to do all the wonderful things the demonstrator would show them. They'd be one up on me. My desire to be "in the know" and be with a cherished friend trumped my departure plans.

With mixed emotions, I put myself through another home demonstration, but this time, I had Chris at my side, beaming her beautiful smile of love and friendship. The demonstrator introduced herself. I folded my arms in nonverbal protest and tried, as much as possible, not to pay attention to her. I did *not* want to sit through another demonstration, yet I loved my friend Chris and valued time with her. My stomach churned at the price of enduring another forced purchase situation while I tried with partial success to focus on my friend's conversation. The internal tensions between violating my personal vow and the delightful camaraderie of friendship created an edge in me I could not rein in. Situations that provide no easy or unobtrusive escape, frustrate me. I was doubly irritated because I'd put myself in this one.

Chris and I got caught talking at least once during the demonstration.

"Now, Ladies," the demonstrator said, looking in our direction, "if you could all give me your attention for a moment, I've got something I'm about to do that I think you're going to like."

Grrrrr … I'd already been through parochial education where I heard daily to keep my hands folded on my desk, feet flat on the floor, and eyes straight ahead. I didn't need to go through it again as an adult. This woman sounded like a mother superior to me—and my Irish was up. Chris and I "behaved" for a few moments, and then continued catching up with each other whenever the demonstrator took her eyes off us.

I can be a stubborn customer. I didn't believe what she said about her products. On several occasions, my commentary sliced the otherwise convivial air. My doubting Thomas mouth shot several questions at her.

"Never in the twenty-plus years I've done this business," she says these days, "have I met a more obnoxious person." A dubious honor, to say the least.

This woman who later became my friend always acted the professional and respectfully answered my questions. She secretly wondered whatever caused me to attend in the first place, and secondly, why didn't I just leave? I, on the other hand, sat there wondering why she told so many stories about her family. Why didn't she stick to talking about her products? I could do a much better job if I were doing what she was doing. Of course, this is the trademark of all excellent trainers. She intentionally made everyone feel that they could do a better job than she did.

Somewhere during her presentation, she stopped for a few minutes and shared the financial aspects of her business. She talked about how she'd started for a little extra money and planned to do it for only three months. When compared to other part-time jobs that paid seven-to-eight dollars an hour, she challenged us to find any that would pay twenty to twenty-five dollars an hour where you could set your hours and vacation time. I remember thinking at the time I was worth twenty-five dollars an hour.

When the show ended, I had a hard time deciding what to buy, the reverse of my Tupperware experience. I wanted many items but restrained myself due to our lean checking account.

"I think I might like to do this!" I whispered to my friend Chris. She told me years later, "When you said that, I thought, 'She is crazy! She still has a little one in diapers!'" She thought the business had no future.

Chris Keuer left long before I decided what to buy. Typical of a customer interested in direct sales, I was one of the last people remaining. Half an hour after the presentation, I went up to the table with my order, but the demonstrator had moved temporarily to another room. A few brochures on the table caught my eye. I picked one up that described how to get started in the business, and I quickly scanned to the end for information about how much one gets paid. Looking at her calculator on the table with a running total of sales, I did the math. She had made one hundred dollars talking about her family and some products. *That's as good as a hooker*, I thought. Prostitutes made a hundred dollars a night, or so I remembered from movies I'd seen. I didn't know the hourly rate of most other people's work.

I completed my order and went home—much later than I had expected. My husband looked surprised that I'd stayed as long as I did, knowing how I felt about home demonstrations. Out of pure love, he patiently endured the litany of stories I relayed of all I'd seen and heard. That night and the entire next day, I kept thinking about how it would be a perfect fit to get me out of the house once a week to enjoy some adult companionship. I'd been out of corporate life for almost five years and needed something to do. I loved being home with our children. I wouldn't trade that for all the world. But my mind was beginning to atrophy, and I worried when my conversational abilities seemed limited to "pee-pee," "poo-poo," and "Sesame Street" episodes. Doubts crept in my mind like cracks on a wall: Could I still maintain an adult conversation on a subject other than children?

Locally, I volunteered at our church as well as Oak Park's Youth Committee, the Chicago Guild for the Blind, and a local nursing home. Still, something seemed lacking. *This stuff could be the ticket.*

At Friday night's presentation, I'd indicated I wanted some informa-tion about the business opportunity. Saturday and Sunday came and went, and the phone never rang. By Monday, I still hadn't heard from her and started to get frustrated that she had not called. If she'd let another day or two go by, I don't know if I'd still have been as receptive. I had little patience in those days. Not that I've gained much since. She finally called and arranged to come to my house the next day.

She almost fell over when I opened the door to greet her the following day. As she tells it, *Oh, my gosh, it's the customer from hell!* she thought. As is often the case at direct selling events like Donna's where there were twenty people, it's hard to put a face to the name on the sales receipt. The demonstrator had apparently not made the connection with my name until that moment. But again, to her credit, this professional woman had a lovely smile that she willed in place as she greeted me and entered my home. I never had a clue she'd have preferred to turn around and go home.

In no time at all, she laid out the details of getting started in the business. She informed me how much more I'd earn when I became a leader. Later in my own business, I would use this subtle word choice in my efforts at recruiting. She had said *when* I became a leader, not *if* I chose to become one someday. I remember thinking at the time, Why the heck wouldn't I become a leader if I would be paid more for doing the same work? I signed on the line with nervous excitement and walked her to the door as a new member of her team. October 14, 1987, was a day that changed my life.

As she walked out, I asked her how to invite people to my first demonstrations. She reached into her bag and offered some packets to get me started until my business kit arrived. As I walked back to my kitchen, doubts began. *What have I done?* It was all so spontaneous. I didn't even pray over it.

I started calling a few people to get my business started. I figured my sister was a lock. She was the first to turn me down.

"Oh, Chris! I would love to help you, but I just went to one a couple of weeks ago in my neighborhood, and everyone I would invite was there! I'm so sorry!"

I felt dejected. I didn't expect her to turn me down. The training back then did not teach us how to address this objection by scheduling her a month or two later. In my mind, her "no" was a dead end. I needed customers now.

My next call was to my best friend, Vicki Shanahan. "Chris, I know all about these home demonstrations. I'm pooped out!" she told me on the phone after I explained how I'd begun this new business. "That's all I've been doing for the past few months, and I need a rest. So do my friends. I'm very sorry. I would love to do one for you, but I just can't right now. I hope you understand."

I certainly did understand, but that didn't help me in my quest to book enough business to order my signup kit. I had already decided to use my home as a practice run before going to other people's homes. After two rejections, my discouragement caused me to hold off from calling anyone else. My sponsor called a day or two later asking how I was doing. I told her my tale of woe, and she took it in stride, encouraging me to think of a few more possible friends. But hurry, she counseled. I can't send in your order until I've got those dates written down!

Spurred on by her encouragement, I made another call, this time to my friend Mary Bromann, a member of our church choir. My husband had been the best man at their wedding. Guitar-playing Fr. Tom had left the priesthood to marry her. I hated to ask her a favor. I didn't want anyone to feel obliged to help me. I made the classic mistake of focusing on what I needed or feared, and not on how I could help others.

After getting the details of what would be involved, Mary happily said yes. Yippee! My first yes! Oh, boy! Oh, boy! With one under my belt, I screwed up my courage to ask another friend from the choir, Nancy Ristau, who also agreed to help me out.

"Oh, thank you, thank you!" was all I could say.

"Hey, it's okay," Nancy said. I could hear her grin over the phone. "Just tell me what I have to do."

Well, that was it. I'd reached the end of my list of friends, at least, those from whom I felt comfortable asking a favor. I didn't believe I knew anyone else well enough to ask. I know, I know. Some might call me a wimp. I felt a bit insecure back then and not altogether sure of my acceptance socially. I figured my closest neighbors would come to my first demonstration at my home, and if they liked what they saw, they'd schedule one. I committed to enough dates and got started.

My first demonstration went smoothly, although I was scared to death. Nervous energy caused my legs to shake like crazy even though I knew all the neighbors were there to support me. I sold around two hundred dollars that night and experienced a profound sigh of relief when the door closed after the last guest, knowing I'd gotten through without making a complete idiot of myself. The next demonstrations brought new things to worry about since I had to travel to other people's home. My easygoing friends, Mary and Nancy, proved extremely helpful and encouraging. Without their yeses, I would probably never have ventured down this path that has been so rich for me in so many ways.

After that, my business, such as it was, came to a dead end. My skill at building future business and customers was undeveloped. My sponsor gave me a lead for a Home & Gift Show in Itasca, Illinois, that cost twenty-five dollars for a booth. The event created a temporary "vendor mall" where various direct selling representatives gathered in one place for the public to shop. This event generated several new leads. By attending my friend Chris' Holiday Brunch, I garnered another lead from Eugenia Calleson when I dropped the words "my business" into the conversation.

"Oh? What business do you do?"

I was getting the hang of how to market my business. At Eugenia's, I experienced my first discussion with someone interested in direct sales. It was my third month in the business.

Before I left for Eugenia's, my family prayed at the dinner table, as we always do, the traditional Catholic prayer before meals: Bless us, O Lord, and these thy gifts which we are about to receive from Thy bounty, through Christ, our Lord. Amen. After that, we added personal prayers out loud, starting with the youngest at the table and ending with my husband. The little ones put in requests for Nintendo and Barbie houses since Christmas was near. I prayed to make lots of money that night. My husband, for the only time I can remember, corrected my prayer. He prayed, "That Mommy gets there safe and sound and has a good time."

As prayers often do, this one hung with me throughout the forty-five-minute drive to LaGrange Park. *What could I do to have fun that night?* I pondered as I drove. Getting out of the house for some alone time without the children had been one of my goals for this new business. Having fun was something Joe kept hoping for me. I still maintained too intense an approach to most things. How could I have a good time at this demonstration? Each audience is unique. Some are quite lively and thoroughly enjoyable; others sit unmoved by attempts at humor, exhibiting doleful politeness. I tried to picture the latter group and what I could do that would be enjoyable for myself. Nothing came to mind.

As I worked that night, I mentally loosened the perfect professional image I thought necessary for people to place their trust in me. I admitted to a few personal boo-boos. Heads nodded as others could relate to similar experiences. *Oh! So I'm not the only one ...* That response encouraged me to air other stories to the delight of future attendees. I gained confidence in sharing my blunders as well as offering free consultations.

When my presentation ended that night, I took my briefcase and moved to the dining room around the corner to take orders. I sat alone for the longest time in that dining room, feeling a little silly all by myself, drumming my fingers. It was only my fifth presentation, and I had yet to learn the art of schmoozing with guests, so I waited uncomfortably, untrained to do anything else while guests decided what they would order. A customer came around the corner, and I sighed knowing that I could finally begin to write up an order. Only she wasn't ordering. Not just yet. She was curious about a few things.

"I think I'd like to know a little more about this business," she stated matter-of-factly, and the pummeling of questions characteristic of her inquisitive nature began. I was unprepared to answer some of them, for I received no training on how to share the business back then. I handed her a little brochure and hoped that would suffice. My mother left a little pink booklet about the facts of life under my pillow when I was a young teen. I followed the same passive "read this and I'll check back to see if you have any questions" approach. We eventually got to her order. More questions would follow in the days ahead. Soon satisfied that the company was stable and fit her lifestyle, she became the first member of my team in January 1988. She brought a whole new dimension to my business, starting me on the path to leadership which arrived five months later.

This new path was unmapped and bumpy with lessons, obstacles, and detours. And one major setback.

CHAPTER 8

THE VOICE:
THE BEGINNING OF
COLLOQUY

*I tell Him in every way possible (using the words that come to me
most spontaneously) that I love Him, that I want to love Him,
that I want to advance in His holy love, and that I wish to prove
my love for Him by my actions, by doing His holy will.*
—Teresian method of colloquy[15]

OUR PARISH IN River Forest offered a variety of educational
opportunities that I took part in whenever I could get a babysitter. I
loved to expand my knowledge about my faith and learn more about
God. Being a musician, I prioritized concerts or liturgical events where
music was the focus.

One Lent, our parish had invited Sr. Kathy Sherman, a musician
and songwriter with the Sisters of St. Joseph, to provide a morning of
musical reflection. Without knowing much about her, I made up my
mind to go. The smell of ripe bananas in my fruit basket enticed me to
make a loaf of banana bread for this little gathering. The recipe page for
this bread looks like a well-loved teddy bear, its edges a little worse for
the wear, the page separated from the binding of the cookbook. Multiple
grease spots and unidentifiable food droppings decorate its borders.

As I stood at the counter mixing the ingredients and looking out the window at the sunny but cold March day, I heard a voice inside my head say, "Give her a hug." I'd been thinking about Sr. Sherman and wondering about the kind of music she'd be singing. Assuming I was talking to myself, my response to this inner dialogue went something like this: *I can't just go up to a person I don't even know and give her a hug. Who would I say told me to do so?*

"Tell her 'I AM.'"

Now, I'd been studying the Old Testament in Bible Study Fellowship class, and we'd just discussed the very chapter where God identifies Himself to Moses as "I am Who am." I dismissed this whole internal conversation as my way of processing what I had been studying. I refocused my attention on the banana bread.

"Give her a hug."

Oh, for crying out loud, I thought. *Will you stop already?*

A part of me began to ask myself just to whom was I talking? *This isn't your own thinking, Chris,* my inner wisdom cautioned. *But this can't be Who I think it is. It sounds too much like my voice, not someone else's.* I tried to shake off this uncomfortable train of thought.

I can't go up to an unknown nun and give her a hug, I protested in my inner dialogue. *Any reasonable person can see that.* Silence was the only response. The echo of "tell her 'I AM'" lingered in my memory. I didn't exactly know what to do with it. I shook it off again and dismissed it. Foolish daydreaming!

I finished baking the bread, wrapped it still warm in aluminum foil, grabbed some napkins and a knife, and rushed out of the house in my usual lateness. The concert took place in the Fr. Fahey chapel with chairs arranged in a circle near the altar. No refreshment table had been set up, so I sat with the warm bread on my lap. Eventually, I decided I'd have to cut it in my lap and pass it around to the dozen women present. I felt a little bit of a goof, but that's never stopped me before.

Sister Sherman sang some of her songs lovingly to us in her soft voice, and I closed my eyes to listen. My heart received them, made them my own, and sent them straight to our Lord in little valentines of love.

Sunlight streamed through the bright red and blue hues of the stained glass windows that grace the long, majestic walls of St. Luke

Church. My spirit drank in the peaceful moment, whispering silent Thank Yous to God.

Sister Kathy's next words pierced the tranquility of the morning. She told us she wanted to play a new song she'd just written. "I haven't recorded it yet and hope you will like it. It's called, 'I Am.'"

She began strumming the guitar and singing her new song, but I heard only the name of the song, "I Am," reverberating words from earlier that morning, with the instruction to give her a hug. My heart quickened. My stomach tightened. The familiar "you screwed up" feeling drew a shallow breath. Such a simple thing I'd been asked to do, and I had ignored it. In truth, I had refused to do it. I suddenly realized with absolute certainty and shame, the Lord's voice had spoken to me that morning. I hadn't recognized it like Samuel in his sleepiness. I wrestled with Him as Jacob had wrestled with the angel. I balked just as aging Sarah did when she heard she'd conceive a child, and I ignored the first direct command He'd ever given me of which I was aware.

Oh, what a fool I was! I tried hard to focus on her song and listen to its words, but all I wanted was the song to end so I could give her this silly little hug God apparently wanted her to get. My first test of doing the will of God and I had failed. Perhaps she'd prayed for confirmation from God that this song was acceptable. Who knew why this hug was important, but I sure went right up to her when she finished and explained that God asked me to give her a hug, which I quickly delivered. I refused to focus on what any of the other women thought about my breaking the circle and interrupting the lovely meditative moment. I retook my seat self-consciously and tried to calm myself by focusing on my breathing. To this day, I don't remember anything else about that morning.

By the time I got home after that concert, I was physically shaking from the realization that God had spoken to me. I replayed over and over again the short "conversation." I continued to be astounded that the "voice" I'd heard sounded so much like my own and not that of the image of God projected in films, the booming male voice we hear when "God" speaks. That's when a little light bulb went off. God lives within me. I had received the Holy Spirit in baptism and confirmation. I receive the Body and Blood of Jesus Christ regularly throughout the week in the sacrament of the Eucharist. He is in me. The whole Trinity is.

And if He's in me, He's probably going to sound like me, not Charlton Heston in "The Ten Commandments."

I felt terrible that I didn't know Him when He spoke to me. I hoped that if there ever were a next time, I wouldn't be as argumentative as my Irish nature is wont to be. I feared there wouldn't be a next time since I'd bombed so terribly on this first one.

The story of Samuel in the Bible soothed me, as I remembered that he, too, didn't recognize the Lord calling him in the middle of the night. "Samuel, Samuel," God called to him. Not knowing the voice, little Samuel got up from his bed and went to Eli, his instructor to whom Hannah, his mother, had entrusted his upbringing out of her gratitude to God for the gift of her son. God must be used to the fact that He's got to repeat His messages several times to us humans since we don't seem to be able to perceive Him at first. He had to call Samuel three different times that night before Eli came to understand that it was God calling Samuel in his sleep, so he instructed Samuel to say, "Speak Lord, your servant is listening," the next time he was awakened by the Voice calling his name. Samuel got to know the Lord intimately from that point onward, and I suspect he enjoyed many colloquies[16] with Him throughout his life.

I didn't get much work done the rest of that day. God's direct contact with me shook me to the core. I felt as though I was in a mild shock. Yes, I'd sung and prayed for years that God would use me for whatever purpose He needed. I didn't expect to be aware of it if it happened or that He would speak from inside me. He didn't talk to me three times the way he called to Eli in the night. I wasn't sure He'd ever talk to me again after not recognizing His voice. I'd soon find out.

This "transcendent experience of God breaking into ordinary consciousness" is the practice of colloquy of Gabrielle Bossis, Sister Meg Funk writes in *Tools Matter*. I had no exposure to this practice of intimate exchanges in the heart. After reading Bossis' *He and I*, it encouraged and solidified my practice of it.

"The first moment is an event that happens to many of us," explains Sister Meg Funk, who also practices colloquy. "We awaken to the real presence of Jesus. Then we participate in that presence by sharing our thoughts with him. We listen 'as if' we hear him, 'as if' through our imagination comes a 'voice.' At that moment we don't consider ourselves in a 'for-real' conversation. But we are in a 'for-real' practice of faith.

"The practice of colloquy is to shift the 'I-thoughts' to thoughts of sharing 'in faith' with Jesus. Self-talk, at first, might seem like auto-suggestion, but as we see it unfolding in *He and I*, it becomes communion. Our prayer becomes a sharing of all our waking thoughts"[17] in the presence of Jesus.

This practice didn't develop overnight. Gradually, I accepted the shocking fact that this inner voice answering me from time to time was not my manifestation, but God's. It was difficult to believe. I had to do some soul searching about why I felt this couldn't be happening. What I believed was what the church and the Bible taught. Was I, for example, willing to believe Jesus Who said, "Anyone who loves me will obey my teaching. My Father will love them, and we will come to them and make our home with them" (John 14:23 NIV). Well … I *did* believe that the Holy Spirit came over me in Baptism with a further dose in Confirmation and that I receive the true, real Presence of the Body and Blood of Jesus Christ in Holy Communion. I believe in the Holy Trinity. So if I accept these "gifts" of God's very presence, grace, and Spirit in my body and soul, why then, would it be so unbelievable that God would speak quietly to me the way one would a child when he needs a little help?

I prayed with fervent hope that I could someday achieve what Cardinal John Newman prayed, that when people looked at me, they would see God's face; when they heard me, God's words would be sensed; and when they felt my touch, they would sense God's caress instead. It had begun, it seemed. Twenty years later, it would manifest in another hug just as eye opening. But I get ahead of myself.

Cardinal Newman Prayer

Dear Lord, help me to spread Your fragrance everywhere I go.

Flood my soul with Your spirit and life.
Penetrate and possess my whole being so utterly,
That my life may only be a radiance of Yours.
Shine through me, and be so in me
That every soul I come in contact with
May feel Your presence in my soul.
Let them look up and see no longer me, but only You, O Lord!
Stay with me and then I shall begin to shine as You do,
So to shine as to be a light to others;
The light, O Lord, will be all from You; none of it will be mine;
It will be You shining on others through me.
Let me thus praise You the way You love best, by shining on those around me.
Let me preach You without preaching, not by words but by my example,
By the catching force of the sympathetic influence of what I do,
The evident fullness of the love my heart bears to You.
Amen.

I was afraid of what the next task might be if He gave me one. Obviously, I had trouble with something as simple as a hug. But it seemed to me most things Jesus asks of us are simple tasks: to visit someone who's sick, to give someone a sip of water or compliment, to take clothes from our closets and give them to the poor.

I began to feel shame at my lofty "do-good" thoughts on Sunday and my subsequent selfish behavior during the week. The buildup of grace was giving my soul better vision and what I saw in my daily actions disturbed my heart. I felt similar shame years later when our community, a very well-to-do neighborhood, expressed resistance to local Grace Lutheran Church who desired to open its doors once a week to shelter the homeless.

"The Son of Man has nowhere to lay His head," Jesus told His apostles in Luke 9:58. One of the most fervent prayers John recorded is: "May they all be one, Father, as I am in You and You are in Me" John 17:21. Surely, we could allow those who find themselves homeless to rest for a night on the floor of one of our churches? This was a no-brainer for faith-filled people. I attended a town hall meeting on this topic and was immediately relieved and excited to see so many of my fellow parishioners at the meeting.

The Village's Board of Trustees was about to hear how many of us want to live out our faith as in Matthew 25, I thought. I sat near Pastor Leuking of Grace Lutheran and glowed at the prospect of all that I was about to hear.

As expected, some people expressed concerns at the prospect of homeless individuals entering our safe and secure neighborhood. I was unprepared for them to be the same parishioners with whom I shared a pew each Sunday. The shock of their harsh words about "those people" may have erased the last remnant of my naiveté about the goodness of Christians. I felt sorry for the homeless who found no room at the inn in our non-welcoming community. I prayed for the opponents of this opportunity to hear the soft voice of God in their hard hearts. I did not judge them, however, for who was I to do so, one who had such a hard time giving a nun a simple hug?

I heard a story many years ago at a Bible Study Fellowship lecture in Oak Park, of a traveling couple tired and weary after a long day. They checked in for the night at a hotel. Exhausted, they immediately fell into bed and a deep sleep. The next morning the wife, being an early riser, got dressed and quietly let herself out of the room in search of a cup of coffee. She made her way down to the lobby, fixed two cups, and upon arriving back on her floor, realized she did not have her key, nor did she remember her room number.

She walked down the hall about the distance she thought she needed, but to no avail. Each door looked the same. She had no idea how to find the one that led to her husband. Baffled and lost in the hallway, holding two hot cups of coffee, she wondered what she could do. She paused and stood still in the silence of that empty hall. No sound came from any room. Suddenly, she heard a cough. She knew that cough. And immediately, she found her room.

When I heard that story, I wanted to have such knowledge of God, such a close relationship with Him, that when He "coughed" or asked for a hug or any other innocuous request, I'd know His voice without a doubt, His sign to me that He wanted my service. Just as married couples learn one another's quirks and preferences over time, accept them lovingly, and often joke about them, my desire to know God more intimately would take years and years. I was ready for that committed relationship. I did not want to suffer the embarrassment of not recognizing God speaking to me again if He ever chose to do so.

Because of thoughts and desires like these, I paid more attention to what makes a relationship intimate. Through reading, Bible study, homilies, and prayer services, I realized I talked too much to God and did not listen nearly enough. I didn't have a clue what it was like to listen to Him other than at Mass or while reading the Bible. Thus began my contemplative prayer life. I learned to be alert and pay attention to God's presence within and outside of me, observing and receiving in silence the loving presence of God, possessing Him in love "whom no one can possess through knowledge."[18]

CHAPTER 9

THE PRISON

I will turn the darkness into light before them
and make the rough places smooth.

—Isaiah 42:16

MESSAGES RISE FROM our subconscious on a continuous basis. We sense the need for food, drink, exercise, or rest. Similarly, the Holy Spirit sends the soul messages for specific actions or works of mercy He desires. I don't always act on such promptings. I think only saints do. Most of us barely notice them, like birds in the sky or white noise in a room. It took years and years of training myself to listen and obey Jesus' Spirit nudging me. First, I had to recognize the nudges for what they were; then, I had to get past kicking myself after the fact, hearing myself say too late, "I know I should have listened to my instincts." I called everything an instinct before I recognized the holy nudges. I usually waited, unsure. The nudges often directed an uncomfortable action on my part. I seemed always late in getting to the table after He had rung the dinner bell. I take small solace in the fact that even Jesus' disciples didn't recognize Him walking with them to Emmaus.

When I bake yeast bread, I knead the dough for eight to ten minutes. It evenly distributes the ingredients, develops the gluten, and begins the fermentation process so the yeast can start doing its work. It takes time to stretch gluten, to become malleable enough to bake into a beautiful loaf of bread. God's graces ferment in us like yeast.

"The work of our interior life is discernment. We discern our thoughts. These thoughts rise first as an inclination and then as an image with a story connecting the inclination to our feelings or desires. Next comes an invitation to act on the desire. This act, at first, is a single moment of enjoyment but can become a habit with repeated fulfillment of the desire, whether in mind or physically in behavior. If this habit is done for some time and affirmed by the intellect, this can soon become stitched together with our innermost identity. The reason thoughts matter so much is that this rising of a thought is where we can discern where, what, who, and how God is acting in our lives." (Meg Funk, *Discernment Matters*)

We read Scripture passages repeatedly and hear the same readings every three years at Catholic Masses. Often, a particular word or phrase seems to jump out at me. When I do the practice of lectio divina, I stop at such a moment, for that is what I'm looking for: the Living Word reaching out to me.

While growing up, I had interests in many things. Prisons weren't one of them. One day in my thirties, as I read Matthew's 25th chapter on the separation of the sheep and goats, I heard the part of releasing prisoners differently. I noted it and nothing more, having no idea what one could do to release prisoners. Eventually, I joined Amnesty International as a supporter, sending small amounts of financial support and occasional letters to and on behalf of prisoners.

Sometime later, I noticed a magazine advertisement for PVS, Prisoner Visitation & Support. Quakers started this organization when some of their members were incarcerated as conscientious objectors during the Vietnam War. I sat with the little ad clipped to a notepad for a while, discerning if this was what God wanted me to pursue. When I sensed the pulse of grace, I responded by sending a request to become a volunteer. Fully expecting to receive a resounding and exuberant response, suspecting that volunteers to this ministry were few and far between, I learned my first lesson in this ministry: waiting.

Eventually, someone contacted me and informed that I would be interviewed to see if I was a suitable candidate. Lesson #2: It can be as difficult to get into prison as to get out.

Jeannie Graves arrived at my home for what I assumed would be a cursory interview. An attractive, middle-aged blonde with a petite, trim body, Jean carried a cane that she didn't seem to need when she walked in. We had similar styles of communicating: direct and to the point. Her eyes felt like an airport's control tower, always scanning my face above a smile. Warm and open in her conversation, laughing easily, Jean focused on her task: to assess if I had what it takes to qualify as a visitor to all manner of humankind in a hostile environment with strict security measures and without an agenda. We sat at the oak kitchen table in my home for what became the most intensive interrogation I'd ever experienced. We did not move from it for two, maybe three hours. Jeannie introduced me to the prison system as another country with a language and culture unique to itself. I mostly sat in awe of her vast knowledge of this world of which I knew nothing.

Meeting her intensity with some of my own, we discovered matching passions and strengths in each other. This ministry was no easy volunteer job. When she had satisfied herself with enough probing questions to appease the CIA, I watched in silent admiration as she walked stiffly with her cane out my front door. What had I gotten myself into?

Weeks later, I received a letter approving me as a PVS volunteer plebe and began the process of getting a security clearance, fingerprints checked, and instructions for prison visitation protocol. These security measures took several months. A few male PVS volunteers took me under their wing and prepared me as best they could for my first visit with tips, stories, and warnings of the need for patience.

From my lectio[19] journal, Feb. 4, 1998:

"Fear is useless; what is needed is trust."

These words of Jesus stood out from the Gospel reading yesterday and are still with me.

I trust. So I say. Then why do I fear the unknown? Why do I fear a new twist in my life? Why do I fear my first visit to prison today?

Poor Peter, I used to think. Such wavering faith that he sinks in the water after being enabled to walk on it. Poor me, for thinking I was any better than Peter.

Trust shall be my active word this week.[20]

Hearing the metal-on-metal bang-echo-echo as prison bars slammed into each other took some adjustment. The sound resonated off the stone walls and floors. I signed in at the front desk as a visitor, receiving a key to store my coat, purse, liquids, and keys in a storage locker in clear sight of the security officer and cameras. Driver's licenses got swapped for an ID badge worn prominently; especially important should a lockdown occur during a visit.

"Take a seat. He'll be down shortly."

Getting into prison tested my ability to wait. We sat on plastic chairs facing the security desk where we watched the officers check in attorneys and visitors until the chaplain came down from his office.

The Metropolitan Correctional Center (MCC) is in downtown Chicago. At the time I was a visitor, the prison chaplain escorted all PVS visitors to the visiting room. Each month he called or emailed our coordinator when prisoners requested one of our volunteers. Only a few did although a significant percentage of inmates at MCC came from foreign lands and had no one in this country to visit them.

The seemingly simple task of scheduling an appointment time for us to come in required coordination with our calendars, the prison and chaplain's calendars, prisoner court times and legal visits. The Bureau of Prisons stipulated the dress code for our visits dictated by safety concerns and common sense. Modesty in clothing showed basic human respect; baggy clothes were discouraged because of contraband concerns.

The chaplain eventually came down and greeted us. When the elevator doors behind the security desk opened, we'd watch him emerge from the inner world of the prison. He had to wait at the gate until the officer opened it so he could greet us in the waiting area. If the officers were signing in other visitors or vendors, he waited. Clang! The gate finally closed behind him. He then stood completely enclosed by bars in a space that held approximately a dozen people in close quarters. Clang! The second gate clicked opened to release him into the waiting room area. A jarring bang of iron bars-on-bars preceded his greeting as the gate closed behind him. Clang! I clenched my teeth and worked to calm my gut. I do not like loud noises.

Protocol required he sign the guest book acknowledging the time he escorted us into the prison. He gave us a nod to follow him.

As a PVS visitor at MCC, I could bring a Bible, a notepad, and pen into the prison. I submitted a report to PVS headquarters after each visit, documenting who I visited and general observations. Before allowing us entry, an officer ran our personal articles through a scanner inspecting for contraband. If other visitors stood in line to enter, we waited in the transition area until the officer signaled the gate to close. The slamming metal sound resonated with greater impact on my ears and body at this closer proximity. Suddenly, my freedom ended. Metal bars surrounded me on all sides. An officer I did not know and who did not know me controlled my mobility. I looked at the chaplain, and he nodded assurance with a small smile.

Turning our backs to the gate after it closed, we faced the gate into the prison, waiting like corralled cattle until it opened. We walked to the elevator and watched the chaplain push the call button. Clang! The gate behind us announced its closure with the subtlety of a sledgehammer. We were inside.

Exiting the elevator on the visiting floor, we walked down a monotone hallway. No one spoke. If they did, the conversation sounded like Morse code: a question, a few words; a one-word reply.

In the visiting room, the chaplain signed us in at the officer's desk and told us who our first prisoners would be. He departed to resume his work. We waited on plastic chairs in this room of concrete blocks covered in institutional bland paint lit with fluorescent lighting. The room held seating for around thirty people, and I observed a few prisoners in orange jumpsuits already in conversation with what I assumed were family members. Security cameras watched us from the corners of the room as did the officer at a desk.

I looked at the three names on my list of prisoners I'd be seeing. I received only one request for a visit from a female prisoner. She told me each female is strip searched before and after a visit. If they were having their period, the officer would toss them a sanitary pad. I understood when she did not request a second visit. Ultimately over time, I gained permission to go to the female floor to make it easier for them for a visit. I saw some women ironing their orange jumpsuits to look presentable when their family came. They primped as they did "outside."

Conversations are privileged. They often start with curiosity about the weather. Some ask if I could get a message outside to family members. The answer is no. Period.

Often a prisoner would share medical or court challenges. We listened. The world of a prison is like another country. Our training taught us to understand, speak, and act in ways that prevented problems for prisoners after we left. Different interpretations of our actions could look like favoritism toward a particular prisoner. That could cause problems.

The chaplain returned to escort us back down after a prescribed time. If something delayed him, we waited. I always felt relief in leaving.

You don't get out of prison until you put in your time as a volunteer, prison employee, or prisoner in the system. You don't get a relationship or an inner life of peace with God without putting in your time as well. As I drove home along the Eisenhower Expressway after my first prison visit, I felt an incredible sense of appreciation for my freedom. I push a lot of limits; the speed limit is no exception. This time, I kept the speedometer to 55 mph. Most of the way.

Fear is useless, what is needed is trust. Trust was my active word this week. I leaned into it in the prison, but that wasn't where He was most interested in working on me. I didn't hear Jesus whispering: "Resistance is useless, what is needed is trust." So after a while, He initiated a little conversation.

CHAPTER 10

THE DOOR

Courage is not the absence of fear, but rather the judgment
that something else is more important than fear.
—Ambrose Redmoon

WATER REMINDS ME to be ever fluid in my interaction with God and His creation. If you've ever swum below the surface, you know that as water gets deep, the sunlight's penetration ends and darkness prevails. You need a light to feel safe.

There are times in one's life, however, when you cannot escape the darkness, not for a while at any rate. You must endure it. You learn to find your way in the darkness with other senses. It develops humility. I certainly don't like asking for help, or surrendering until I break free into the light once again. One of my hardest lessons involved disciplining my will to let go of an attitude or self-serving approach.

Darkness shows up in many ways. My persistence in getting others to see things my way may have darkened Christ's light in my life. Joe used to say to me, "It must be nice to be right all the time." I dismissed his not-so-subtle pushback and gentle teaching, feeling glad he saw things my way.

Fear is a dark obstacle on any path. In the early days of my home-based business, it prevented me from inviting people to join my team. I was afraid I'd displease them by appearing as the perennial "pushy salesman" and they wouldn't like me (if they even liked me to begin with). In my spiritual path, it kept me from intimacy with God.

What was there to be afraid of? Why would I hesitate to get closer to God who loves me with an unfathomable love? Well, plenty of reasons. He can do anything. So there's a little fear of that power. Next, He could ask something I don't want to do. Think of arrogant Saint Paul unable to see for days. He'd been living in darkness. After Jesus spoke to him, he couldn't see because of the light. Boy, can I relate to him being full of himself, stuck in self-righteousness. And proud of his work, so sure it was the right thing to do, getting rid of those terrifying Christians. I didn't want that kind of an experience.

With all the gifts and talents God gave me, I feared He would ask something huge in return. How do you say "No, thank You" to the Creator of the universe? You get knocked down with a blinding light (that wasn't the first time God tried to talk to Saul, now, was it?); you receive an offer you can't refuse. So the way I figured it, by avoiding close contact with Him, He wouldn't have the opportunity to ask, and I wouldn't have to decide how to answer, or face the consequences if I tried to turn Him down. I had it all figured out.

> *Divine revelation cannot be discovered in the same way as the beauty of a work of art or the genius of a man are discovered ... It is the opening of a door that can only be unlocked from the inside.*
> —Karl Barth, Christmas sermon, 1931

I'd known for a long time that the ache in my soul was for God and God alone. Nothing else would assuage it. I felt like James Earl Jones in the movie *Field of Dreams* as he responded to the invitation to follow the baseball players into the cornfield. He walked right up to the cornstalks and stood there, hesitantly, looking into the dense growth of seven-foot-high plants, trying to see where the others had gone. He reached his hand in gingerly and pulled it back quickly, afraid of what might happen to it. Reaching in again, he held it in place, and then pulled it back slowly. Nothing happened to it. He was still fine. Then, with one look back at his friends, with a huge grin on his face and the last chuckle of delighted surrender, he stepped in. And disappeared.

> *Do the thing you fear to do and that's the death of fear.*
> —Mary Kay Slowkowski

I remember a time when I was deep in prayer, wordlessly sitting with God. I felt drawn down a long hallway. I followed the urge and found myself wandering toward a door at the end of the hall. As I approached the door with a bit of hesitation, I slowed and began to wonder what was beyond that door. Cautiously, I opened it. It swung out into black space. Nothingness. I wanted to withdraw, pull back, but something—I barely recognized God's movements in my life at this point—something kept me there, encouraging me to keep coming, to step forward.

Oh, I don't think so! I thought aloud to this Encouragement. *If I take a step, I'm going to fall!* I didn't like this version of the "Knock, and it shall be opened unto you."

"Do you think I would not catch you?" asked the Invitation to the dark unknown.

"Well ..."

"Do you trust Me?"

"Yes, most of the time ..."

"Then come. Take a step."

"Nooooo, I don't think so." Fear gripped me. There was nothing, nothing beyond the threshold of this door. Black space. Nada. Nothingness confronted me.

I was on sure footing as long as I stood there. If I took one step out into the nothingness, I knew beyond any doubt that I would fall. And the fall was the only thing on my mind.

I shook my head like a little girl afraid to jump into the water with her Daddy standing waist deep, arms outstretched to her, beckoning, beckoning.

"Just one step ..." came the whisper.

"I want to, but ..."

"Just one step. I'll catch you."

I froze in this doorway. Time suspended itself. There was no hurry. The door remained open, and Nothingness waited beyond it. I wasn't willing to step out to where nothing supported me under foot. Reason and will battled in my head.

I wavered. I moved to take a step back. Maybe another day ...

"I will not let you fall. I will catch you. Do you trust Me?" the One Who loved me asked.

Oh, there's the catch, I thought. *He's got me on this one. The fundamental question.*

"Yes, You know I trust You." *I just haven't had to trust You this much before!*

He said nothing more. If I trusted Him, then proof required stepping out into nothingness, knowing beyond a doubt that not only would I fall, but that I would be caught. That I would experience no harm. *I do trust Him,* I rationalized to myself. *This is just so scary.* This had to be a dream. I couldn't move.

"Please come." I don't think I heard this so much as felt it. His heart was speaking to mine. I knew His desire. He wanted me to step outward into nothing and trust Him. It was a free decision. I did not feel pressure to take any action whatsoever. I felt His longing, His desire for me to enter the nothingness, to enter Him. To take that one step out in faith. To show by my actions that my trust in Him was complete.

"Come and see."[21]

"Okay," I consented. I knew I had to do this. My feet shuffled in that doorway, waffling forward, then pulling back, forward, then back. A part of me knew way down in my subconscious that I was going to step out. My dilemma was getting past the fear of doing so.

I released my desire to be in control with solid ground beneath my feet. My wish to please Him overcame my fear. I stepped out.

Into nothing. The sensation felt similar to a sudden dip in an amusement park ride: a sense of falling; stomach queasiness; a closed throat as the queasiness rises; heady lightness and expansiveness. The stomach tightens in anticipation of the landing.

Only I wasn't falling.

Soft as a feather, I found myself floating, not falling. Peace surrounded me. With exquisite tenderness that comes from a Love I can't even begin to approach with words, I felt supported from underneath as if on a cloud of angel wings. Nothing touched me, yet something held every part of me in some way in ultimate security and safeness. Every limb, my back, my neck, my head, all were suspended in space without any sense of gravity. I felt weightless and caressed as a baby in this new place, this supernatural lesson in trust by a patient, encouraging Father. "See, I've gotcha! You were a good girl to trust Me. You have nothing to fear."

> *What I need is this élan of surrender; you must go out of the door*
> *of yourself to enter into Me.[22]*
> —Jesus speaking to actress Gabrielle Bossis, *He and I*

Although more than a decade has passed since this act of surrender, I still sobbed as I wrote this. A deep feeling of unworthiness for the warm bath of Love I received lingered in my heart until He Who Loves Me removed it.

CHAPTER 11

THE FOUNDATION OF TRUST

What I say to you in the dark, tell in the daylight;
what you hear in whispers, proclaim from the housetops.
— Matthew 10:27

WHEN THE DISK arrived in the mail, I avoided it. Silly, I know. Whether it was a generalized fear of all things technical or an unrecognized prescient sense of foreboding, I couldn't tell. I didn't care. I wouldn't touch it. I'd agreed to receive it because my beloved father wanted me to try something. I slid the disk to the far reaches of my desk in a passive attempt to delay the inevitable. Facing my fears is something I have disciplined myself to do. I took the strongest action I could at the time. I stalled.

I bought my first computer in 1991, two years after Fr. Thomas Keating and founding members of Contemplative Outreach met at Our Lady of Grace Benedictine Monastery in Beech Grove, Indiana. They discussed plans there to introduce Centering Prayer to the world. I knew nothing of this at the time. I was about to encounter one of Keating's contemplative associates on an Internet bulletin board and would visit that monastery a decade later where ghosts and a stinging confrontation awaited me. At this point in my life, I didn't even know there were bulletin boards in cyberspace. I still struggled with how to touch my computer and not feel as though I were doing something wrong. One wrong key and I feared I'd wipe everything out. Email and cyberspace were unknowns to me.

It's hard to imagine living without email now, just as it is hard to imagine life without television, phones, and electricity. In the early 1990s, I waited for mail every day and relied on long distance phone calls to stay in touch with out-of-state friends, relatives, and my sales force. My father, Don Sauter, an electrical engineering professor at the University of Pittsburgh and Division Manager for Westinghouse, broached the subject of email with me.

"I would like you to try it."

The request was straightforward, the way he approached most things. Direct. Efficient. No mincing of words. Effective use of time and energy. Talking to each of his six children one at a time finally had an alternative. He no longer had to call each of us to relay either personal or family news. With one email, he could deliver a message to all his children at once, something we take for granted today. His challenge invited me into his world of electronics. My heart raced. I trusted my father; I just didn't trust myself with computers. Too many buttons. Too many ways to screw up.

As Dad explained electronic mail in his usual organized approach, I heard the logic of using this method of communication. One email note sure beat six phone calls. I remembered the days my mother would type us letters on her Underwood typewriter when we were in college. We'd open our mail and find yellow carbon copies. "Dear Christine, Michael, Jean-Marie, David" they'd start, with a litany of misdeeds and mishaps that had occurred on the home front with the two little ones, Richard and Kevin. I remembered, too, how it felt when everyone else had heard some new detail of our family life, and I hadn't. "Oh, didn't I tell you?" would come the reply. "It's so hard to keep track ..." my mother's voice would trail off as another interruption broke our conversation. Life was always busy in our household.

"It's a very simple procedure," my father continued in his usual teaching mode. I tried to stay focused while he inserted the disk into the computer's hard drive, but a litany of computerese followed. My mind balked as my stomach tightened. My friend, Mary Bromann, had brought me up to speed on how to turn a computer on and off and open a few documents. I was competent at that. Adventuring farther into the complex world of the computer, let alone the Internet, seemed like an invitation to walk on hot coals. I feared becoming one of the lost boys of Neverland if I ventured into the vast universe of the Internet. I get easily distracted as it is. Would I ever find my way home?

Counterbalancing my fear was a solid-as-a-rock trust of my father. Both of my parents were highly intelligent, well-read, generous, and loving. Their moderate risk tolerance equaled their adventuresome approach to learning. They always looked for ways to encourage and support us in following our dreams. Dad, I would learn much later, had purchased some of the first computers and introduced them to his peers at Westinghouse. These early machines had memories of only 300 megabytes, but he foresaw their potential. I, on the other hand, didn't enter the computer world until I bought my first Mac at the age of thirty-seven.

That enduring trust, which had never failed me, fueled my agreement to try this email thing, but only if Dad put the disk into the computer and did whatever needed to be done to get it all started. I was too afraid of doing something wrong and bollixing it up. It was months before his travels brought him to our home in Chicago where that disk sat waiting for him. Dad popped the disk into my computer and walked me through the various start-up questions, all foreign to me. I felt relieved he would show me the way. But way too soon, he said: "Okay, you're all set up. Now go explore." And he walked away, as was his custom when it was time for us to discover a new part of life he had carefully carved out for us to experience. God has a similar pattern of teaching His people.

After Dad went back home to Sun City West, Arizona, I timidly turned on the computer and opened up Prodigy. I started pushing different categories, buttons—I didn't know what I was doing—and found plenty of places to lose hours of my time. I turned the computer off, grateful I hadn't screwed anything up or imploded the thing on my first try. Overwhelmed by the endlessness of the Internet, I realized I needed some focus to explore it. I grew up with television channel dials physically attached to the TV that required us to get up from our chair, walk to the television set, and turn them to the three or four channels from which to choose. I needed to reduce the options the Internet provided.

I found my way to the Prodigy Religious Concourse, which had two bulletin boards. The topics of one held little interest, like crystals and witchcraft. I clicked on the other topic. It contained Judeo-Christian subjects with which I was more comfortable. I eventually found a Catholic board with headings like "Ask a Deacon," "Ask a Priest," "Death and Resurrection," "Communion in hand – No!" Twenty to thirty different topics were listed. I read through most of them, some having only a few notes posted on the subject, others evidently established for a length of time. *Who are all these people?* I wondered. Ah, there's the rub. You don't know. All you see is a name. It could be anyone. You don't know whether they're liberal, conservative, fallen away or cafeteria Catholics. It was challenging to read their commentaries without knowing anything about them or how they had formulated their opinions.

Reading the bulletin boards relieved my isolation from being a stay-at-home-mom. It was like getting personal mail. It would take a day or more before anyone responded.

I clicked on Ask a Deacon once and read a string of questions about the Our Father. One man wrote he had to preach about it in the upcoming weekend. He posed a simple question about the phrase "Thy kingdom come" and I typed in a quick response spontaneously. The answer seemed obvious to me at the time so what the heck, I decided to share my two cents' worth. He replied the next day.

We had a few short exchanges; then he asked me if I was a priest. The question took me by surprise. He didn't know me as a woman because of my name. When I replied on the Ask a Deacon site, I guess he assumed that some of the writers were, indeed, deacons or priests. I wanted to say yes, that we are all called to be priests (see Hebrews 7:6; Psalm 109:4) to give honor and glory to God, but I replied I was a layperson. *Perhaps I better get out of this particular topic.* I clicked on "About Contemplation."

I had skipped this topic previously. It topped the list but sounded lame. I liked intrigue and challenge; doing the impossible appealed to me. I don't like sitting still too long. God gave me many talents, and I felt responsible for using them well and often. Contemplation sounded too sedentary.

When I began to read the discussions there, I grew very still inside. I think I stopped breathing a few times. These people were discussing the God I knew. Not in some high and mighty language, but in one that showed familiarity with a God Who was within.

Dr. Mercedes A. Scopetta created the "About Contemplation" topic in October of 1994. This compassionate Cuban-American, who read Thomas Merton as her Bible growing up (Castro banned Bibles), felt the Holy Spirit saying something like, "We must reach out to more people. We must teach this way of praying so I can reach into their hearts and bring my Kingdom to the world."

Mercedes was a member of the Executive Board of Contemplative Outreach at the time. Trappist monk Thomas Keating founded Contemplative Outreach[23] to teach centering prayer and create a spiritual network of individuals and small faith communities committed to living the contemplative dimension of the Gospel in everyday life. This prayer (also called The Prayer of Consent or third-eye praying) is considered a pure gift from God. Individuals pray it by consenting to be in God's presence without words, very different from the way I learned and memorized recited prayer. "It opens the mind and heart—our whole being—to God, the Ultimate Mystery, beyond thoughts, words, and emotions" (Thomas Keating), "in which the soul, purified by His infused love, suddenly and inexplicably experiences the presence of God within itself" (Thomas Merton).

"It is what leads you to a silence beyond thought and words," says St. John of the Cross[24] and what makes your prayer simple and brief. "It is what teaches you to forsake and repudiate all that is false in the world."[25] Mercedes told Fr. Keating of this new small community of contemplatives she'd begun on the Internet, and he gave his blessing.

I know God is everywhere. I just didn't think I'd find Him in cyberspace. High tech stuff existed for business, nerds, and scientists, my convoluted former thinking told me. I had viewed my computer as a business tool and separate from my spiritual life. I associated God more easily with nature, churches, or meaningful talks with friends.

"Surprise! I'm out here, too, and inside you," God seemed to say. "What part of 'I'm everywhere' do you not grasp?"

Two memories stand out about that first discovery of these souls in cyberspace who experienced God as I did. The first is a reference to OMOH in some entries. What could that be? OMOH ... Some mantra? It held the key to explaining many of the experiences I had during my prayer time, as well as the fruits of that prayer time. It gave me a name: a contemplative, a term with which I was only vaguely familiar.

The second significant moment in meeting this online community occurred after reading its postings for a day or two. I quietly typed a comment to introduce myself, feeling quite bold doing so. I still was not used to writing anything publicly about God. Mercedes, the founder of the group, remembers it differently.

"You didn't come into the group quietly, Chris," she chides me. "You wrote a quotation from Matthew: 'What I say to you in the dark, tell in the daylight; what you hear in whispers, proclaim from the housetops'" (10:27).

Okay, maybe a little excitement had been sparked at finding kindred hearts and minds. If you are familiar with the still and quiet nature of contemplatives, that was quite an entry. I didn't know a thing about contemplatives, but I would soon learn.

CHAPTER 12

LEARNING BALANCE

We are not human beings having a spiritual experience.
We are spiritual beings having a human experience.
—Pierre Teilhard de Chardin

AT THE BEGINNING of 1988, one new consultant joined my team each month. I stepped into a leadership role seven months later due more to enthusiasm and desire than actual skill. No company classes trained us in recruiting at that time. Enthusiasm has gone a long way in many areas of life with passion often trumping technical know-how. The latter can be taught and learned; the former is intrinsic.

After living on one income for four years, the extra dollars my business generated for our family felt luxurious. My hard-wired ambition, which hibernated during baby-making years, re-awakened and happily stepped into a steady jog. This driven, Type-A achiever shrugged off her flabby stay-at-home-Mom-skin and stretched new muscles of freedom and business building.

I loved having something on which to focus besides the children. Building a business gave me what volunteer jobs could not: measurable gains in success, income, power, and status. It granted me critical flexibility to nurture my family in a safe, loving, stable environment and still utilize my leadership skills and intelligence.

My children were one and four years old when I started in direct sales. My strong work ethic and identity as the eldest of a large family fueled a desire to grow a wide team and extensive customer base. These qualities helped me through the tough, recessionary times of the late eighties and tapped my creativity when my children wanted attention during customer phone calls.

I took my business seriously and did a lot of things, but I did not have balance. The workaholic in me did not know how to relax. Whenever I sat in the family room to watch TV and spend time with my family, my mind drifted to the work sitting on my desk. My drive to achieve quickened its pace in this no-glass-ceiling opportunity. It was my first experience of being able to accelerate a career without others evaluating me as a woman (e.g., less capable than a man), and it felt as invigorating as riding a zip line.

My husband once found me at my desk during a lull in entertaining neighbors at one of our monthly potluck pool parties. "What are you *doing*?" he rightly questioned. Indeed! Working from my home gave me access to my desk twenty-four hours a day—not a good thing for someone like me. I had yet to learn the self-discipline of separating work and family.

The challenges along the way—the important ones, perhaps the only ones—required internal transformation. Maintaining balance between my drive to achieve and my love for my family remains a challenge to this day. The German work ethic hard wired into my genetic code proves difficult to turn off at times. My Irish stubbornness tied to this achievement-driven DNA carried a price. I pushed my body into an accumulated stress syndrome from which it would take months to recuperate. Depleted energy reserves and exhausted adrenals would not recharge. I had to suspend playing guitar in church choir. Fatigue reigned. After singing the opening song, I had to sit in the pew while everyone else remained standing, something only the ill and physically challenged do at Mass. I used up what little energy I had with that first song like a phone battery that couldn't hold a charge. My body stunned me by calling a timeout. It had its limits, and I had ignored them, staying up too late, working whenever the children gave me a break, never resting except for too little sleep.

One day, my beloved husband insisted I take a three-day vacation away from the family.

"What do you mean?"

"You need to get away," he confided with quiet, loving concern. "You need some time to yourself to rest."

"There's no way, honey. That's very sweet of you, but I couldn't possibly. The kids ..."

"I insist," he said. A look followed that meant no further discussion. A look full of love and concern for me.

With no idea what to do or where to go, I clearly got his message and loved him for it. My body sank deeply in the chair. What woman who runs a household, cares for little children, cooks most if not all the meals, pays the bills, volunteers at church, and throws a business on top of that couldn't use a break? After researching some possibilities, I decided on a bed and breakfast in Saugatuck, Michigan, and slowed down enough to canoe a river and smell the roses for three days.

I learned from that experience the importance of being proactive in taking time for myself. My doctor had been asking about my stress level. Denying anything had changed much was true. It never dawned on me to consider the cumulative effect of sustained stress over several years. Because I was near a collapse from work and devoid of down time, the doc told me he'd put me in the hospital if it weren't for my two little ones at home. I got the message.

At a meeting around that time, a key industry speaker asked everyone to stand. She asked us to lift one leg off the floor, balancing as best we could on the remaining leg. While she stressed the importance of balance, we continued to tip back and forth unsteadily, putting our hands on the table to keep ourselves balanced and occasionally dropping the lifted foot for stability. When she finally allowed us to put our foot down, she told us balance was a dynamic process, a constant shifting of one's schedule and activities just as we adjusted different muscles to stand on one foot. The illustration of the nature of maintaining balance stuck with me. As our bodies and circumstances change throughout the years, we need to make multiple mental and physical adjustments.

As a result, I bought books and studied stress management, ultimately teaching it as a workshop at several conferences to make sure I learned the lesson well. Still, it would take me years before balance wobbled into place between working and relaxing. Like a toddler learning to walk through many falls, the continuous effort to find balance sustained my health and enabled me to mentor similar high-achiever team members in the years ahead.

Learning the violin had been on my bucket list for years. After finding it listed among the stress-reducing activities I studied, I bought one and started lessons. For some, learning an instrument sounds like more work. When I make music, my heart sings. In the basement, I practiced by bowing between the low-hanging rafters to reduce the impact of my beginner squeaks on the rest of the family.

As I recovered from my exhaustion, I thought about the cost of being out of balance. Being a workaholic in love with the sense of power and achievement I accumulated had put stress on our marriage. My body physically broke down. Because I worked late at night when the children were finally asleep, tiredness kindled a short temper that created tension in the family. Subsequent poor decisions led to a frustrated mom and slammed doors. My neighbors complained they never saw me. We incurred $2000 in medical bills for physical therapy on muscles held too long in place from computer time, violin playing, and hour-long phone trainings I conducted without a headset.

Inspirational speaker Les Brown once said that if you like what you're getting, keep doing what you're doing. If you want something different, then you're going to have to change. Taking responsibility to change my imbalance, I began adding healthy supports to my life such as daily centering prayer, daily Mass, a hydraulic desk to prevent re-injuring my neck muscles, a new physical exercise plan, and hiring a professional organizer. I read one or two self-improvement books each month, listing them in my monthly newsletter to keep me accountable and to model the behavior I wanted others to emulate. I invited my team to join me for quarterly telephonic goal sessions since we were in so many states; I set weekly dates with my husband; and I devised a long-term goal to find a place to live by the water. I knew it was a lot. I had no intention of ever going back to that imbalanced place again.

CHAPTER 13

CENTERING PRAYER

When you give Me a token of your love, you give Me so much joy.
If you could only know! No longer to feel a stranger,
the one left out in the cold as I am for most people.
—God addressing French actress Gabrielle Bossis in *He and I*[26]

1995

IT FELT A little odd when I first began praying without words, especially when Mercedes suggested I try praying this way in a group. Paying attention to the presence of God without thinking, without agenda, without judgment, simply being with Him was a bit like an old couple content in their rocking chairs. At first, you want to talk as usual, but when the Other chooses silence, you settle into rocking and listening.

Taking Mercedes' advice, I joined St. Edmund's Centering Prayer group in Oak Park. I had some reservations about shifting from private prayer to some "Kumbaya" group experience. Sitting in a circle of twenty or so people on metal folding chairs in the basement of the rectory, I watched as a candle was lit. The lights clicked off. Someone voiced a relaxation exercise to start us. Being used to the silence of my home, new sounds distracted me during the first group meetings: tiny breaths from those close by, bodies moving and chair creaks, a cough, a sniffle. It took a few weeks to get used to praying with others. The difference in energy, however, was an important lesson for the maturing of my spiritual senses. A strong sense of God's Presence hovered around us.

Type A's like me balk at doing nothing attentively. We multi-task. With the agenda of Centering Prayer belonging to God instead of me, I used my sacred word frequently in the beginning to release thoughts of doing something, for nothing seemed to be happening when I tried this prayer at first. I'd take a quick peek at my watch. It had only been three minutes. Releasing the thought about time seemed to take up half the twenty minutes sometimes. I gave up using a timer after a few weeks. It was too much of a distraction. Praying on my own, I'd be surprised when forty-five minutes sometimes disappeared from my conscious awareness.

"We are so often tempted to give up," says Pascaline Coff. "The practice is so boring, since there is nothing at all for the senses to do. It is difficult for us to welcome an experience that is non-self-reflective, because we are so good at self-reflection! In meditation, we are forced to realize that we are only who we are in the now, in this present moment. This is the only place where God is, where grace is. We tend to analyze, criticize, plan – and thus, miss the grace of the present moment, Reality Itself. There is a time for these activities, but it is not during the sacred moments set apart for special Presence."[27]

It took me a while to release myself from the desire to analyze the prayer method, the physical sensations that sitting still brings, and the maze of thoughts that present themselves during prayer time. My mind loves to analyze things. Martin Laird, Professor of Theology and Religious Studies at Villanova University, helped me with his perspective:

"... cultivating a contemplative practice, such as using a prayer word, the breath, sitting in stillness, is not to reduce prayer to a technique. Techniques imply a certain control and focus on a determined outcome. Contemplative practice is a skill, a discipline that facilitates a process that is out of one's direct control, but it does not have the capacity to determine an outcome. A gardener, for example, does not actually grow plants. The gardener practices finely honed skills, such as cultivating soil, watering, feeding, weeding, pruning. But there is nothing the gardener can do to make the plants grow. However, if the gardener does not do what a gardener is supposed to do, the plants are not as likely to flourish. In fact, they might not grow at all. In the same way, a sailor exercises considerable skill in sailing a boat. But nothing the sailor does can produce the wind that moves the boat. Yet without the sailing skills that harness the wind, the boat will move aimlessly. Gardening and sailing involve skills of receptivity. And so it is with contemplative practice and the spiritual life generally."[28]

As I learned this practice, it had many applications to my life as a leader of independent contractors. For example, Laird states that "the practice does not have the capacity to determine an outcome." In my business, I could not determine the outcome or success of anyone on my team. I could inspire people and plant seeds of encouragement as God does for us. But I could not *make* someone do something or stick to a goal or submit any sales. It gave me some empathy for God's relationship with us.

I remember a friend once told me she had reached a point where she could not read anything. God directed her to be still with Him. It seemed odd to hear this, for I read for hours every day. I couldn't imagine not reading. At times in my life I found myself willing myself to do whatever God wanted of me, only I hadn't a clue what to do. So I sat in my boat and waited for the wind, the Holy Spirit.

If you observe a circle of people doing Centering Prayer, especially in the early morning hours, you may see a few of them draped in shawls and blankets. When the body is still, its temperature drops. Some, like me, sit still more comfortably with a shawl, sweater, or blanket draped over the shoulders. Bread dough rises better with a towel covering it to cut any drafts.

Gardens tug at my soul. My eyes check for weeds, blooms that need dead-heading, and signs of insects or plant distress. My Irish and German ancestors were farmers. A part of me comes alive when I can work a while in the earth's soil. Plants' ability to regenerate and re-seed fascinates me. They naturally seek and bend toward the light.

After planting seeds, a learning period occurs while I discover which new leaves are weeds and which are "good" plants needing protection, fertilizer, and water. I pulled up a dozen poppies once, not knowing their leaves, thinking they were weeds. Just as we know a tree by its fruit, weeds become known by a gardener who has spent enough time in the garden to recognize them. Discernment comes when recognition occurs, and we know which plants to pull out and which to keep. A daily walk in the garden lets me know what plants need water, which need to be trimmed or staked with a strip of old fabric or a twist tie, and which I should move to a new location for more or less sun. It frustrates casual observers unwilling to commit their time to the garden.

"How do you know which is which?"

"I can never get mine to grow ..."

My prayer time with the Lord is the time I give Him to walk in the garden of my soul and water, trim, and stake what He sees there. He improves the soil in which I grow. My spirit can't "see" Him doing this, of course, but I sense His work afterward. Spiritual fruit grows and ripens within all of us when we let the Master Gardener have a walk in our soul. The more time I spent with our Lord in Centering Prayer, the more I was drawn to Holy Communion the way a couple in love is drawn to one another every moment.

My work during the day imitated gardening: cleaning up mental or physical weeds; noticing where something was stagnant in its position and discerning how and when to transplant it. My job included nurturing people; scrutinizing for their weeds and helping them pull them, or accepting them as they grew alongside me, wheat and chaff together. Sometimes, standing tall as the flower God made me offered a glimmer of His joy and peace to others that day. In the evening, the Master Gardener walked through my garden, trimmed my wayward branches, and pulled the weeds that choked His light and life. I loved His touch, even when it was a sudden cut. I knew it was to help me grow and trusted how He tended my soul. My protests became fewer.

My energy levels bounce on such gross, high levels all day long that I used to miss most of the fine, subtle energies of God's presence. Silence soothes and teaches. "Silence is holy," says Catherine de Hueck Doherty in *Poustinia*, "a prayer beyond all prayers, leading to the final prayer of constant presence of God, to the heights of contemplation, when the soul, finally at peace, lives by the will of Him Whom she loves totally, utterly, and completely." But patience is required because the work of this prayer has profound depths. Many of us are used to everything being available instantly. We'd rather buy a loaf of bread than bake one. We'd rather surf for a new church and preacher than sit silently in the presence of the only One Who matters.

"Silence is ... always the act of listening," de Hueck Doherty counsels. The lack of noise (without our listening to the voice of God) is not silence. "Stand still and look deeply at your true motivations if you want to achieve solitude," she says, "... lifting your hearts and hands to God, pray that the mighty wind of His Holy Spirit may clear all the cobwebs of fears, selfishness, greed, narrow-heartedness away from the soul that His tongues of flame may descend to give courage to begin again. All this standing still can be done in the midst of the outward noise of daily living and the duties of state in life. For it will bring order into the soul, God's order, and God's order will bring tranquility, His own tranquility. And it will bring silence."[29]

Father Thomas Keating describes centering prayer as a simple method of opening ourselves to God and consenting to His presence and action within us. He teaches that God actively works with us during the prayer, often granting the contemplative gifts of wisdom and understanding. His method suggests we use a word as a sacred symbol to remind us of our consent. We return to our sacred symbol when we become aware that thoughts have come into our consciousness.

The method of centering prayer is receptive, not concentrative like Transcendental Meditation. It does not require us to have no thoughts, simply to disregard them, a practice that I'd been utilizing as I studied the human potential movement which fascinated me. I couldn't get enough books on the subject. Norman Vincent Peale's *The Power of Positive Thinking* and W. Clement Stone's *Believe and Achieve* moved me greatly. I understood the tremendous power of my thoughts and that I could manage them instead of the delusion that they managed me. My team often heard me teach this. It applied to one of the hardest tasks I had to learn to grow my business: how to ask for a booking of a demonstration on my calendar. Some of the thoughts that often blocked me included *I probably shouldn't say anything right now. I don't want to be pushy.* Or, *this is probably not a good time to call.* Or, *she doesn't seem like the type of person who'd host a demonstration in her home.*

The gifts of the Holy Spirit really didn't register when I studied them before Confirmation in the second grade. When I reviewed them again thirty years later for Bible study and pre-Confirmation interviews of catechetical students, they still remained a memorized list of perks from which I felt little connection. The gifts felt stored away and untouchable, like the sacred oils parishes collect from the bishop during Holy Week or box seats at the theater. Gifts for privileged people. Not me.

Something clicked as I read of the contemplative gifts of the Holy Spirit with the online contemplative group. With newly awakened spiritual senses, I found myself wanting these gifts and wondering if I could, indeed, receive them through contemplative prayer.

The Word of God would soon show me it was alive and well in my life. By prioritizing Him first thing in the morning with centering prayer, heavenly fruit began blossoming on my branches.

We judge our time spent by the results it produces. We try a new diet, job, or routine, and if it's not getting us where we want, we move on and try something else. Centering prayer produces abundant fruits. Like most fruit trees, it takes a few seasons for the fruit to appear. In the meantime, we are counseled by the founding teachers of this method not to judge the prayer time. It is God's time to do what He wills. He's building His house within individuals, and the initial construction work does not show above the surface. It requires time to be patient, to "wait upon the Lord" for "He does marvelous deeds." And He began doing them to me, with me, within me, like living yeast that produces carbon dioxide causing dough to rise.

Learning to trust Him (one acid test I experienced was to stick with this centering prayer method when I didn't initially see any results), not knowing how or when it would take place, I counted on one day being different … transformed. Here's how it manifested in me. I could no longer harbor feelings of anger toward a person, my patience increased to an endurance that surprised me. No longer could I speak an untruth. See for yourself. Whatever you discover, the change will be from nothing you have done other than sitting with God. In point of fact, you may have tried to change to no avail in the past. And then one ordinary day, you're different.

"Don't judge centering prayer on the basis of how many thoughts come or how much peace you enjoy," counseled one of my centering prayer friends. "The only way to judge this prayer is by its long-range fruits, whether in daily life you enjoy greater peace, humility, and charity." She told the online contemplative community that she had been a strict disciplinarian at school. After centering prayer, she became more compassionate. Her students approached her with problems—something they hadn't done before. She didn't know when she changed; she knew only that she was a kinder person and her students benefited greatly from the change.

In Michener's book, *Hawaii*, dozens of pages describe the very beginnings of the island. Molten lava bursts forth from the ocean floor and hardens. Time passes. Lava erupts again and adds to the first outpouring, then sets immediately in the cold, cold depths of the ocean. Hundreds of years pass with more lava breakthroughs, build-ups, and cool downs. And then one seemingly ordinary day, a point of land appears in the waters of the Pacific Ocean. Centering prayer, fortunately for us, doesn't take anywhere near that long to show itself on the surface of our life. But it does test our patience initially as we sit in silence day after day with the Lord, as author Catherine de Hueck shares below.

"This silence will come and take possession ... of lover, bride, mother, worker, nurse, apostle, priest, nun—if only the face of their soul, in the midst of their daily occupations, is turned to God.

"At first, such silences will be few and far between. But if nourished with a life of liturgical prayer, mental prayer, with the sacramental life of the Church, slowly, slowly," like lava building up from the ocean floor, "silence will grow and come to dwell in a soul more and more often. Then suddenly, it will come to stay one day."[30]

These words of Catherine de Hueck's encouraged me when I could sense no progress toward being a kinder, gentler person, when all I could see were my rough edges, like newly cooled lava rocks that kept bruising those whose paths I crossed. While I lived in hope, it seemed improbable that I would experience this silence staying with me one day. Then again, more than one surprise lay in my future.

I learned to wait upon the Lord, often impatiently and reluctantly. It is a marvelous thing He does with and for His children. Keating calls God "the Divine Therapist." His time with me in this prayer resulted in a general cleaning up of the "junk" I'd held in my unconsciousness that prevented me from being happy.

If you can't keep your thoughts on Me, come back to Me as soon as you notice this, gently, without bitterness against yourself.[31]
—Jesus speaking to actress Gabrielle Bossis in *He and I*

It's not easy to be a contemplative or to understand and value contemplative prayer without experiencing it. I was attacked once for this very reason. During one direct selling conference, I shared my hotel suite with another attendee. Part of sharing a room involves negotiating who gets to shower when, and the timing of getting ourselves up and moving for each day's events. I pray first thing in the morning, I told her, by propping pillows up behind my back in bed so I can sit straight and be alert to God's Presence. I do this for twenty to thirty minutes, I carefully explained.

"It's like offering my first fruits of the day to our Lord. After that, I'll be available for conversation."

Early the next morning, I followed my usual routine, sitting upright in bed with a pillow tucked slightly beneath my tailbone for a straight spine. I placed another hotel pillow behind my back for support. My roommate was still asleep in the other bed when I began my quiet time with my Lord. I breathed in peacefulness in slow, restful breaths. I placed myself in the arms of our Lord. Time seemed to stop in my consciousness. My heart filled with God's love.

Thump!

My head jerked backward by some physical force that bluntly, suddenly tackled my upper body. My heart raced. I tried to shake myself into present time consciousness. My mind braced itself in a primal fear at the sudden blow.

What ... ?

I shook my head to try to make sense of what was going on. I struggled to reorient to the present moment. My heart raced. My awareness rushed to the surface from the depths where it had been resting. Blinking at the light stinging my eyes, I saw a pillow in my lap. My roommate stood at the foot of my bed.

"Are you done yet?" she asked impatiently, her hands akimbo.

I looked at her uncomprehending, taking in what had transpired. Consciously calming my racing heart, a rush of compassion filled me. My roommate had no idea. Never in a million years would she have thrown a pillow at me if she'd known where I had been. She sensed "something" sacred and didn't know how to break in and connect. She wanted to get my attention and knew not how to approach. She kept a respectful distance and used the softest thing she could find to break the spiritual dimension separating us. We all long for relationship. She wanted to continue hers with me. Patiently waiting and honoring another's prayer time wasn't part of any etiquette she knew. My own quandary of spiritual etiquette lay waiting in the future.

CHAPTER 14

TRANSITIONS

Happiness is not something you acquire; love is not something you produce; love is not something you have; love is something that has you.

—Anthony de Mello

THE GOSPEL STORY of Mary sitting at our Lord's feet and Martha working her butt off to prepare food for Him instead of drinking in His presence resonates with contemplatives. We struggle with finding a balance between the Mary and Martha parts of our lives. Our hearts long to spend time with God, yet He calls us to bring the fruit of that contemplation into action in the world.

Martha criticized Mary for not helping in the kitchen instead of sitting at Jesus' feet, listening to Him speak of God's kingdom. I can relate to Martha because I'm a doer, preferring to get things done. I think I could be happy emulating Mary as long as I could pass along what I learned. Like Jesus, I have a teacher's heart. Jesus chastised Martha for being too busy and missing His teachings right in her own home. Finding that balance felt like a lifelong endeavor. I loved the challenge.

As I struggled to integrate the Mary/Martha elements of my life, I eventually developed a loose structure of early morning centering and spiritual reading to water my soul daily. It was rarely smooth going.

Lovely peaceful moments in prayer occurred in the morning, followed by temper tantrums at dinner as if I were an adolescent. I never allotted enough time to take care of what I needed to organize myself during my young mother stage of trying to get out of the house to do my work. I prioritized taking care of everyone else. This choice, of course, led to feelings of frustration when I experienced no time left to be the cool, calm professional person I wanted to be. Instead, I became the Tasmanian Devil racing around to find products, changing clothes at the last minute, doing makeup at stoplights, eating leftovers as I drove faster than the speed limit. In between, doors got slammed and not-so-nice words sputtered from my mouth to no one in particular as I tried to do everything without enough time, doing little well and much poorly. I couldn't think about sacrificially offering up my frustrations. I was too much in a tizzy. As a goalie in front of my soul, I'd failed; the opponent often scored.

I always seemed to miss the usual steps everyone else covered: lipstick, brushed teeth, shaved legs, deodorant, earrings. Trying not to act harried, I would get to the customer's front door, take a deep breath to calm myself, and ring the doorbell. Darn. Whose house is this? I can't remember her name for the life of me. Now I greet her namelessly and compliment her home. I start setting up and hope a guest will arrive to speak her name.

Somewhere along the way, surprising insights began to open in my mind the way sections of cooled lava drop into the red-orange underground molten rivers of Hawaii. Aerial flyovers reveal these temporary holes. They look like missing sewer covers on gray, barren lava fields. Within days, the openings close, and pilots scan for the next ones.

God's presence is always with us, but most of the time we cover it by our hardened, cooled love or indifference. We don't want to see below the surface. When we welcome the Trinity into our heart without restraint, the heat of God's love melts that hardened love. It falls away and we "see" a tiny glimpse of how the Trinity moves through life, touching everything.

I have come to bring fire to the earth, and how I wish it were blazing already!

—Jesus in Luke 12:49

The number of parallels between the spiritual and the ordinary overwhelmed me as my spiritual senses awakened. Like eyes sensitive to light, or bodies vulnerable to over-stimulation, my heart's eye closed protectively from the overload, and I'd forget them. Eventually, the parallels converged, spilling upon each other as two rivers meet to form a new, stronger union. I could no longer distinguish them. They merged and flowed together, like the hand-stacking game where several people make a tower of stacked hands, one hand atop another until all are on the pile. The bottom hand pulls out and goes on top. The new bottom hand then moves to the top, and so on. It doesn't matter who's on top or bottom; they're all from the same Source, the one stack, the one Body: Christ's Body.

The seeming implosion of my career from corporate manager to stay-at-home mom might have made some feminists cringe, but each transition felt right and organic at the time. I had no intention of missing the inglorious, character-building, snuggly moments of parenting two beautiful children (I refer to their inner beauty although they were easy on the eyes) with all the love and Catholic values in which my parents bathed me.

When I entered the direct selling industry, my ego took a bruising. Tupperware represented America's suburbia in the 1950s. By the late 1980s however, people were "Tupperwared-out." They'd roll their eyes or look away in an attempt to avoid an invitation. People would say something small like, "Oh, you do the Tupperware-kind-of-thing?" with a tone of voice that indicated they were as interested in you as an empty beer can. After that kind of reaction, one either got discouraged or worked hard at creating a different image, or both in my case.

For years, I struggled with this low-status image of direct sales; other aspects of the transition from the corporate world flowed easier, such as vacation time, work hours, and not having to be careful about what I said about fellow employees or bosses since there were none. I reduced my commute to a walk from the kitchen to my office in the next room.

I also reduced my language to certain word choices. Since I now worked in various homes with a vast range of religious and social values, my words affected customers as well as my young, impressionable children.

Like live entertainers, I never knew who was in a particular audience. Within any twenty-four-hour period, I could experience a prim and proper customer who invited me to her home or a potty-mouthed, ill-mannered guest. One could transition from a millionaire's home to the home of a pastor's wife who wanted to make a good impression on her husband's parishioners. Some people found casual slang language unacceptable and a turnoff to future business opportunities. I remember several incidents when the word "hell" created some commentary among guests, and I'm sure, caused me to lose some business. (To the delight of my children, my father would often exclaim: "What the hell!" I never found the expression offensive.) While I had the freedom to be myself for the first time in my professional life, I strove to maintain a pristine reputation and positive impressions for those judging whether or not they wanted to invite me into their home.

Jesus' ministry carried little prestige as well when He "changed careers" from carpentry to forming apostles and teaching about His Father. He had some language problems, too. He had to teach in parables for no context existed to understand His subject matter. Some of His word choices and metaphors alienated people. Most walked away when He spoke of Himself as flesh to eat, for example, as "living bread."

When I mention making homemade bread, I get as many rolled eyes as excited ones. "Who's got time for that?" I often hear. The answer to making time for bread or prayer is the same. You make time for what's important.

"What do you do?" is a common question in social gatherings. It created a dilemma for me regarding identifying myself as someone in direct sales. When I mentioned my company, I'd get a dead-end, "Oh, that's nice." The person turned for conversation elsewhere. I was unaccustomed to this reaction. Respectful nods occurred when I mentioned my past corporate titles. Shared common ground created comfortable camaraderie. No such luck when I mentioned a direct selling company. Most people had a cursory understanding of our business, which didn't rank much higher in their minds than selling Girl Scout cookies door-to-door.

Standing on my own without a corporate identity made me uncomfortable at first. I could no longer take shelter behind the protective armor of a corporation. As an employee, little of my identity needed to be known; my employment depended on representing the company professionally, managing my department prudently, and contributing to the company's growth and profits.

Looking upon an audience—and they looking at me—without such an identity was about as comfortable as asking for a first date. But I knew my stuff. I had studied my products and company policies just as I had for high school and college classes. I liked to prepare in advance. Confidence followed naturally. It took a while to realize no one would check on me; there would be no performance reviews; I was free to work as I pleased.

To thwart the poor image people had of direct sales companies, I tried a variety of ways to describe my business. Until I received my first thousand-dollar paycheck, however, I didn't believe I could change attitudes from disdain to respect. By the time I accumulated a million-dollar team, I had learned (and earned) self-respect in this industry and, as a result, found multiple ways of describing what I did that elicited further conversation. Money changes attitudes, mine included.

"What do you do?" now generated answers like:

"I run a million-dollar business from my home. What do you do?"
"I help people earn six-figure incomes."
"I'm a recruiter for a multi-million-dollar company."
"I look for people who have natural leadership skills and know their current position underutilizes their talents. Do you know someone like that?"
"I make dreams come true."

Just as I bristled at the direct sales label, I pushed away the mystic reference when someone applied it to me. The word had all sorts of holy unworldliness associated with it that didn't feel comfortable. I began reading about them and related to the loneliness attributed to mystics. They experience things differently, and I could relate to that. The definition of a mystic I liked most referred to someone who had direct experience(s) of God.

The Catholic label created another box people placed me in. "What do you do?" questions sounded like: "What church do you belong to?" These questions provided a safe way of asking my denomination. After I had answered them, the conversation would take a significant shift if the questioner was not Catholic. I'd bounce a question back: "Why do you ask?" The reply always came back the same. "Just wondering...."

I'm still an infant when it comes to Catholic evangelization. Someone needs to teach me how to ask the next probing questions, just as I needed helpful details about how to recruit in direct sales. It's one thing to know about a business or a particular denomination. It's eye-opening when someone tells you what others think about your company or faith life.

I learned of a perception that we don't make real money, we only earn free products in direct sales. Not true. I earned an average of $80-$100 per presentation in the beginning of my career. I learned non-Catholics think we worship Mary or the saints when we pray for help, among other misconceptions. Scott Hahn's book, *From Home to Rome*, gives some examples of this. Not true again.

We are all children of God. Every mother who loves her son wants to help him in every way she can. As a Catholic, I pray to Jesus' Mother in heaven when I'm struggling or in need, as well as the saints. When our journey gets difficult or lonely, it seems perfectly natural to seek out friends among the communion of saints for help and guidance. God gives the saints a share in His power. It pleases Him to let them help us. To not ask for their help is akin to the way men sometimes refuse to ask for directions. Mary always points us to Jesus. "Do whatever He says," were her words to the servants at the Cana wedding where He turned water to wine. They echo within me often.

St. Anthony helps me find lost things, for example. Pat Gaunt taught me her version of praying to him. "Tony, Tony, look around. Something's lost and must be found."

"You call St. Anthony, Tony?" It sounded irreverent to me.

"That's how the nuns taught me. Isn't that what the nuns taught you?"

"Certainly not," I replied. Now I can't get that version of praying to him out of my head.

An inspirational speaker I once heard changed how I expressed my faith in public. The speaker asked us to imagine the eulogy we would most like to hear if we had a chance to "visit" our funeral. After some thought, I decided on the words I most wanted to hear: a loving mother, a loving wife, and a good, Christian woman. I pondered that last phrase unsure of how many people knew I was a Christian or a Catholic. I had kept my faith private through my twenties. Sure, I went to church every Sunday, sang in the choir, and did Bible study. But was that enough to be known as a good Christian? Many of my friends wouldn't know that about me, and certainly not my business associates, because I didn't want to bother them about matters of faith, theoretically out of respect for their chosen religious practices. I rationalized it as respecting others' privacy.

My only image of evangelists came from television. The few enthusiastic born-again Christians I'd met wouldn't stop talking about Christ as their personal Savior, repeatedly asking: "Are you saved?" This caused me to want a different approach. More like Jesus' quieter way of sharing meals and spending time with the shunned and stigmatized. It dawned on me I'd have to learn how to talk about my faith and my relationship with God if I wanted to be called a Christian woman by the time it came to bury my remains. In my position as a leader in my company, I knew many eyes were upon me. My actions, demeanor, and inclination toward either kindness or sarcasm would reveal enough about my faith life. I didn't have a clue how to do this, but I focused on it and asked God for guidance. The Holy Spirit's fire always looks for kindling, and I'd just given Him some. Sure enough, all sorts of spiritual moments suddenly influenced my consciousness.

I'd slice a cucumber extremely thin, for example, and see the exquisite beauty in the symmetrical seeds within it. I'd hold the slice up to the light, remarking on God's beauty in the simplest of things. I would marvel how each seed in a flower, an apple, a pinecone, a stalk of wheat, or a cucumber bore the power to create new life. I'd allow those little moments to happen as the Spirit prompted me and shared them with whoever was with me.

Some companies draw the line at spiritual discussions in business meetings. Employees receive a communication that "that sort of thing" is just not appropriate. Since I was not an employee but an independent contractor, it dawned on me such restrictions did not exist for me. As I devoted more time to spiritual matters, my conscious awareness of God's intimate presence grew internally and externally. I even started listening to Christian radio stations in the car to avoid some of the crass DJs and music selections that were becoming increasingly aberrant to my ears. I recognized much later, of course, the Holy Spirit making Himself known to me.

But when he, the Spirit of truth, comes, he will guide you into all the truth. He will not speak on his own; he will speak only what he hears, and he will tell you what is yet to come.

—John 16:13

I gave myself permission to speak with courage about God if and when I felt comfortable doing so, telling myself not to be afraid of offending anyone. This transition took some time to accomplish. Just as I had to overcome the lower caste image of a direct sales person, I had to overcome the image of the superficial, overly enthusiastic televangelist before I could start speaking about God publicly. In the first case, I feared becoming the salesperson everyone avoided. In the second case, I had no solid examples of how to talk about God gently, naturally, as part of regular conversation.

Fear exerts a strong influence on behavior. Because of my fear of being pushy, I kept the mute button on my home-based business for years, a common behavior in our industry. On the spiritual side, my fear of becoming an in-your-face-evangelist caused me to hold back from sharing my faith.

"I didn't know you were Catholic!" would resound to my chagrin, until I learned how to overcome this fear.

> *Our fears must never hold us back from pursuing our hopes.*
> —John F. Kennedy

Slowly, interspersed throughout my product demonstrations, I allowed myself—pushed myself even—to speak of God. Timidly at first, I found ways to share my love and appreciation for God in all I did, just as I learned to introduce the benefits of my business at my shows to expand my team.

God is the center of my life. He gifted me with a husband who helps me experience a sliver of His unconditional love. Joe's love and trust shocked me when, while engaged and living in two different cities, he'd tell me to date others if the opportunity presented itself so I wouldn't be so lonely in Chicago where I didn't know a soul. He trusted our love. He wanted only my happiness. He has shown this Christlike love for me all his life. Joe and I co-created with God two children who gave me greater insights into who and what I am as well as breaking open the most tender part of my heart to love as I've never known. Gratitude filled my heart, and I began to say so publicly. Acknowledging the source of my life and happiness opened a level of consciousness I had not known before.

Sometimes it would be midnight or one in the morning before I'd return home from working with customers who would linger afterward to talk, their spiritual appetite whetted by references I'd made during my presentation. They hungered to speak of God, and I served up whatever I could. These warm, openhearted discussions would confirm for me over and over that I should continue this course of sharing my faith out loud and remove the "privacy please" sign from my heart's door.

Priests exhort us from time to time to "pray for vocations to the priesthood and religious life," but it's my experience that the subject of evangelizing others to the Catholic faith reverberates from the pulpit less often. Although I attended Catholic grade school and college, the only instruction I remember receiving in this regard came from one teacher.

"Invite someone to go to Mass with you."

Until we moved to Florida in 2004, we did not find a vibrant faith community whose pastor regularly invited non-Catholics to study our faith and consider joining us, encouraging his parishioners to do the same.

It took me a while to realize that both my company and my church encouraged and expected me to share what I'd found. Grasping the business side came quickly because of the monetary reward associated with it and the available materials to pass along. Grasping evangelism took longer despite the rich reward promised in heaven. I knew money. I didn't know heaven. The Catholic church did not teach me how to "go and preach the Gospel to all nations, baptizing them"[32] and inviting them to join our church. I received no encouragement to carry around tracks or pamphlets as I had received from other believers. The last one I received came from a lovely teenager on a plane. She was no more than fifteen years old and apparently had a supply of them in her carryon bag or purse. As rooster Foghorn Leghorn from Looney Tunes cartoons would say, "There's a ... I say, there's a training opportunity there!"

In direct sales, we encourage team members to bring guests to meetings to take a closer look at the business. It is rare to hear a priest at Mass ask: "Who's brought a friend today?" Some ask visitors to identify themselves by raising their hands so we can greet them, but rarely was the expectation voiced in any parish I attended that we, the lay people, should invite others to come (to Mass) and see. In my experience, that expectation remains mostly silent and unsupported.

Expecting people to perform at a level that is beyond what they've been trained to do creates frustration. An illuminating series of DVDs that provides an inspiring look at our faith in breathtaking and high-definition cinematography is Bishop Robert Baron's *Catholicism: A Journey to the Heart of the Faith*. My heart swelled in gratitude as I watched the graceful revealing of the church's art, music, cathedrals, saints, and multi-colored faces in this moving story of our faith. In it, the universality of our one, holy, catholic and apostolic church resounds of the Mystery Who came to transform us.

For those drawn to Catholicism, parishes provide RCIA (Rite of Christian Initiation for Adults), a process to become Catholic or complete any sacraments not received as a child. Filled with life-changing instruction and resources about sacraments, saints, Mary, grace, Jesus, the Trinity, the rosary, and the Real Presence in the Eucharist, it reviews centuries of rituals, signs, and symbols that make the universal liturgy a life-giving drink for thirsty souls. Most Catholics know little about it because they grew up in the faith and learned it as a child. They would be in awe of the layers of understanding revealed by attending a class or two, which I highly encourage.

What God has spoken to me, how He purified my heart, words that poured forth from my mouth without thinking, seemed meant to be shared like fresh baked bread. How much less of a struggle our lives could be if more of us shared our "private" moments with God and opened ourselves to the workings of the Holy Spirit. Satan and his minions love to sow weeds of doubt and fear in our minds to curtail such sharing.

Similar resistance to sharing occurs in the direct sales business. Some companies call it sponsoring or recruiting, and people resist it because of fear. Pushy salespeople have caused negative associations to be attached to an invitation to join the company. We don't wish to be perceived as pushy so we back away. Recruiting has little to do with sales, more to do with service. Many people are looking for jobs or extra income these days, and everyone in direct sales has business opportunities that can help others. Our pride or our fear, Satan's two biggest weapons, usually hold us back from asking others to consider joining the business to meet their needs.

It seemed almost sinful in my opinion to enjoy the autonomous freedom and financial security I had found and keep it to myself. I learned to focus my thoughts on how selfish I felt when I didn't offer the business opportunity to others. Most of us would not eat a full plate of food at a table where others sat with empty plates.

The fruit of the righteous is a tree of life
and the one who is wise saves lives.

—Proverbs 11:30

When we contemplate God in solitude and listen to His voice within, He allows Himself to be found. We return with food on our plates, manna from the Bread of Life.

"It takes the guts out of you to share because God touched you," says Catherine de Hueck Doherty (*Poustinia*). "We don't want to share it with others. But if we don't, we'll never hear it again. What you hear is part of the Good News … you are meant to share it."

I didn't like thinking of myself as a recruiter when I started my new business. And I didn't identify with evangelism as something I should be doing as a Catholic. Just as women sometimes sarcastically ask a man, "What part of 'No' do you not understand?" I could imagine God asking me, "What part of 'go and make disciples of all nations' do you not understand?"

Then I heard the voice of the Lord saying, "Whom shall I send, and who will go for us?" And I said, "Here am I. Send me!"
—Isaiah 6:8

The Lord has been calling His people to share His love and faithfulness for centuries. In 1 Peter 3:15 (ESV) He exhorts, "But in your hearts revere Christ as Lord. Always be prepared to give an answer to everyone who asks you to give the reason for the hope that you have. But do this with gentleness and respect."

My good friend Alan Bern taught me this lesson in high school when he asked me how I knew that Jesus was the Messiah. Ever since then, I knew I needed to be ready to speak up for my faith in a loving and caring way. It took a while to receive the gift of courage. As I moved in that direction, I experienced a few challenges.

CHAPTER 15

PREPARE TO BE CHANGED

For the word of God is living and active, sharper than any two-edged sword, piercing to the division of soul and spirit, of joints and marrow, and discerning the thoughts and intentions of the heart.

—Hebrews 4:12

IN JEFF CAVIN'S "Welcome" section in *The Great Adventure: A Journey Through the Bible*, he cautions students to keep in mind that the Bible is divine revelation: a book authored by God and written by the inspiration of the Holy Spirit. It imparts not only knowledge but also illuminates the mind and spirit.

Never read the Bible without first preparing to meet God there and hear Him speak, and always prepare to be changed.

—Jeff Cavin

I thought I *was* ready to change when I engaged in Bible study. I felt the prick of His truth in my heart, but I wouldn't hold still long enough for it to get in. Deep in my prideful doo-doo, I thought I could change myself.

The more I read about the contemplative life and participated with the online community, the more I began to realize I fitted the description of a contemplative. The label felt like a wool shirt, scratchy and uncomfortable. I struggled to know what it meant. The Irish in me gets prickly when anyone tries to label me or box me in. I'm a bit of a rebel, and I've been known to take an action sometimes only because everyone else is taking the other. I don't like to think or act like everyone else, which gets me into trouble from time to time. Most of my closest friends and family admonish me to "Behave now" before we enter certain events. That requires a significant effort. I'm not always successful. Let's just say I'm more like actor Jack Nicholson than Audrey Hepburn, which smacks of pride and ego, I know. I'll get to that later. For now, let's stick to the fact that in my prayer life, I found a home in the deep, silent stillness of God's Presence within me. In my work life I ran like a garrulous roadrunner. A lovely life of contrast and contradiction. Perfect company for Jesus.

Part of my motivation in studying the Bible in my thirties and forties, and growing a closer relationship to Jesus, had its foundation in fear. I knew at some point in every life we descend the mountain into a deep, dark valley. Hearing once that we build our faith in the good years so that it sustains us in the dark years, I used that truth to motivate my studies and prayer time. I had been faithful to God and dedicated time to serving Him and sometimes, though inconsistently, spent time in prayer with Him. As I read Keating's *Open Mind, Open Heart*, I began to recognize prayer practices that had evolved naturally on my own. I never knew they had a name.

Discovering this inner life filled me with mixed emotions. As a Catholic, I studied the many mysteries of our faith. But while I felt excited about the closer relationship with God, I also felt sad that I was only now learning about contemplation. Why was it so mysterious? Why did it seem so secret? Why aren't we taught that this beautiful inner life with God exists richly within many faith traditions including Catholic? Why hadn't I heard of this type of prayer practice in a homily, even once in my lifetime? Why don't we commonly know that the pope asked all the monastic leaders of the world to find a way to re-teach this practice to lay people? (The Church taught contemplative prayer to her people until the sixteenth century.) Maybe I had heard of some of these practices when we studied the lives of the saints in school. Perhaps I dismissed them as inapplicable. We often don't "hear" things when we're not ready for them. One thing is for certain: No one in my life asked me to try centering prayer until I found this online contemplative group of Christ-bearers.

It irked me that no one taught centering prayer in the schools or parishes of my youth because I, too, had an appetite for more than the Mass and prayers before meals. Most of us feel this longing when we get quiet enough to pay attention to it.

> *Contemplation is the awakening to the presence of God in the universe around us. Contemplation is knowledge by love.*[33]
>
> —Bede Griffiths

As my home-based business grew, I attended workshops to develop better time management skills. In one workshop, the trainer asked us to list our top five relationships and prioritize them. I chose God, Joe, my family (children, parents, and siblings), work, and friends. Then we had to estimate the amount of time we spent with each. I had a little problem there. The number one spot got an hour at church on Sunday and not even five minutes a day between grace at meals and bedtime prayers if I remembered them. That opened my eyes. I renounced that allocation of time and dedicated myself to spending more prayer time with God. To say that God was the highest priority in my life while He got the least amount of my time created a personal integrity problem for me. Establishing my early morning half hour of prayer helped me rebalance my time with my highest priorities.

A similar pattern of thinking I could change myself with a little extra effort showed up when I moved to Florida and resumed playing tennis after twenty years. I couldn't seem to win many points or return balls over the net consistently. I signed up for lessons, learned some new techniques, then practiced on the ball machine, expecting to have those new strokes automatically click in when I played competitively. Of course, they didn't. Irritated at my slow pace of learning, I immediately resorted to old habits of playing. Trying harder and harder to make the new stroke stick resulted in bad swings or imbalanced steps. Mentally I tried too hard and analyzed too much. The obvious solution? More practice, which of course, took time.

I practiced every week until my muscles learned the new way to swing. Once I accomplished the strokes, I had to learn the fine art of keeping my feet moving and knowing where to run, when to plant them solidly, and how not to play every shot for a winner. I'm still learning.

It takes patience for God's grace to work just as it does to train a body for a sport. I could only hope that someday, somehow, the lessons would click, and I'd have the patience the herons show waiting in ready alertness on the oyster reef by our home.

Tennis, my relationship with God, and building my business took time to develop and bear fruit. One problem stood in the way. I wanted everything now.

At one conference, I was called onstage to be honored for the exemplary work I did that year. After receiving the surprise award in front of 2,000 people, a microphone was placed in my hand and I was asked "to say a little something."

One usually freezes in such moments. What can you possibly say? You don't have your wits about you. You've been completely surprised, your emotions are overwhelmed and, as you think about anything to say, you see thousands of expectant faces looking at you through bright lights. The blood rushes to your face and away from your brain. Only one thing popped into my head: a phrase I'd read in the hotel Bible by my bedside the night before. It applied perfectly to the situation.

"I planted the seed, Apollos watered it, but God gave the increase," I quoted Paul from 1 Corinthians 3:6. "You can do it, too!" I added. I don't remember saying much more than that. For once in my life, I kept my speech short and sweet.

I received some letters afterward thanking me for creating a model of a successful Christian business executive unafraid to share her faith publicly. Some told me of their spouse's impression hearing and seeing that testimony. My heart swelled that God had used me as He saw fit to pass a message along. I felt sure the Holy Spirit worked through me at that moment, for, unlike my Protestant friends, I had few Scripture passages memorized. As He promised, God gave me the words. (See Luke 12:12, 21:15; Exodus 4:12)

Having attended Mass every Sunday since I was a child, absent only if ill, I grew to love the liturgy, the beauty of its prayers, readings, and mysterious transubstantiation of bread and wine into the Real Presence of Christ's Body and Blood. My pastor, Fr. Moriarty, asked me to form a liturgy planning committee after daily Mass one morning, commenting that he saw the Holy Spirit at work in me. I cherish that memory, for it confirmed what I'd been experiencing internally, not knowing until that moment the name of the Divine Artist at work. The moment he spoke those words, Truth nodded within me.

To prepare myself for this work, I studied the sacramentary, read books on liturgical planning, and attended liturgical conferences. I loved learning the meanings and historical connections to the symbols and rituals at Mass, the sacraments, even the various colored vestments worn by the priest, deacon, and altar servers. My roles as lector, extraordinary minister of Holy Communion, sacristan, musician, catechist, and homilist for the children's Masses brought deep joy as well, for my intention was purely to serve the Lord as He directed me.

It surprised me one day at Mass to hear a prayer the priest prayed, probably an opening or offertory prayer, and find it wanting. These prayers at a Catholic Mass are scripted for the presider each Sunday and holy day, approved by the office of the Congregation for Divine Worship in Rome. I'd heard them for years. Now, however, as God made Himself more at home with me, I could hear His voice respond internally as the prayer was read by the priest. For example, in Lent when the priest prayed "… be with us, Lord, as we prepare," I heard God whisper, "I *am* with you, now and always." For a year or two, He spoke to me during these prayers at Mass, teaching me His Truth and deeper ways to pray to Him.

Being receptive to the promptings of the Holy Spirit grew slowly. I resisted going to confession, for example, again mostly due to pride. Non-Catholics have difficulty with us Catholics on the topic of the sacrament of Reconciliation. They don't understand the need to go to a priest to confess sins when you can ask God to forgive you in private prayer time. I understand the dilemma because I used to focus on the confessing part, too. It's how we were taught in preparation for the sacrament. There's a broken relationship with God when we sin and we need to confess those sins to be right with God again.

Yeah, yeah ... I understood the theory just fine, but that kind of teaching never reached my heart. Since I hadn't experienced a close, intimate relationship with God when I learned about confession as we called it as kids, the fact that sin broke that relationship didn't seem to matter much. When I chose the dark path, I didn't know how personally God took it; how I abandoned Him and walked away from our relationship. How much He wanted to love me and be near me and He couldn't do so while I stood in the mode of "God will understand if I just do this one thing...."

When a priest said he cherished the look of joy and happiness that comes over the faces of those absolved of their sins in the sacrament of Reconciliation, it dawned on me that confessing the sin might not be the only important part of the sacrament. Perhaps the most important part occurred when we heard that our sins were forgiven. "I absolve you of your sins in the name of the Father, and of the Son, and of the Holy Spirit." We need to hear these words spoken by the priest as he makes the sign of the cross over us after we confess our sins and say an Act of Contrition. We need to see the actions. It's why Jesus told the crippled man, "Your sins are forgiven." He needed to hear those words, not "You are healed." And Jesus knew the importance of showing His mercy even if the others observing the miracle did not. God's grace pulses into our souls when we express contrition, transforming many faces into joy that priests have the privilege of seeing.

If we do not intend to change our ways, we cannot make a good confession. One of the most gifted priests in the past century, Padre Pio, a recently canonized Capuchin mystic, confessor, and stigmatic for fifty years (bearing the five wounds of Christ's crucifixion), knew how to read hearts.

He spent most of his day in the confessional. "Padre Pio's charism enabled him to know when someone was being deceitful in confession or simply had forgotten a serious sin, perhaps through lack of an adequate examination of conscience. In such cases he was able to tell the penitent exactly what they did and when, as well as any relevant circumstances. This drew many hundreds a day to him, moved by the grace of sincere repentance and the knowledge that Padre Pio could guide them with the wisdom of God.

"He also drew those who did not believe in his gifts or who intended to test the Padre. He unmasked these invariably, often in harsh ways. In the end they often repented, made a sincere confession, and renewed their lives, despite their initial intentions."[34]

God used an herb recently to teach me the power and need for confession. I always end up with a clump of parsley in my vegetable bin of my fridge because it's sold in clumps larger than I need. For years I would throw out old wilted parsley. One day, someone taught me to trim off the dead ends of its stalks and place it in a cup with an inch or two of water. Within a few hours, the parsley that had drooped over the cup's edge pitifully, with no sign of life apparent, stood straight and tall, green and perky. The grace of the sacrament of Reconciliation works with similar efficacy. We trim off what's dead in us, what's preventing us from receiving the water of life from God, and step into the life-giving sacrament that immediately refreshes our soul; our body responds happily with the removal of the weight of the sin(s) we carried. Our heads and hearts no longer droop.

The inner work necessary to reach the state of contrition, though important, can be tiring. It reminds me at times of Moses, who led his people through the Red Sea, and shortly after that, found himself attacked by Amalek. He sent some men to fight him and told them as long as he held his staff over his head, they would win the battle. But his arms grew weary and whenever he lowered his staff, the battle turned against them. Fortunately, Aaron and Hur served him well and helped him hold his arms up with his staff until his men claimed victory.

I don't know which saints may have helped me keep my arms outstretched to God, but I was shocked to hear one of my leaders refer to me as unselfish and humble when she introduced me at a meeting. It didn't register at first for I was all-too-aware of the selfishness of my thoughts and the depth of my pride. She didn't seem to be joking. Her words rang with sincerity and respectfulness. Somehow others perceived qualities within me that had been hidden from my eyes. My head bowed in humility and astonishment at an internal change God had sculpted for others to see. The last words of our Lord's prayer floated from my heart: "… for the kingdom and the power and the glory are yours, Almighty Father, forever and ever. Amen."

God had more work for me to do, but I wasn't ready to hear that yet or to sacrifice my goals for His will. Finding new ways to gain customers, business associates, and new leaders dominated my thoughts when they weren't focused on our family.

Our relationship became strained as I continued to follow my will instead of His. He soon decided it was time for a little talk. When He did so, I would find myself prostrate on a stone floor of a monastery chapel crying uncontrollably.

CHAPTER 16

CLIMBING THE LADDER

I will give thee places to walk …
—Zechariah 3:7 KJV

MY TYPE A orientation always thinks: Where's the head of the line? How do I get to the top? Who's in charge? Maybe I could be in charge someday. My mind always wants to know the limits in any given situation. I regularly push right up to the edge and test it. I tend to look at what has been accomplished to figure out how to exceed or achieve something greater. My daughter showed a similar proclivity at an early age. Walking a path in Glacier National Park, a magnificent wilderness wonderland in Montana we'd never visited before, she would continuously push past the three of us on the path to assume the lead position. She was seven years old.

Despite interesting jobs early in my life in film production, product management, and hosting a cable TV show, none of them changed me much or made me a better person. Most allowed me to pay the bills and live comfortably.

Direct sales felt different. The service aspect of the business appealed to me. The first level of service involved standing before an audience and "edutaining" them in a way that generated sales and requests for more. I learned that skill in 1988 and fine-tuned it throughout the years.

The second level of service occurred by offering the business to others and helping develop some into leadership roles. Eight months after starting, I achieved the first level of leadership in the company—someone who'd encouraged and trained others into running their own home-based business. My most embarrassing moment took place while seated in the front row of the company's conference in 1988. The atmosphere ricocheted excitement and high, happy energy.

At the beginning of the conference, an announcer named each of the company leaders who were asked to stand as they heard their name. All received warm applause. I waited but didn't hear my name. *Oh, no!* I thought. *I'm such a new leader no one remembered to include me.* Perfectly understandable, I reasoned. So many details converged in preparing for a conference. My promotion had occurred only weeks before. It could easily have been overlooked among the myriad details being managed.

My heart started pounding in my chest as I realized my recognition moment was passing by. My palms began to sweat. Time moved to an alternate state.

They're not going to call my name! I kept thinking. *They're going to feel so sorry about missing my recognition when I tell them later.* Full of myself, I thought: *They're going to say that I should have said something* ... I made a decision. I couldn't sit still a moment longer. I decided to help them.

Jumping to my feet, I proudly proclaimed: "And Chris Manion!"

A great big smile crossed my face, knowing I helped save an embarrassing omission. I beamed with pride at my achievement. After a momentary pause to recover from the interruption, the gracious speaker smiled and continued, "As a matter of fact, I was just about to announce the newest leader of our company: Chris Manion."

Polite applause followed. My face flushed hot with embarrassment. I didn't hear the brief description of my statistics and other complimentary accolades. I sat and melted into my seat. I wanted to become as small as a mouse and scurry out of there. Obviously they hadn't forgotten me at all! I was too new to the company to know what a big deal they made of every new leader.

My ego was so grand, my need for recognition so great, I couldn't even wait five seconds. Mortified at my vanity, I wince when I recall its naked public display. No matter that I came from a large family where there's little time for individual attention and recognition, there's always something to be learned from every affliction and painful experience. I learned beyond a shadow of a doubt how important recognition of one's achievements is and from that time forward I made a concerted effort each month to recognize my team's accomplishments.

Increases in commission as well as a passive stream of income on team members' sales mark two significant perks of achieving leadership in most direct sales companies. My new goal focused on growing my team from five to fifty.

A year into the business, I typed up an address list on my Selectric typewriter. It'd be four more years before I'd buy a computer. The list contained seven or eight names of team members in one column, and the words: "Help me fill up this side!" handwritten in the other. Coming from a large family, the desire for a large team seemed natural. The more team members, the more money I'd make, and we had many needs as a young, growing family subsisting on one income for the past five years. Our family made do in practical ways: I sewed curtains for the dining room and bedrooms and clothes for the children; I shopped garage sales and bought items when they were discounted. I used coupons and created lists of what we'd buy when we had more money. I looked forward to getting a new roof on the house and fresh carpeting for our bedroom to replace the bright orange shag carpet, wildly popular in the seventies.

The transition from former corporate manager to direct seller required a few adjustments. Lack of job status stung. As an independent contractor, I had neither life insurance nor office hours, both a blessing and a self-discipline challenge. We accessed group health insurance through the Direct Selling Association (DSA).

The benefits, on the other hand, provided many enticements: time with my children whenever they needed me, or I needed them; complete flexibility as to how and when I worked; time off whenever I wanted it with no need for a reason or excuse. I had job security; freedom from downsizing; well-planned, exciting annual vacations; control over my income with no glass ceiling; choice of a boss (me); and politics played no part in promotions.

Not having to submit an MBO report (Management by Objective) or receive a yearly review felt delightful. The power to promote myself to the next management level was tantalizing. Getting passed over and wondering for the umpteenth time if being a woman had anything to do with it belonged to the past. If I missed a meeting, I suffered no career penalty other than my loss of information; I could run my business my way in my style in my preferred location and that would never change.

Dressing for work each day held no restrictions; I could choose any clothes I wanted for my demonstrations, maintaining my own standard for professional appearance. Gone was the stress and wasted travel hours that rush hour snagged. Tantalizing incentive perks offered by the company could be mine by increasing my sales or recruiting, or not.

The survival behaviors from my corporate executive days had to be turned off. That world was behind me; I didn't have to please anyone but myself, my family, and God.

It took a few years to grasp the fact I had no boss to please anymore. Savoring each bite of freedom, I decided to pursue an award or goal if it benefitted me, my family, my career plans, and desires with no real long-term negative consequences if I decided not to play at any given point. I liked the freedom to choose.

Most people find the perks and income in direct sales independent contractor leadership quite rewarding. I wanted others to experience the same delights, vacations, and extra income I earned. By helping others, I kept getting bigger and better rewards. It seemed like a no-brainer to keep going. I recalled the biblical saying: What you give will come back to you tenfold. Or was it a hundredfold?

Being a servant leader evolved as my best way to build a team. Focusing on what was in it for me made me feel self-conscious and selfish. Serving others, as Christ showed His apostles at the Last Supper, felt much more authentic to my soul: focusing more on others than myself; finding ways to inspire them to reach *their* goals, not mine; and gently guiding them like a shepherd so they didn't fall off the side of their mountain. Encouraging each person to face his or her fears, overcome personal obstacles, stay focused on goals, or pick herself up and start again came from hard-earned personal experience and diligence.

Along the way I met personalities who rubbed me the wrong way, pushed my buttons, or puzzled me. Nothing I learned in high school or college prepared me to work with them. The unique position of being in sales for the first time as an independent contractor and leader of independent consultants meant I had no real power to alter their behaviors. The same applied to my customers.

It irritated me when I allowed a customer to get under my skin, especially when I knew I was right. My tone of voice spoke louder than my professional words. How did I allow certain people to get under my skin? I realized I needed to figure out what pushed my buttons if I wanted to behave as a professional in all circumstances. Although we cannot control events, we *can* control our response to them.

After taking several courses on personalities, I discovered Dr. Tony Alessandra's[35] cogent explanation of different behavior styles that improved my understanding and communication, especially with family members and business associates. Amazement filled me when my strained discussions with a company leader eased as a result. Following the golden rule, I had been using direct approaches with her the way I liked to be "done to"; this professional, however, was an indirect person and appreciated building relationships first, with business matters to follow. The golden rule approach did not work with her. I thought I was saving her time (my preference) by cutting to the issue that concerned me. Doing so, however, bypassed critical connecting moments (her preference). Alessandra's Platinum Rule saved me: Do unto others as *they* would like to be done to. After that, I internally asked a couple of his questions to pinpoint each person's personality style with whom I worked and discovered smoother sailing whenever I took the time to apply it.

Unfortunately, before I discovered Dr. Alessandra, my actions simulated a bull in a china shop. I'd ramrod my ideas and training techniques across all personality types. Being almost always right, of course, I battled verbally to get others to see the wrong of their ways. It's amazing I made any progress with that approach.

My team grew as I applied and taught Alessandra's teachings. What a heady feeling to invest time and effort in others and watch it bear fruit. Not all chose to learn, of course. Certainly each team member owned their personal accomplishment. Learning how to work with them according to the manner with which they best learned and listened, and not how I wanted, proved a significant breakthrough.

One rule I emphasized to leaders: Do not take their team's issues personally. It's one of the Four Agreements.[36] Our teams consisted of independent contractors. We could not make them do anything they didn't want to do. The key word in their title was independent. That meant we could not claim responsibility for their success (which belonged to them), nor their failures (they owned these, too). We could only be responsible for our own business and setting a good example for others to follow.

We also could not motivate them. I was shocked to learn this. What *can* we do? Inspire them to do the best they can with what God had given them. Motivation had to come from within. Not everyone on a team was capable or ready to do the inner transformative work to claim confidence, healthy self-esteem, and success in this business. Discovering this fact was a sign of progress. My job, it seemed to me, was to become the best possible person I could and pass along to others what I learned. In the process, I modeled how I improved myself, how I walked my talk.

> *Do what you can, with what you have, where you are.*
> —Theodore Roosevelt

CHAPTER 17

AIMING FOR THE TOP

If you want to be happy, make other people happy.
If you want to be rich, help others become rich.
—Anonymous quote used by speaker Jean Russell Nave

MY GOAL TO get to the top focused on adding enough people to my team to have two or three at a time desiring a leader's paycheck. Caring enough about others to help them achieve *their* goals, believing in them until they do, and holding them gently accountable showed the future leaders what to emulate to their team. In direct selling, a role shift occurs from boss to mentor and coach. Whether parent or leader, developing strong, faith-filled, confident individuals requires encouraging, inspiring, training, coaching, modeling, and believing in those you're leading. Building a happy family or a large team is like planting and cultivating a tree: You can enjoy its fruit and shelter from the sun for decades. Holding this image in my mind helped me through the hours, months, and years of nurturing leaders to find their areas of strength. Nothing inspires more than rewards and recognition from someone who cares, believes, and communicates with you.

In 1994, when I reached the top leadership position after seven years, I didn't feel quite up to the status of those already there. It seemed everyone would be looking up at me as if I had all the answers. I was still the same me, though God had been working on softening my heart during Bible study and prayer time in the years preceding my promotion. I certainly needed it. My direct approach hurt others' feelings. My impatience made me snap at my family. My poor time assessment left me constantly amazed at how long it took to get ready for a show. I'm certain my entire family breathed a collective sigh of relief when I finally walked out the door (they made bets on how many times I'd return for things I'd forget). Let's just say calm did not reign in my house before a show.

A sense of humility flooded me with this new promotion, a new and uncharacteristic feeling for me. I didn't recognize it as a tangible sign of God's grace at work. I was still "too dense," as my mother would say. With awe and wonder, I observed humility's calming effect on my high-spirited ego. It also seemed to affect other areas of my life, such as my desire for flair and dramatic effect in fashions and style. I began to dress more modestly.

One becomes a leader in the direct selling industry because others have made a decision to experiment with entrepreneurship. One becomes a top leader because others stretched themselves past their comfort zones to lead and grow teams of their own. Without my team, I was simply a salesperson doing her business.

"Self-sufficiency is an illusion," writes Brother David Steindl-Rast. "None of us would be what we are if it were not for our parents, teachers, and friends. Even our enemies help make us what we are. There never was a self-made person. Every one of us needs others. Sooner or later life brings this truth home to us."[37]

After this hard-to-achieve milestone, I rested for three-quarters of a year. Rest for me probably equated to business as usual for others. I was tired. My business cycle transitioned from building mode to maintaining until a new top level of leadership was established.

As I moved through multiple changes on my way to the top, I reorganized often to keep things running smoothly and reestablish balance. I learned how to think and act more strategically to manage the responsibility and demands of a larger team, multiple leaders, and colorful personalities.

One conclusion became apparent: I needed administrative help. Bringing someone into my home where my young, impressionable children observed everything and formulated their values, language, and habits, made this a delicate task. My children were eight and eleven years old when I began hiring neighbors and referrals by word of mouth as part-time office assistants. It took some of the pressure off me.

In August 1999, my beloved father was diagnosed with stage 3B lung cancer. The doctors gave him six to nine months to live. My body sagged under the weight of the emotions. I began grieving his impending death and praying for his healing.

As I approached a future without my father and a new pinnacle of achievement in my career, I noticed that it seemed once I reached the top of the success ladder, my energies shifted more intensely to God. My desire increased to do whatever God wanted me to do.[38] I had accomplished my desires; now I would expend my energies for what God wanted.

"The irony of this 'psychological reversal' is that the more deeply you commit to the purpose or aim of the Christ Body, the more you are called upon to develop yourself to the fullest, because you want all of your activities to be passivities of growth for Christ, not passivities of diminishment.... Your activities become not so much a matter of developing yourself as developing the Body of Christ." —Teilhard de Chardin[39]

Reaching the top was not limited to my work. My spiritual journey experienced new heights as my faith grew deeper.

Strive eagerly for the greatest spiritual gifts.
—1 Corinthians 12:31

Divine union. The first time I read those words, I thirsted for that union. But the more I read about it, the more it seemed accessible only to holy people and saints. Since I was neither of those, I felt discouraged and sad.

Lacking the experience of divine union, we feel alienated from
ourselves, God, other people and the cosmos. Happiness can be

found only in the experience of union with God, the experience
that also unites us to everyone else in the human family and to
all reality.
—Thomas Keating, *The Mystery of Christ*

I first learned of divine union in my deepening hunger for God on the Prodigy bulletin board for the About Contemplation community of which I'd become fond. Since discovering it in 1995, I went online to this group the way some people divert themselves with a computer game or television. I found myself exclusively reading and sharing with contemplatives, fascinated by what they wrote, hoping maybe they could shed some light on divine union. Some people wrote of their loneliness or frustration at not being able to find time for God in their life among work, their children and spouses, groceries, homework, cooking, and laundry. My dear friend and spiritual director, Mercedes Scopetta, Ph.D., always gently steered the community's aching hearts to the Lord through centering prayer. She'd remind us our Lord "is within and without and all around us, closer than we are to ourselves." She'd teach us that "our spiritual senses needed to develop so we could become aware of His life and His presence, His love and His blessings in the midst of our brokenness so that our lives may be renewed." She was the first to introduce me to spiritual senses and to say we "can only grow into healthy mature human beings if our hearts are centered on God. Then we will be free to love and be loved."

If our hearts were centered on God, maybe divine union could occur. The teachings were deep in this community as we read and discussed Fr. Keating's books. I learned a new dimension to the Trinity. When I asked Mercedes, "Where does centering prayer come from?" She cited this beautiful passage from Thomas Keating's *Intimacy with God*:

"Its source is the Trinity dwelling within us. It is rooted in God's life within us. We do not reflect about this truth nearly enough. With baptism comes the entire uncreated presence of the most holy Trinity: Father, Son, Holy Spirit. We participate as human beings in God's life just by being alive, but much more through grace. We participate in the movement between the Father giving Himself totally to the Son, and the Son giving Himself totally to the Father. They empty themselves into each other. The Spirit of Love reconstitutes them, so to speak, so that they can keep surrendering forever. This stream of divine love that is constantly renewed in the life of the Trinity is infused into us through grace. We know this by our desire for God. That desire, however battered by the forces of daily life, manifests itself in the effort that we make to develop a life of prayer and a life of action that is penetrated by prayer."

As new people joined the About Contemplation community, they asked familiar questions. The repetition of the basics of centering prayer and lectio divina, or divine reading, were repeated so often that I began to understand them and practice them. Some in the community shared the change they noticed as a result of these prayer practices like finding patience which before never existed, or finding tolerance for people who annoyed them. Some wrote of "wonderful experiences," which made me curious. They were quick to say there were also days and weeks where they felt nothing was happening.

The community felt like a house of Love, full of people desiring to stop talking "at" God and to begin opening to Him, allowing Him to fill them with His endless, compassionate love, healing their hearts' wounds and filling them with grace.

While searching for more about divine union, I learned that centering prayer was a contemplative way of praying that goes back centuries in the church.

Since much of my success in direct sales centered on attitude and motivation, I paid attention to this quote that Mercedes shared, again from Thomas Keating:

"Motivation is everything in the spiritual journey. God, I think, cares less about a change in lifestyle or ideal circumstances than about our attitude toward what we are doing. Our motivation can be inspired by the false self system dressed up in religious, spiritual garb. This letting go into the unknown, this submitting to the unloading process, is an essential step into the mystery of our own unconscious. Hidden there is not only our life's history, especially the emotional wounds of early childhood buried in the warehouse of our bodies, but also the positive elements of our potential growth in faith, hope, and divine love, and where the Divine Indwelling is also present. We must gradually recover the conviction, not just the feeling, of the Divine Indwelling, the realization that God – Father, Son, and Holy Spirit – is living in us. This is the heart of the spiritual journey, to which Centering Prayer is totally in service."[40]

Perhaps this Divine Indwelling had something to do with Divine Union.

Little did I know when I read Keating's words that a mystical experience awaited me in Sister Pascaline's Forest of Peace that would unequivocally teach this lesson.

CHAPTER 18

I Don't Know How
I Know, I Just Know

*Our spiritual nature is notable for its intuitive capacity to know
things directly, at least some things.*

—Thomas Keating

IN THE EARLY years of coaching my team, when someone called
saying she was struggling with something, I used a Band-Aid approach
for a solution. Reaching into my files for a training flyer on the topic, I'd
assure my team member I had the answer. I'd share the top ten tips on
the topic and send her a copy. "Do these and you'll solve your problem,"
I'd say. I'd hang up feeling satisfied I'd helped another person.

My intentions were good, but I didn't know how to coach back
then. The questions I ask now to guide others to their inner wisdom I
knew nothing about then. How counterintuitive: Ask questions to lead
others to find their own solutions rather than trying mine and reporting
they didn't work.

The term "best practices" began in the early 1990s in the medical
field. Spending daily time alone with God is such a best practice. As my
silence with God accumulated, His presence within me washed off the
hard crusty sleep from the eyes of my heart, a heart I had surrendered
to Him in 1970. He softened, opened, and filled it with many graces.

Somewhere in the years of coaching my team and promoting leaders within it, I received the contemplative gift of wisdom. I do not know when I received it. Silently, like an underground spring, the Holy Spirit released it within me.

One day, as I listened to a team member share her struggles over the phone, it surfaced. I heard the essence of her problem as she told an emotional story. Ping! Clear as a bell, sharp as a light in the darkness, it made itself known to me. She kept talking. In the past I would have let her continue, patiently waiting until she finished before taking a stab at actions to resolve her problem. On this particular call, when this gift of wisdom manifested itself, her continued story gave me metaphysical indigestion.

Interrupting phone conversations makes me uncomfortable. I cut her off as gently as I could.

"Stop!" I spoke the word clearly and strongly for effect.

I knew, from an inner knowing, I needed no further details. She had revealed the problem area. It resonated in a unique way the moment she spoke it, which had never happened before. I gave advice on the phone that day that proved to be the solution to her dilemma. The words just flowed. I didn't have to think them. She confirmed I had hit the nail on the head when I spoke my counsel.

After she had hung up, I shook my head in amazement. That "knowing" came from nothing I'd worked on, studied, or perfected through practice. I have enough ego to take credit for the hard work and achievements I've accomplished. This knowledge was not from me or any of my folders. This was not something I had learned.

Additional phone calls from team members searching for advice confirmed this "Ping!" experience over and again. I began to coach differently, listening now for something new: the ring of Truth. Probing with open-ended questions, I listened for the sticking point, where thinking darted awry. When I found no fault down one vein of questioning, I'd shift direction and probe in another. I didn't buy my team's stories anymore. I didn't know their truth, but I knew its sound. They'd tell me their story and somewhere in the telling of it, I'd hear truth's ring. They didn't realize they'd just touched the source of their dilemma. They'd talked right over it. When I stopped them, and they had a moment to reflect on what they'd said, truth revealed itself like dawn. I didn't have to do much work after that. Silence, followed by a voice choked with emotion, revealed they had begun processing a truth God's grace revealed.

> *It requires less effort to love God than it requires to eat, or sleep, or breathe, or to perform the simplest and most instinctive acts of our natural life: because it requires no energy at all to make an act of will, and when our wills are possessed and moved always by His grace, charity becomes as spontaneous and constant and continuous as breathing itself.*
>
> —Thomas Merton

This knowing came from God, a gift from the unpredictable Holy Spirit. The Lord had purified my heart in my twenty- to thirty-minute prayer times, opening my senses to new levels of sensitivity and perception. I sat in wonder at it. I'd studied the gifts of the Holy Spirit[41] and memorized them in preparation for the sacrament of Confirmation: wisdom, understanding, counsel, fortitude, knowledge, piety, and fear of the Lord. These concepts remained conceptual—in my head, not my heart—and meant little to me as a young one. I had seldom thought about them since. It startled me to see some of them opening in quiet competence within me.

When I reached the top level of leadership in my company, like Solomon, I asked God for wisdom. The Holy Spirit seemed to answer this request, bestowing His gifts as He saw fit. From His generous bounty, He gave me more than I requested.

> *It is the Lord your God who gives you bountiful harvests and blesses your work.*
>
> —Deuteronomy 16:15

Once I became aware of this silent gift of "knowing," I felt an increased desire to offer myself as a coach to team members and encouraged other leaders to schedule one-on-one sessions with those on their teams who wanted private help during my annual visits. I wanted to share and use this gift. It did little good sitting dormant within me. When others shared their heart's concerns with me, it opened naturally like the sun's light opened my favorite Heavenly Blue morning glories.

"There is a higher way of knowing God," writes William Johnston in his Introduction to *The Cloud of Unknowing,* a spiritual classic. He quotes Dionysius the Areopagite, a Syrian monk of the early sixth century who influenced the unknown author of *The Cloud of Unknowing.* "Besides the knowledge of God obtained by processes of philosophical and theological speculation, there is that most divine knowledge of God which takes place through ignorance. In this knowledge, the intellect is illuminated by 'the insearchable depth of wisdom.'

"Such knowledge is not found in books nor can it be obtained by human effort," continues Johnston, "for it is a divine gift. Man, however, can prepare himself to receive it; and this he does by prayer and purification."[42] It is given and not taken, waited for with long-term willingness. You cannot study for it, will it, or earn it,[43] according to Gerald May in *Will and Spirit,* a book we discussed in the online contemplative community. You cannot get this knowing by trying harder, says Richard Rohr, which is difficult for most people to accept.

In his 1998 apostolic letter "On the Dignity and Vocation of Women" (Mulieris Dignitatem), St. Pope John Paul II remarked that "the church asks that these invaluable manifestations of the Spirit (see 1 Corinthians 12:4) be attentively recognized and appreciated so that they may return for the common good of the church and humanity."[44] It's important to recognize the charisms of the Spirit and to have teachers who help us understand them. This kind of valuable work took place in the online contemplative community I'd joined in 1995.

Questions about these invaluable manifestations rose earlier at the time of the Second Vatican Council in the late sixties. Author Mary Catherine Hilkert references a change-maker from Vatican Council II, Cardinal Suenens, in *Speaking with Authority.* The Cardinal "made a significant intervention in the development of the Constitution on the Church (Lumen Gentium, hereafter cited as LG) by calling for inclusion of a section on the share of all the baptized in Christ's prophetic office and explicit reference to the Pauline proclamation that 'to each person the manifestation of the Spirit is given for the common good' (see 1

Corinthians 12:7). Cardinal Ruffini objected, arguing that charisms were limited to the early church and given as rare gifts, and warned that an emphasis on charism could endanger the institutional church. But Suenens insisted that charisms were neither the extraordinary endowments of a few within the Christian community nor the prerogative of the ordained or religious institutes. Rather, the gifts of the Spirit are bestowed lavishly on all the baptized. Recalling the promise of baptism, Suenens maintained that 'we all receive the fullness of the Holy Spirit, the lay [person] as well as the priest, bishop, or pope. The Holy Spirit cannot be received more or less, any more than a host is more or less consecrated.'[45] Suenens' view won the day on the question of charisms with the Council's recognition that the Spirit allots gifts to the church as the Spirit wills (see 1 Corinthians 12:11), and distributes special graces among all the faithful to make them 'fit and ready to undertake the various tasks or offices advantageous for the renewal of the Church' (LG #12)."[46]

Suenens' universal interpretation of the charisms of the Spirit energized me. For too long I'd heard how rare these spiritual gifts were. Inwardly, I cheered for Suenens decades after his courageous stance during the Vatican Council.

An unusual experience brightened one morning when I honored and obeyed God's nudge to get up early and continue writing this book. My preference would have been to keep sleeping. But after thirty minutes of centering prayer, I got up and wrote, then went to daily Mass. I was aware that I had pleased God by doing so. An experience that morning helped me see that all creation is made for us to admire and, by admiring it, we gladden the One Who made it for our delight. As I walked out of church, quiet and peaceful and filled with God's love, I saw a Monarch butterfly darting about the flowers by the church steps. It alighted on a leaf as soon as I saw it and stayed there, letting me look at it for quite a while. That butterfly was just as obedient as I was that day, for I am quite sure God asked it to be still and let me admire it. Again, I don't know how I knew this. This knowing dropped upon my mind like morning dew. I started to move to my car but became aware that God wanted me to know He'd made that butterfly just for me, so I bent to admire it.

Butterflies usually flutter away when I want to see them up close. This one just waited for me. The moment reminded me of one of Gabrielle Bossis' colloquies with God when He told her that He'd made all of nature for her so she could be surrounded by beauty and love every day of her life. I paid attention to the markings on its wings. It remained still. Suddenly, I was aware it was waiting until I moved away. The best I can explain this knowing is that it was like intuition, when something pricks your consciousness, only this was instant and sure knowledge, nothing to question or ponder. It happened the way Betty Eadie described in *Embraced by the Light* when she conversed with Jesus after her near-death experience. The butterfly, like me, obeyed instructions to allow his beauty to be a feast—visual food and soul nourishment—for another one of God's creation, me. Silently thanking the butterfly for its obedience, I lingered to enjoy what God had placed before me, noting every marking on this beautiful creature. I knew I didn't have to rush to drink in its elegance before it flew off. This butterfly would wait for me like a waitress attentive to her tables, not rushing her customers. I bent closer and admired the three black circles at the base of each wing. Its attention focused unhurriedly and unafraid upon me as I marveled at God's inexhaustible creativity and masterful designs.

My desire to move on was leftover energy and habit from years of taking quick notice of beauty around me and then dismissing it to focus on the all-important work I thought I had to do. Like many Type A personalities, years and years of rushed moments had accumulated as I climbed the success ladder, starving my soul of these long drinks of God's beauty and delicate aperitifs. It amazes me how throughout all of history, our Great Chef continues to place one delicacy after another before us. We mostly dismiss them and never partake, never even taste them. When we do indulge a nibble, it's momentary or often while we're doing something else: talking to an associate, reading and writing, working at our computer, or walking.

A couple walked by my window the other day at my home in Florida. The man cradled a large slice of pizza drooping over the napkin beneath it, taking bites as he walked along. That symbolized the late twentieth century's soul-draining, multi-tasking actions I chose. Tasting life on the go.

Finally, when I'd had my fill of the butterfly and decided to walk away, I knew the butterfly would move too. It did. I smiled and marveled at the gift of knowledge as it continued to unfold.

CHAPTER 19

DYING AND RISING

I am most myself
not when I resist God,
not when I try to become God,
but when I surrender to God.

—Bishop Robert Barron

DURING THE CHRISTMAS holidays of 2002, my siblings and their families flew to Phoenix to celebrate my parents' fiftieth wedding anniversary. Their actual anniversary would take place six weeks later on Valentine's Day. With thirteen grandchildren at every level of schooling, the holidays proved more conducive to the clan's gathering, where speeches resounded and cameras clicked. We raised glasses in toasts to their union that had produced seven pregnancies (a miscarriage sent one angel daughter or son to heaven ahead of them), thousands of days of happiness, and a strong family who loved one another. My parents toasted to their love, to the six of us, and to the six extraordinary people we married, whom they considered as equally great gifts of friendship and love.

Weeks later, my lovely mother fought for her life as sepsis roared through her immune-deficient body. For seven weeks the battle raged, with Dad faithfully at her side in the ICU room of the hospital. My sister flew out to join him for a while. Ever grateful for my flexible business, I flew to her when she got out of the hospital. We enjoyed each other's company for a week as she tentatively walked the road of recovery in her walker. The days flowed in love and gentleness as Dad and I attended to the woman who had given me life and love all of my days. I am forever grateful for them. We spoke loving words to each other, which we already knew in our hearts. Two days after I returned home, she succumbed to a resurgence of the sepsis. My father called with the news.

"Your mother's gone, Chris."

How ironic her death, for she had been preparing us for Dad's passing. He had been diagnosed with inoperable lung cancer in 1999 and given a six-to-nine-month life expectancy. She'd taken the news hard and had become depressed at the thought of life without him. The debilitating effects of her advanced rheumatoid arthritis caused her to rely on him for physical assistance. She told me it took fifteen minutes to pull up one nylon knee-hi with a grip stick. She could no longer manage more than a few short stairs or get out of ordinary chairs on her own. Because of her fragile grip, Dad created a large wooden handle into which he inserted her car key so she could start the car.

Her love of medical research drove her to explore dietetic approaches to healing. She put Dad on a macrobiotic diet. He plowed ahead with weekly chemo in his typical German stoicism while she looked ahead to life without him and saw only pain, loneliness, and debilitation. I recognized God's mercy when He took her home first.

She "visited" me a few weeks after her death during daily mass on an otherwise unremarkable day. Gazing at the altar, as if in a dream, I became aware of looking out through her skull. I recognized the shape of her eye cavity which varied from mine; I could sense different wrinkles at the edges of the eyes, a different nose. Great happiness and contentment surrounded me. It lasted only a few seconds, but I felt her joy and peace. I sensed no pain or anguish, only joy. It softened the grief, but my heart still hung heavy, my energy as flat as palm trees on the ground after a hurricane.

One month later, I faced the challenging task of writing a six-minute speech for a conference at which I was to be honored for achieving the highest level of field leadership. I found the task impossible. Having a teacher's heart, I desired to use those six minutes as a teachable moment. I knew the company recorded our speeches; they'd be passed on to future generations. My awareness of the enormity of this opportunity burned like a candle's flame in the darkness. The teacher in me recognized that I could influence a large number of people, so I did not wish to waste the opportunity to pass along an influential lesson. Much had happened as I rose through the ranks; many lessons had been learned. I tore up page after page of attempts to consolidate my experience into six minutes. It wore me out. Week after week I tried, but to no avail.

In desperation one day, I swallowed my pride and turned to my husband. I confessed my inability to complete the task.

"Do you want me to try to help?" he gently probed. I nodded.

"Why don't you go for a paddle in your kayak then while I see what I can find?" He opened his laptop and started looking through his files. When I returned an hour or so later, he turned his laptop toward me.

"See what you think of this."

I read a gorgeous piece of prose. "Where did you get this?" I asked.

"I wrote it," he replied in his usual, humble way. That surprised me. I didn't remember he could write from the heart. He authored a book, professional articles, and training materials in his field of medical and vocational rehabilitation, but nothing like this. Not since our engagement.

God answered my prayer through Joe. Combined with what little usable content I had written on my own, my speech became our speech. Since I could never have reached the level of upper management without his quiet, behind-the-scenes support throughout all the years of my career, our combined effort felt like sacramental grace. I submitted the speech on deadline.

Reaching the top level is a very big deal in direct sales. It gets seriously celebrated. My grief from my mother's death, however, left me with little energy to prepare for or enjoy its official acknowledgment. I bought a skirt at a consignment shop and found a cocktail vest on sale, hoping they looked adequate for the occasion. In my grief, I had no energy to go to a department store and shop. I wanted to keep this as low key as possible to get through it. My heart still silently grieved.

Then and now, the sales force in our company understood that our work made a difference in the world. When thousands of us descended upon various cities for annual conferences, our passion filled the air with palpable, contagious, and overwhelming excitement.

Mixed emotions surrounded the celebration of my milestone achievement at this particular conference. I'd changed into my formal clothes for my big stage moment. My longtime hairdresser, Sandy Ross, had driven downtown on her own accord to touch up my hair. Aside from my children's weddings, I didn't get my hair done. Cutting it every two to three months was enough for me. So Sandy's touch up felt luxurious. Excitement radiated from friends and family. The heaviness of grief still weighed me down.

Backstage, I stood where the stage manager indicated and breathed deeply in a dismal attempt to keep myself calm. Before me stood a piece of stage scenery about to be lifted so thousands of my peers could see me standing atop a staircase. I wanted only to get through this moment without tripping or making a fool of myself. The moment felt huge. I was uncomfortable with this much attention.

A minor smile spread over my lips. The irony of the juxtaposition of my current wish to be anywhere but stage center, and the years I had spent longing for recognition, working hard to earn it, auditioning for plays in high school and college, was not lost on me. Miss Sarah Bernhardt, my mother used to call me, when she'd observe me in a flailing, dramatic swirl of adolescent emotions, wreaking havoc at the dinner hour or straining the patience and tolerance of my father in a discussion about my curfew.

"Please help me give a great big welcome ..."

Checking myself in the backstage mirror, I knew I looked okay after receiving an unsolicited compliment from one of the most stylish leaders in our company.

"Very nice, Chris," one of my friends said backstage in her usual, understated way. I smiled and noticed some inner part of me relax. At least, I knew I looked good before my special moment on stage. Oh, the vanity in such moments. I'd already had an internal conversation about who determines what looking the part means. As an independent contractor, I got to make that determination for myself. But more rode on the moment of this appearance on stage.

The official acknowledgment of my promotion at this conference represented the materialization of the dream of reaching the top of the ladder in my company; the Cinderella moment in a career. Many in the audience pictured themselves someday in the very place I stood. Many dreams would be linked to the image I presented that night. I needed to appear transparent enough that anyone could project her face onto the scene and visualize herself receiving the award.

This whole night made me jittery and nervous. I'd worked so hard for so long. My ego had hungered for the recognition of reaching the top. My mom's death, however, blanketed the moment with a soft sadness of bittersweet loss. I didn't feel strong or full of confidence any longer. I preferred to stand from my seat, give a gentle wave at the polite applause, and sit back down. But that wasn't going to happen.

The position I'd achieved takes years of recruiting large numbers of people, shaping, guiding, and encouraging dozens of them into key leadership roles, and in that process, generating millions of dollars in sales annually.

Just don't trip. I repeated this to myself several times as I stood atop the staircase still hidden from the audience. The announcer's voice reverberated my name through the theater. A cheer rang out from the audience, and the applause started as the scenery hiding me slowly rose.

Don't do anything stupid or dramatic, I said to myself. It didn't feel right standing there accepting all that applause looking all full of myself. A tuxedoed gentleman began to climb the stairs to escort me down. I took a step forward, and in a spontaneous moment, lowered my head, bent my knee, and dropped to a deep bow before the audience that included many of the very people whose efforts helped me achieve this recognition. I have always had a profound sense of gratitude toward the leaders of my team who built us into the second strongest organization in the company.

Tuxedo man smiled as he approached the top step and offered me his arm. The descent went without incident. A sigh escaped my lips. Cameras flashed as I made my way onstage. A staff member crossed the stage and placed a bouquet of exquisite red roses in my arms. The "Queen for a Day" moment culminated with "Somewhere over the Rainbow" crescendoing through the convention center.

It touched me to be given an opportunity to thank my leadership team publicly for how much they meant to me. My family sat in the audience on this auspicious occasion, beaming pride at their mom and wife. We exchanged I love yous in sign language.

The moment created a cherished memory.

Later, I was cued onstage to deliver the speech Joe helped me write. It took every ounce of my strength. It came from the deepest parts of us, not a safe speech touching lightly on career stepping stones. I felt so weak-kneed afterward, I could barely walk offstage. I was spent. It was a good spent. With Joe's help, I'd given all I had.

> *Everyone has inside her a piece of good news.*
> *The good news is that you don't yet realize how great you can be!*
> *How much you can love!*
> *What you can accomplish! And what your potential is!*
> —Anne Frank

The following is an excerpt of that speech.

> *The greatest discovery of my generation is that man can alter his life simply by altering his attitude of mind.*
> —William James

I've been studying and learning about attitude nearly all my life, thanks to my outstanding parents. My mother lived in pain—sometimes pretty intense pain—all forty-eight years that I knew her. She never complained. Not once. She had an attitude of redemptive suffering for others. My dad has inoperable stage three lung cancer now. He's an elite cyclist who rides fifty to one hundred miles across the Arizona desert on his bike. He was misdiagnosed. Instead of suing the doctor, my parents forgave him. It's been two years now since the doctor said Dad would no longer be with us, and Dad's going strong! He exercises every day, does what he loves, what brings him joy, including intensive workouts on Thursdays and Sundays. I'm very proud of him.

Personally, I didn't have such a very positive attitude when I first started this business. As a matter of fact, I'd vowed never again after attending my first and only Tupperware show. But God has a way of opening my eyes to see things from a different perspective when I set my mind—my attitude—against something.

From the beginning I've only wanted to do my best. It's what most of us want. It's what we teach our children. Mediocre is so beneath the greatness we each have been born with; for God made us a little lower than Himself. Doing just enough to get by is so easy and a fairly common attitude. Yet, it is an insult to the gifts God has given us. Who among us, upon receiving a dozen roses would let them lie on the table and never put them in water?

After studying many books, authors, and speakers about achieving a happy, successful life, I did two things that had a significant impact on my career, which was supported by a team who produced in excess of $100 million in sales. Those two things?

1. I trained my mind to reject all negative thoughts, and

2. I prioritized time each day to be with God.

Each of these commitments took time. Researchers tell us that hundreds of thousands of negative messages hit us by our twenties. Recognizing those we've allowed to take root in our minds and then slowly, systematically, kicking each one out took many months, but when they were all out, there was a lovely increase of energy and a fresh CAN DO attitude that took permanent residence in my mind.

I'll never forget the story of the crabs that Bart Breighner, CEO of Artistic Impressions, told us years ago at another conference. "Do you know why you don't have to put a lid on a bucket once you have more than one crab inside?" he asked. "One crab can climb out by herself, but when there is more than one crab, whenever she tries to climb out, the other crabs will pull her back down."

I don't associate with crabby people anymore. It's part of my commitment to a positive mental attitude.

I still have rough edges to me and will always have areas in which I just won't do well, just like you. But that's where my daily half hour with God has seen its best fruit: increased compassion and wisdom that is not my own but has been a treasured gift as I have grown in my leadership roles and counseled others on their roads to success.

Paths to success are simply opportunities to learn and grow. Any little or big step we make in the learning curve of life is a success. If we choose an attitude of sharing, of passing on to others what we've learned, then we've discovered the secret of a single drop of water in the pond of life: the ripple effect.

The world in which we live tends to overemphasize success as a large accomplishment that will deliver us from all of the woes and anxieties we face day in and day out. Actually, it's the little things that do. The first time we quiet a baby from crying with a tight hug and a gentle kiss ... the first time we hug our spouse and say the words, "I love you" ... the first time we hold someone in need and encourage her to learn from her mistakes ... the first time we recognize the value of life in the midst of personal tragedy ... the first time we take responsibility for our own words and actions is a success ... the first time we stand up for our own self-respect and self-worth ... learning to forgive others who have hurt us ... choosing positive over negative thinking ... getting out of the driver's seat and letting God steer....

My successes in life have been just those. I cherish each of them and all of the others that I have known ... My message to all of you ... treat what you do no matter how large or small as a personal, family, and faith success by choosing a positive mental attitude.

Life is precious, and what we accomplish through our little successes adds little ripples that affect the rest of us. Each ripple that touches us lifts us up and energizes us to do a little more, to pass on a little kindness, to reach out to another person. One ripple touches another ripple and soon clusters, families, whole communities are moved and touched and encouraged by our little successes. Pretty soon, those ripples turn to waves, and although it is my first choice to kayak in smooth waters, there is nothing more exhilarating than paddling in the waves.

I hope my ripples have been strong enough to touch you in some way, for it was only a few years ago that I sat there listening to someone encourage me. Now make some ripples back. Make them big to challenge us all. We all need those ripples for inspiration and momentum. So inspire me and I'll do the same and together, who knows how far the force of our waves will go—one positive attitude at a time!

Many approached me later that day in tears, some shaking their heads saying they didn't know why they were crying. I knew. The God Who blesses our marriage and lives within it, the God Who loves and fills softened hearts, the God within me Who was revealed in the truth of the few words I spoke, touched the same God within them. His touch is exquisite. They felt it and experienced the overwhelming feeling that His presence creates in hearts. I smiled and hugged and cried with them.

Responses to this speech came via emails as well. My favorite may be the one I received two years later.

5-25-05
"Dear Chris,

"I was thinking of you as I prepared to attend the conference. When you were promoted to NED and shared your heart, the founder also mentioned faith issues in comments that year. I spoke with you for a moment on the phone after conference to tell you how my friend's life was affected.

"Immediately following the session when you gave your promotion speech, God was working powerfully in her heart. When we returned to our room, she commented, 'I don't feel like I'm at a company conference. I feel like I'm on a retreat!' As she poured out her heart, it became clear that she was at a decision point. We prayed together for Christ's Lordship in her life. She is Roman Catholic and calls it her spiritual epiphany.

"I think it is two years later now, and I thought you would enjoy hearing an update. She continues to be very involved in her Catholic church. When she returned from conference that year she participated in, and then helped lead, an Alpha program at her church. She also joined her first Bible study through Community Bible Study and has done wonderfully. This year she was asked to be a children's teacher with Community Bible Study for next fall.

"Thanks again for your time and especially ... giving us a window into what matters to you. Though we don't know you, we won't ever forget that amazing moment in my friend's life and how God used you."

Comments such as these are what matter most to me, helping people change their lives for the better, opening their hearts to the tender love of the Lord.

At the other end of the spectrum of this new level sparkled the world's jewels: luxury, prestige, privileged stays in five-star hotel suites with chocolates, Tiffany jewelry, Coach purses, and the latest hi-tech toys as gifts of appreciation. The rarefied view from the vistas of privilege, perks, and responsibility was breathtaking, to be sure, but the excess and luxury made me uncomfortable at times, if truth be told. As we walked out of extraordinary dinners, I'd hang back and watch the group move toward the exit. A part of me remained hungry. These perks did not feed my soul.

CHAPTER 20

I WANT MY TWENTY MINUTES

Tell Jesus how much you love Him.
—Fr. Tom Collins, former pastor at
St. Rita Catholic Church, Miramar Beach, Florida

TWO GREAT ATTRACTIONS pull at our souls according to St. Teresa of Jesus. One is solitary, silent prayer that immerses the soul in God and His mysteries. The other is helping others, sacrificing our work or sufferings for the salvation of souls.

As we work toward finding the balance between action and contemplation, we lean toward one or the other, sometimes doing too much, sometimes not praying enough. Certain moments of correction—events in our life, words spoken to us by others—act like the punching down stage of making bread. Punching down the dough makes the bread finer and occurs after the dough has doubled in size. One or two punches will release the air bubbles; then the baker kneads the dough gently for a short time. This removes large air pockets in the dough for more even texture. The baker then proves the dough a second time.

If you've ever sliced into a loaf of bread full of holes, you know the challenge. You make do, of course, but there's less space to butter, less space to hold the contents of a sandwich, and less to dip into savory oil to satisfy one's palate. Here lies a clue to the perennial question we sometimes ask: Why is this happening again?

It does no good to be in a hurry to bake bread or to grow your soul. Each has a timing worth enduring. Just as our physical senses engage in waiting, watching, smelling, and tasting warm, fresh baked bread, so our spiritual senses engage in learning how to walk and talk and listen to God as He transforms us.

God is our teacher walking with us much the way our parents or guardians encouraged us to try, try again after each fall we took when we began to take our first steps. We do not remember our falls. We only know that now we walk. So it is with our loving Father. His mercy is endless, and He remembers not our sins. He picks us up, gives us the strength to go on, and claps His hands in thunderous encouragement to take another step. The more air pockets of sin and error He can work out of us, the more useful we can be to Him.

St. Teresa of Jesus describes mental prayer as "friendly intercourse" during which the soul "converses intimately" with God, an intimacy born of the knowledge that God loves it. "The soul speaks with Him whose love she knows."[47] But how does one do this?

We learn how to pray the way we learn how to make bread. Active parts and restful parts marry one another. Prayer is not only an intimate conversation with God; ultimately, with meditation, it is our whole day and how we speak, think, react, and wait upon the Lord as we listen. It is what we have done and what we have failed to do. It is our intention, our will, our love.

Meditation books teach practices that move prayer into position to breathe for the soul. Many souls shrivel near death for lack of prayer. Think of the kneading process of making bread as deep, relaxing breaths that stretch and expand the soul, forming strands of connections to God and all creation, just as the proteins in flour develop and form strands of gluten. Kneading bread gives it its texture. Consider the punching down stage similar to what physicians and emergency responders do to stimulate a heart that has stopped beating. "It is now the hour ... to rise from sleep" Romans 13:11-14.

In 2006 during a challenging time, I found myself trapped in emotions of unfairness due to a particular situation. Sleep came fitfully.

One Sunday morning when I awoke with thoughts about this dilemma, I decided I had had enough of my obsessive thinking on the subject and decided to get out of bed and busy myself to distract my thinking. I broke my habit of spending my first twenty minutes in centering prayer. Restless and distraught, I decided I couldn't quiet my thoughts enough for prayer right then. I'd pray later.

After singing at Mass at St. Rita Church that morning, our choir had arranged to meet at a local restaurant in Miramar Beach to celebrate the contributions of one of our singers, Linda, who was moving to Tampa. On the way to the restaurant, I stopped to put gas in the car. At the restaurant, we ordered Bloody Marys and Chianti until Linda arrived.

"Surprise!" several shouted as she walked in. Our attention and celebration delighted her. I offered to buy her a drink. When I pulled out my wallet, the credit card was missing. There was only one slot in my wallet for that card. It was empty. *Uh-oh.* I checked my entire purse. Nothing. I ran out to the car thinking I must have put the credit card on the seat when I got in after gassing up. Nope. Not on the car seat. I checked the center console of the car, the only other place I'd have put it. Not there. I looked between the seats in case it fell out of my pocket. Nothing.

Thinking back to the gas station, I couldn't remember what I did with the credit card once I swiped it. I was on autopilot when I filled the car with gas, my mind elsewhere.

Walking back into the restaurant, I went through my purse again, then decided to drive back to the station and see if the credit card lay on the ground somewhere. I hoped I'd placed it on the roof of the car momentarily while pumping the gas. The drive would take about ten minutes there and ten minutes back. I scanned the menu and told Kitty, our choir director, what to order for me.

I didn't want to think about canceling the card if I didn't find it. My business card had dozens of automatic payments debited monthly from it.

As I drove the car out of the parking lot, I asked God for an explanation. *What are You doing taking me away from this lovely group of people I'm just getting to know?* I began singing and playing guitar with them only a month earlier, having recently moved to Florida. I wanted to meet new people and make new friends. I had looked forward to spending time with them enjoying a lovely Sunday meal.

I pulled onto Highway 98 and began driving back to the gas station at the intersection of Route 30A. *I'm asking for Your help here, Lord, in finding this credit card.* I called on a few of my favorite saints, as well as Mary and Joseph, too, for their help and intercession.

My mind felt anxious and started spinning grim scenarios about the missing card. I rejected those thoughts and tried again to think of the last memory I had of the card. I could picture nothing after paying for the gas. I worked at remaining calm for the next ten minutes until I got to the station. When I feel anxiety due to fear, uncertainty, or confusion about what's going on, I place myself in God's hands, which I did in the car. As I watched the miles go by and felt my thoughts rise and fall, I remembered I hadn't done my twenty minutes of prayer that morning.

At the gas station, a car occupied the pump area I had used earlier that morning. I pulled into the space on the other side of the pump. As I slowed to a stop, I saw a rectangle of something on the ground that caught the sun for a moment. I got out and walked to it. My credit card lay in a spot where cars would cover it up when they stopped at the gas pump. No one saw it because it lay under their vehicle when they got out.

"Thank You, Lord!" I breathed in relief. I slid it gratefully into its slot in my wallet, then wasted no time pulling out of the gas station to return to the restaurant. I wanted to get back to my group of potential friends.

As I drove, I thanked God again for helping me find the credit card. My thoughts returned to the twenty minutes of prayers I had skipped that morning, now that my anxiety was dissipating. The drive took me twenty minutes in recovering the credit card. In the stillness of the car, it dawned on me that God had used this whole little credit card thing to get me alone for His twenty minutes.

A slow smile formed at this realization. I shook my head. My Lord and Master had given me evidence of how much my prayer time meant to Him. I knew my Father loved me passionately and intensely as He does us all. I knew how my heart ached when my husband returned to Chicago every two weeks during the days of transitioning our life more fully to Florida. Our intimate conversations added much to my life. I missed them when he left. How our Father in heaven must miss similar time with His loved ones. With you and me.

It didn't matter that I'd spent an hour in rehearsal that day singing Him praises, and then an hour at Mass leading the congregation in those same songs of prayer. We didn't have our alone time. He wanted time with me, just as we all do with those we love. My smile grew at this new awareness. Well, You certainly got my attention, Lord!

I checked the car's clock. I've never been a good judge of time and how long something takes. My husband is excellent at this and always surprises me at his precise estimates of when he'll arrive home. I'm usually off by fifteen to thirty minutes easily, always thinking it will take less time to do something. In this case, however, I was right on the money. Highly, highly unusual. Eighteen minutes had transpired so far, and I was almost there. "Well, Lord, You got Your twenty minutes," I silently said, "and I got Your message."

CHAPTER 21

KEEP GOD OUT OF IT

To do the useful thing, to say the courageous thing, to contemplate the
beautiful thing: that is enough for one man's life.
—T. S. Eliot (1888-1965) American Poet

ONCE I WAS asked to provide an inspirational quote for a calendar. I felt honored. There were, after all, only twelve of us who'd be chosen, one for each month. I'd been collecting inspirational quotes for years to keep my internal fires burning. Some days I'd search through pages of quotations until I found one that moved me and then recorded it on my voice mail, which added value to anyone calling me. Those quotes reached a dozen people or so on any given day. Tens of thousands would see this calendar.

The quote I submitted went something like this: "Think big. Take action in little ways. There is nothing you can't accomplish when you put your mind to it. After all, you are a child of God."

Weeks later I received a call asking me to tighten up the quote a little, that we really couldn't say "child of God." Could I come up with something else?

I didn't understand how there could be an issue and said so. The answer I received cleared up nothing. Basically, I had to decide if I wanted to be included in the calendar or not.

"I'll work on something new," I acquiesced. "But I'll do it sadly. I put serious thought into this request for a quote. This is who I am, a child of God, and this belief is partly what got me to where I am today."

Reluctantly, I sent in my revised quote: "Always strive for excellence and a positive attitude. Think Big. Listen deeply. Give more than is expected. Be compassionate. And never give up!"

Avoiding a statement that we are children of God in a land whose currency pronounces "In God We Trust" points to a growing problem in this country that I'm sure doesn't belong to the United States alone. We've become so full of ourselves and our power that we think we can push God out of the way and stand on our own two feet.

In her business advice book, *You Can Have It All*, Mary Kay Ash wrote: "Our belief in God should never be checked at the door when we punch a time clock. Faith is a twenty-four-hour-a-day commitment. Many women have made the mistake of changing their beliefs to accommodate their work; it must be the other way around. No circumstance is so unusual that it demands a double standard or separates us from our faith."

No matter what anyone tells you, never keep God out of anything. The moment you do, darkness and fear slip in. I regret changing the quote. I failed this little pop quiz and learned an excellent lesson from it: The enemy is seductive, happy to use our pride or ego (in my case, wanting to see my name in print) to pull us off God's course.

The rewriting of the quote wasn't the only pop quiz. I did better on the one my husband gave me. In a discussion one night, Joe mentioned that I was his highest priority. I knew what he meant but immediately heard a warning bell inside. I thanked him for putting me at the top of his list and then gently told him I couldn't remain there.

"Why not?" he asked with a frown, not understanding. "You are my highest priority."

"I can't be," I told him. "That spot belongs to God. I can be in second place," I said, smiling.

He looked hurt and confused. In his mind, his wife and his family had always been his highest priorities. He loved God and always acted with the best of intentions. He was and is a stellar husband and father. I don't think the list of his priorities needed to be rearranged. I think he simply had to rearrange his thoughts about them. He looked away and sat to do some thinking.

God had another pop quiz in store. This one was much bigger.

CHAPTER 22

HANDLING GOD LIKE A PENNY

Longing for God is the most important factor of this prayer because only on the basis of this inner urge to surrender to God is there hope for progress on this path.
—Sister Ludwigis Fabian, OSB

IN 1970, A Young Life local leader had intrigued me with his personal relationship with Jesus. Thirty-five years later, my personal relationship with Jesus had become a reality. I started seeing God everywhere in the most familiar things. How did that happen?

The relationship mattered to me, and I'd raised its priority. Every relationship has two sides. Having one-way conversations limits how much one can know another; I'd changed the way I prayed. Spending time looking only at my side prevented me from seeing the other.

Americans handle pennies all their lives but rarely study one. They flow through fingers without much attention and are so common most people don't even pick one up from the ground. The same is true of our relationship with God. We study Him, memorize His words and learn His ways, or we handle Him like a penny, letting Him flow through our life with barely a notice.

I love the story—whether it's true or not, I do not know—of a leader known for picking up pennies. It seemed a bit ridiculous for him to do so since he was well known for his wealth and possessions. Someone brave enough asked him why he picked them up. "You can see God's name on each penny," came the answer, "in fact on all U.S. coins thanks to an act of Congress. God's name is holy and should not be allowed to lie on the ground," he said. He honors God's name by picking up the coin, looking at His name on it with reverence, and then carrying it in his pocket where he can touch it for the remainder of the day. Our country adopted the wonderful phrase, "In God We Trust," as the official motto of the United States in 1956. It has been on the penny since 1909 and the dollar bill since 1957.

Another phrase equally worthy of attention appears on the back of the penny. For several centuries "E pluribus unum"—"from many, one"—stood as the de facto motto of the United States of America until "In God We Trust" became official. We state in our Pledge of Allegiance that we are "one nation, under God, indivisible ..." ("that all of them may be one," John 17:21; "many parts, one body," 1 Corinthians 12:12). With maturing eyes of faith, I saw and heard God's presence in all things.

The thirteen letters, "E pluribus unum" are part of the Great Seal of the United States of America, kept by the Secretary of State in a locked glass case in the Exhibit Hall of the U.S. Department of State. The design on the front of the Great Seal represents our national coat of arms. Used for the first time in 1782, it authenticates documents, such as passports, military insignia, and U.S. embassy placards. Since 1935, both sides of the Great Seal appear on the reverse side of the dollar bill.

The eagle, commonly recognized worldwide as a symbol of the United States, is prominent on the front of the Great Seal and holds the motto e pluribus unum in its beak. Its head turns away from the arrows and toward the olive branch to symbolize a preference for peace. Because of its far-seeing vision and upward soaring, the eagle also stands as a symbol of the resurrection of Christ as well as John the Evangelist, the more mystical and theological of the Gospel writers.

The Eye of Providence, or the all-seeing eye as some call it, rises as the prominent feature on the reverse side of the Great Seal of the United States, above an unfinished pyramid of thirteen steps representing the original thirteen colonies and the future growth of our country. On the seal, the Latin words *Annuit Cœptis* surround the Eye. They translate as "He [God] is favorable to our undertakings."[48]

God reminds us of His presence everywhere. Life in the United States gives reminders of Him even in the currency, if you have eyes to see.

Being a leader of independent contractors helped me understand God's relationship with us. He gave us free will. We are not required to love Him or go to Him or even acknowledge Him. As a leader, not a boss, I couldn't make my team like me or talk to me or even return my phone calls.

I learned not to worry about those who didn't respond to my calls or emails. I trusted they knew I was there for them and respected their independent status. I assumed they were running their business just the way they wanted or needed to, since I didn't know the particular details of their lives (they chose not to talk to me). I gave them space and stepped in when they were about to fall off the cliff. God, on the other hand, "thinks" about us all the time. Just as the sun's light never stops shining in our universe, God's tender love can't help but hold us in its radiance. It's what Love does. He gives us room to make all the mistakes we want and then tosses grappling lines to us when we ask Him to save us from our dark, foolish ways. (And even when we don't ask.) They're there all the time really. Some call them grace. Sometimes we can see them when we're desperate.

My team members' relationships with me usually fell into one of three categories:

1. They wanted something from me.

    This describes the most common type of relationship between leaders and their teams. A leader has knowledge, experience, and, often, the inside scoop. The team knows this and the smart ones reach out to their leader in times of need, growth, or struggle.

    Surely, this also describes the most common and primary relationship we have with God. We go to Him when we need something. The intensity of our communications with Him—the core of our relationship—is often in direct correlation to what we need at a particular moment. We hope and pray fervently that He can get us—or someone we love—out of trouble.

A sub-theme of this level of relationship can be "he/she owes me something." In direct sales, we get paid a commission for our team members' productivity. Some of the team's thinking seemed limited to "she's making money on me," and "the very least she can do is...."

It irritates some people that their leader makes a small commission on their sales, although it doesn't irritate them when a salon owner makes a small commission on their haircut or manicure, or the grocer makes a salary on their weekly grocery purchase. But there it is. We do the same to God: "I've been a good Catholic ..." we begin in supplication, implying we earned a favor. We did not.

2.   They cared about me as a person.

Some of my team sought a deeper relationship beyond training and recognition. They wanted to spend time with me; asked about my health and family; and expressed concern, not judgment, when my behavior deviated from the norm. Having taken the time to know me, they could say, "That's not like her." They thought about my life and what it must be like to go through whatever trials or joys I experienced.

These cherished relationships are salve to our isolated lives and weary souls. We all know the absolute delight of receiving an acknowledgment or simple thank you for a gift. We are fond of saying in America, "You just made my day!" when someone shows he or she cares about us.

God is no different. These days, the "through Him, with Him and in Him" preface to the Great Amen in our liturgies pulls at my consciousness. When I think of the absolute delight that God must experience when He receives a tiny acknowledgment or simple thank You, and realize that we are one, not separate from one another, tears overflow in His/my/our response.

3. They didn't need me.

    No real relationship existed with some people. I provided a key to open a door into the company. My usual follow-up phone calls for their training generated no response. Likewise, some of us have no real relationship with God. Some are bold enough to assert to anyone listening that they don't need God; others never bother to think too much about Him one way or the other. They are blind to the ways God tries to reach out to them, or they intentionally ignore Him when they get "nudges" (as I call them) from the Holy Spirit (see man born blind, John 9). I do not judge them. I had plenty of moments of my own when, like Jonah, I intentionally walked the other way knowing without a doubt where God wanted me to go.

CHAPTER 23

THE GIFT OF TEARS

I pray ... that you may be filled with all the fullness of God.
—Ephesians 3:16, 19

DAVID STARTED IT. The magnificence of his naked body took my breath away. He stood splashed in sunshine falling from the skylight above him. My breathing stopped as my gaze transfixed on the work. Moving out of the way, my steps slowed to a halt. The hallway in the museum in Florence took way too long to reach him.

When I was twenty-one, this magnificent work of Michelangelo slowed my senses to a crawl. As I walked around the marble statue, tears began to fall. I didn't know art could cause a person to cry nor that it was acceptable to shed tears for art in public. I slipped behind one of the stone pillars and wiped my eyes quickly in a slurry of embarrassment and astonishment, something I would repeat a dozen times or more before I could walk away.

Tears can be a sign of joy as well as sadness. This I knew. The fact that tears are sometimes a gift from God I didn't know until almost thirty years later. Weeping sometimes accompanies spiritual growth and causes embarrassment or guilt if the experience is different from that of others around us, or we simply don't understand it.

Let me clarify the kind of tears about which I'm talking. Emotional and physical triggers generate tears. Strong emotions, such as frustration, anger, sorrow, or self-pity, can cause us to shed tears. Feelings of gratitude or overwhelming happiness can trigger tears we often see at weddings. (*Why* are you crying? Because I'm so *happy* for her!) We also have the ability to laugh so hard that we cry, a common occurrence in my family.

Physically, pain produces tears. Irritating vapors cause a tear-reflex; vitamin deficiencies or hormonal imbalances cause one person to be more tearful than another. Tears are considered by some to be the new Prozac.[49] They provide release when you cannot put complex emotions into words, as Gwyneth Paltrow found when accepting her Oscar, or Elizabeth Gilbert, author of *Eat, Pray, Love* found on the floor of her bathroom when her marriage ended. Crying helps us more quickly restore our equilibrium after an upset. "If we do not weep on the personal level, we shall never understand other human beings," writes Joan Chittister.[50]

We are "citizens of two realms": the physical and "the spiritual in its unfathomable mystery," says author Paula Huston.[51] The gift of tears is of this spiritual realm. These tears fall without any reddening of the eyes and flow without strain or effort.

Throughout the New Testament, the Holy Spirit acts in diverse ways (e.g. filling people, falling upon them, anointing some). According to the late Right Rev. John Richards, Bishop of Ebbsfleet: "The gifts of the Holy Spirit are not rewards for our goodness, nor badges marking our maturity, nor are they favours which we have merited. If you have ten such gifts, you are not thereby a *better* person than one with none. If you have the gift of *service* that does not make you inferior to or more mature than someone with, say the gift of *miracles*. There can be no prestige or pride in testifying to any that one has received, therefore, only gratitude."[52]

The spiritual gift of tears was an unknown to me. I didn't understand them. Because they embarrassed me, I brushed them away and suppressed thinking about them. This gift wasn't listed among the gifts of the Holy Spirit in 1 Corinthians 12 that I studied for the sacrament of Confirmation. I never heard it mentioned in a single homily nor any class I took despite eleven years of parochial education. It felt like a secret. I added it to my plate of whys—already including contemplative prayer—that had not been taught to me or mentioned as I had grown up.

Ah, church of mine! Share more generously your wondrous secrets with us. Our hearts long to hear them. When you do not teach them, we suffer and hunger needlessly. Body of Christ, learn to share better. Let us help one another to go within to find "the Kingdom of God that Jesus preached up and down the land of Israel, day in and day out, throughout His entire ministry."[53] Teach us more about the *inner* Kingdom of God (see Luke 17:21).

Thank goodness for Sister Meg Funk whose book, *Humility Matters,* revealed the secret to me for the first time. She discussed it at my online community's first retreat in her Indianapolis monastery. Other attendees besides myself showed relief to hear an explanation for the tears we experienced.

She referenced the gift of tears with compunction about which I knew nothing. In case you're in the same boat as me, I'll share what little I've learned. Compunction is a piercing of the heart with an intense awareness of how grievous is our sinfulness to God's heart. While I shed a great deal of tears when I experienced compunction (more on that later), my gift of tears usually occurs in a much quieter and calmer manner.

> *First pray for the gift of tears,*
> *to soften by compunction the inherent hardness of your soul.*
> —Evagrius of Ponticus

"Compunction is not rare," Meg Funk wrote, "but the gift of tears that often accompanies it seems to be a rare gift. The morbid sorrow of dejection is replaced by the purity of having experienced being forgiven. Starting over is natural and graced, as full emotional energy flows from within and without. These tears are full of joy, marvel, and awe, and the proper emotion is to cry. The teaching is that we may not receive the gift of tears, but we should pray for the grace of compunction. The memory of our moment of compunction keeps our hearts soft, and we do not return to our previous ways of dead living."[54]

Gratitude flooded my heart when I read these words in Sister Meg's book in 2005 and heard her teach it at our retreat. I had been wiping tears from my face at Mass and during prayers for years. When the tears fell in public, they always embarrassed me, for I did not understand them. Tears were associated with extreme sadness in my mind.

I disagree with Sister Meg's opinion that this is a rare gift. From my lay perspective, I've often witnessed the Spirit's presence and effect on others, filling their eyes and rolling down their cheeks.

On the other hand, perhaps she's right. Perhaps that is why I never heard of it before reading her book, nor have most people with whom I've approached the topic. Many have witnessed these tears, however, most recently during the televised 2015 visit of Pope Francis to the United States. We may not have heard of the gift, but we have witnessed it. My hope in raising this and other topics is to increase our common vocabulary to be able to discuss these spiritual gifts, improving our awareness and understanding of them.

My tears at Mass often fell during the consecration. They were not sad tears. I didn't feel I was *crying*. They seemed as though they came from Jesus—Who resides within me—from His sadness at the Last Supper when He looked around at the faces He loved, knowing this was His last meal with them, and they did not know it. They did not know the depth of His love nor the sacrifice to which He would surrender. They probably participated in this celebratory meal in a jovial mood, remembering the special relationship the Jewish people had with God, Who saved them from Pharaoh. Perhaps they discussed what transpired that day. They had no idea what lay before their Lord and Master. Jesus knew. He had a prophecy to fulfill.

He knew what He had to do that night. His sacred heart surely ached at the distance between the people and Himself and His Father. The human condition and the ease with which we rationalize disobedience to His Father's Ten Commandments were all too well known to Him. How tenderly He and His Father loved all whom They had created. Laying His life down in one of the most humiliating and painful deaths possible provided a perfect sacrifice of pure, supernatural love with the power to break through the stone cold hearts of His people. Such an act of love would expiate all sins forever.

He broke the bread to start the meal as usual. But it wasn't usual. This simple act created a new covenant between God and His people.

Many thoughts and centuries must have washed over Jesus. The ache of abandonment perhaps magnified hundreds of thousands of times within Him as He reflected on all the lost relationships since the beginning of humankind He and His Father had experienced from those who, once born, rarely gave Him another thought.

He'd already shed tears looking over the city of Jerusalem before entering it for Passover for the last time. Did His thoughts flicker to the pain and torture ahead of Him? Did He feel frustrated that His actions, words, and miracles failed to convert most hearts there? Were His tears similar to the ache of love from knowing loved ones are hurting but won't accept your help?

Don't they know how much We love them? His Spirit must have cried out countless times within Him. *Why don't they see all the gifts We offer them each day?*

"To Shavon, from Jesus" is what could be printed on a gift card tacked to every tree you walk by each day. "To Sarah, from God" could be an invisible note attached to little artistic scraps you find for your collages. "To Tom, from Jesus" could hang from every sunset and crescent moon.

It's impossible to know Jesus' thoughts the night He broke the bread for the last time with His apostles before His death. But I sense my tears at the consecration at Mass have their foundation in His sadness that night, that poignant, cherished last meal with His friends. I feel what must be His heavy heart when the priest raises the Host and repeats Jesus' words at the Last Supper.

"Take this, all of you, and eat of it, for this is My body, which will be given up for you." I picture Him looking at the disciples' uncomprehending faces and then turning to give a long look to His Mother, also present in the room. For some reason, the words of Jesus spoken by the priest at Mass when he raises the chalice cause even more tears to well up.

"This is the chalice of My blood, the blood of the new and eternal covenant, which will be poured out for you and for many for the forgiveness of sins. Do this in memory of Me."

The cup held strong meaning for Jesus. He prayed later that night in the garden to His Father: "Take this cup from Me; yet not My will, but Yours be done" (Luke 22:42). The moment is His complete surrender.

His Father tenderly sends an angel from heaven to strengthen Him for what He is about to endure (see Luke 22:43). That's an amazing moment. It teaches us without words the extraordinary powers God grants His angels. I'm guessing Jesus felt sorely tempted to walk away, for He warned His disciples to "pray that you may not undergo the test" (Luke 22:40).

I also considered the tears could have their source from Jesus' Father, my Father Almighty, Creator of heaven and earth Who resides in my soul with His Son, and Who aches at each consecration for the pain that He knows His Son experienced on our behalf.

> *God wants nothing other from us than our love,*
> *through which we spontaneously learn to enter into His feelings,*
> *His thoughts, and His will....*
>
> —Pope Benedict XVI

Catherine Dougherty reports that "... the Russians pray ... for the gift of tears, which they believe wash away their sins and the sins of others. This is because Christ shed bloody tears in Gethsemane."[55]

"The religious traditions honor the gift of tears and have found ways to ritualize it. During the Passover Seder, when Jews remember their escape from Egypt, they bring salt water to their lips to symbolize the tears of bondage. When a person died in ancient times, mourners put their tears in bottles and sometimes even wore them around their necks."[56]

As I let God into my heart little by little—releasing the notion He was in some distant heaven where He could look down and grant me an occasional wish—I began to experience tender moments of unconditional parental-like love in my prayer times, love that communicated how much He cherished me. Love does to your heart what a rich, perfectly torched crème bruleè does to your palate. It's so delicately sweet, you can barely stand it, but you go on and on and eat the whole thing, as slowly as possible, savoring every moment, licking your lips repeatedly and sometimes even groaning softly in appreciation of the pleasure. And every time it's offered, you want more.

I've never been loved like this before: pure, unbridled love of the sweetest, most exquisite tenderness. Unlike food that fills you up, His love overwhelms me. It overflows in tears, sweet, beautiful tears. Tears that I feared would be misunderstood.

Tears are to the mind the border, as it were, between the bodily and the spiritual state, between the state of being subject to passions [emotions] and that of purity....
—Isaac the Syrian, the 7th century saint

They came during choir rehearsals at St. Luke Church when I would open my heart fully to our Lord in song. The music and lyrics moved me deeply and softened my heart, swinging its door wide open to our Lord in pure adoration and love. At the end of a song, my face wet with fresh tears, I would turn to blow my nose and wipe my cheeks, or pretend to need something from my guitar case to cover the actions of wiping my tears so I wouldn't attract attention to myself. I didn't want anyone asking me why I was crying, for I couldn't explain it then. I knew it was an intimate moment with our Lord, but I had no language or knowledge of this gift to articulate it. As warm bodies in a cold car cause its windows to steam up, so God's love warmed within me.

When she feels the presence of my eternal Godhead, she begins to shed sweet tears that are truly a milk that nourishes the soul in true patience. These tears are a fragrant ointment that sends forth a most delicious perfume.
—St. Catherine of Siena

Rev. John Richards, Bishop of Ebbsfleet, reports the occasions of the coming of tears are the "times when God is particularly present by his Spirit. They come in times both of receiving and giving ministry; in times of prayer; in times of worship."[57] He describes his experience.

"I find it easy to share about my own gift of tears, because as I have stressed, such gifts are nothing whatever to be proud of. They are *not* signs of maturity, nor rewards for goodness. Having certain ones does not indicate any seniority, having other ones does not imply inferiority. It is *the Spirit (Who) allots to each one individually just as the Spirit chooses.*

"I had, for many years, found that I wept gently, but with no real emotion or sobbing or facial contortion, whenever a Christian gathering moved together into real praise of God, or whenever there was teaching or singing that drew us nearer to the Cross of Christ. For decades, I've simply been unable to sing 'When I survey the wondrous cross.' It is as if my eyes take over from my voice! The tears flow when my voice cannot.

"As a public speaker, it was not a gift I would recommend! At a personal level, it was a nuisance. (I did not find it embarrassing, though, since my years of stammering as a Christian had taught me to believe that anyone who felt impelled to ridicule me because I was a stammerer was displaying as much weakness as I was, but of a different sort!)

"Tears appeared to have no purpose in a public speaker other than to hinder him/her in the job. But whatever it seemed at a practical level, I know for certain that at a spiritual level it was *mightily* used by God. It was in a decade when there was widespread stress on *power*: power-evangelism, power-healing, and power-leadership. My tears seemed to have provided an antidote. It displayed my own vulnerability and was used, I think, to lead people to realize that there can be no Pentecost other than through the Cross of Christ.

"It was as if there was growing separation of Pentecost from the Cross, and that God wanted some leaders to be seen to express the necessity of vulnerability, and that I was one of those so privileged. Like St. Paul I experienced a paradoxical ministry where God's power somehow came through weakness."[58]

It seems He pours Himself into my heart when I open it to Him, and it fills up and cascades over, time after time after time. I used to hope that my heart would grow bigger to hold it all someday, to be a vessel He would fill up, and I would pour out. Now I think of myself as part of His holy fountain through which He pours His life-giving Love onto the world.

Sometimes, I think He gets carried away. He can't help Himself if the door to my heart or your heart is wide open. It is so pure, so exquisitely pure and sweet and tender and gentle, that it just melts me. It was a good thing that I knelt or sat when this first happened for I'm not sure I could have continued to stand. I've stopped brushing the tears away these days. I let them fall, figuring most people are looking at the altar, not at me. I carry a handkerchief now.

Benedict of Nursia, the founder of Western monasticism, wept almost continuously in response to the goodness of God, writes Thomas Keating in *Open Mind, Open Heart*. "Similarly, there are times when ... the only response is to dissolve in tears ... Tears may express joy as well as sorrow. They may also indicate the release of a whole bundle of emotions that can't find expression in any other way. In prayer if tears come, treat them as a gift ... which is both painful and joyful at the same time. Joy can be so great that it is painful."[59]

When the Holy Spirit opens the panorama of the world and its pain to you, it will be tears rather than tongues that will be given, says Catherine de Hueck Doherty in her widely-read book, *Poustinia*. He may grant you different gifts at different times, or take them away as He did with St. Teresa of Calcutta or St. Therese of Lisieux near the end of their lives.

What follows is an excerpt from a letter by Bishop John Richards to a person who asked him about the gift of tears. "It expressed what remains to be said," he wrote, "so I have simply quoted it just as written.

"... Thank God for it [your gift of tears], but realize that such a gift is unlikely to be a permanent adornment. As you grow, you change, your situation changes and what God is calling you to be and calling you to do is likely to change also. Watch out for new gifts as the Spirit deems necessary and don't cling to old ones like sports trophies!

"The outworking of your gift will not be identical to anyone else, for God has made you unique and treats you accordingly. Don't feel guilty by comparing what God is doing with you with what He is doing to someone else. That's hardly relevant!

"Don't focus on the gift. Watch out that you do not indulge in it. Never boast about it, but promptly witness to it if the Spirit leads you to do so, for your sharing is likely to bring great reassurance to others and will free them from false guilt that the expectations of other Christians may have forced upon them.

"It is likely that life will have for you deeper pain, not less, as you see and feel things increasingly more from God's view.

That is a special calling, and is, I think, linked to our sharing in some way the sufferings of Our Lord.

"Very often, in situations where God is felt to be present, the tears will have no emotional upheaval behind them, nor will they be accompanied by sobbing. The gift of tears is not the gift of sobbing one's heart out!

"Spiritual sensitivity is two-sided. Sin, your own and others', will pain you more; beauty and goodness will move you more. Both the wonder and goodness of God, and the horror and enormity of evil, will perhaps seem too big for you to cope with.

"In practical terms, you may have to take steps (unnecessary to many other Christians) to reduce seeing the deluge of evil that comes into your life via newspapers and TV.

"If you have the Gift of Tears, as I think you may, do not feel that every tearful overflow is spiritual! Don't encourage tears. Beware of getting over-tired. If you are ministering in public, you may have actually to move your thoughts deliberately away from God(!) in order to cope better. (Rare advice from a Christian minister!!) Don't feel guilty about this. If you have a job to do, do it, the best you can. If tears get in the way, take practical steps to keep them in check. (If I am giving a talk, I have to go through it aloud half a dozen times or more to get the tears out of me first, if I'm to have any chance of getting through it smoothly in public!) I'm reminded of Joseph in Genesis 43:30 [Joseph hurried out because he was overcome with affection for his brother, and he was about to weep. So he went into his private room and wept there. Then he washed his face and came out, and controlling himself said ... Genesis 43:30]. Not quite the same thing as the Gift of Tears, but a good example nevertheless!

"If, in spite of all you do, you experience tears in public ministry, don't let it bother you. Just let them fall and keep going. I can assure you it will not distress people. They will move people, and when that happens it may be a means by which they can respond more wholly—not just their minds—to God's ministry to them.

"Tears is, I think, a very 'spiritual' gift, and so it is important (as with all spiritual things) not to let the devil divert you into being over-spiritual! The over-spiritual are a pain to God and man! Keep the balance of your life right. Keep the secular going strongly and move as the light of Jesus within it. Keep your spiritual life 'earthed' - and a sense of humour is near-essential.

"Whatever gift(s) you have, never rest on past abilities, expect to grow, and earnestly desire day by day any new good thing that the Lord has for you."[60]

This last advice got my nod. Resting on past abilities was not my style. You're either green and growing or ripe and rotting is a favorite quote inferred from a rhetorical question by Ray Kroc (McDonald's entrepreneur). There isn't a day I don't expect to grow in some way. I'm always reading to learn more, and looking for new things to try. It's a little more difficult to "earnestly desire" any new good thing the Lord sends my way. I still have to correct my old thinking that I can figure things out for myself.

Just as I learned that tears didn't always mean sadness, I was beginning to grasp that God was pursuing me more than I was pursuing Him.

CHAPTER 24

LETTING THE NETS DOWN IN DEEP WATER

Jesus said ... Push the boat out further to the deep water ... and let down your nets ... Don't be afraid ...
—Luke 5:4, 11

WHEN I'M FOCUSED on a task, I don't pay attention to my body's warning signs that it's time to take a break. Growing up with five siblings honed my ability to tune out all sorts of distractions. I broke a metatarsal bone in my foot once because of my intense focus while co-teaching a leadership workshop. I took copious notes as my co-presenter taught her portion. It was perfect content to use for a future leader meeting. The next thing I knew, twenty minutes had flown by. I heard her say: "Chris and I will be happy to take any questions for the next ten minutes."

Popping up from my seat in the front, I took a step toward her. When I put my weight on the foot, an internal warning flashed. The foot didn't work. It bent sideways in a nauseating lurch that dropped me to the floor. A cold wave of sweat rushed an alert to my entire body. I knew the drill from past injuries and kept my head near the ground, hoping to avoid fainting. Chairs squeaked as peers jumped to their feet.

"Are you all right?" echoed all around me from too many concerned faces.

"Please, go on," I said from the floor. "I'm fine. *Really.*" I put on my best reassuring face. Raising myself to a chair when the cold sweat stopped, I felt relief I'd avoided fainting. Two hundred eyes were no longer looking at me.

My foot had gone asleep from sitting with legs crossed in a dress and heels. I have no memory of the tingly sensation from the foot that is usually hard to ignore. Off came my low heels to ease the throbbing; I laced on a pair of cross trainers for the rest of the conference. Because I had to walk slowly to avoid pain, I agreed to be wheel-chaired through two airports to return home. X-rays revealed a metatarsal fracture that healed after wearing an AFO (ankle foot orthotic) boot for six weeks.

In spiritual terms, I was equally unobservant in reading my soul's warning light. I held too casual an attitude toward the sacred at times. A close relationship, at least, a response from God, still needed to be established. I felt an internal warning for reassurance or redirection; a nagging urge to find Him pressed on me. Although it could be pushed away, it boomeranged.

I learned the limitations of pouring myself out for others without filling up from time to time. A car needs fuel and oil to run; otherwise, it stops. The soul that does not access God's grace and love hardens, dries up, and shrinks like a weak vein threatening to collapse during a blood transfusion. When my bucket ran dry, I learned that retreats could fill it up and soothe my soul.

My first retreat occurred with Young Life in Bloomington, Indiana, on a woodsy property with a small lake. I remember little about it. I was in my mid-teens. My soul searched to fill the longing in my heart. My only clear memory is of a walk to the end of a weathered deck. I sat with my feet dangling above the water and reached out to God in the stillness. He didn't seem to reply, or I didn't recognize His voice amid my inner turmoil and emotions. My spiritual senses were immature. I took in the sounds of nature, the bird calls in the air, the fertile waiting of the water's threshold. Was the hand of God in the wind on my face?

We need to find God and He can't be found in noise and
restlessness. God is the friend of silence. See how nature — trees,
flowers, grass — grows in silence; see the stars, the moon, the sun, see
how they move in silence. We need silence to be able to touch souls.

—St. Teresa of Calcutta

Two decades later, I did a few weekend retreats through my parish that concentrated my time with God and introduced me to the graces of Eucharistic Adoration. We were encouraged to sign up for one hour of adoration before the Blessed Sacrament sometime between 9 p.m. and 6 a.m. I was getting closer to the Divine like an adolescent hovering near the one he or she fancies. But I hadn't figured out how to ask for the date yet. It seemed like a non-working cell phone connection. I would be on my end saying, "Hello? Can you hear me? Hello?" And God would be on His end saying, "I'm here. I'm here."

While on lunch break during an NCEA (National Catholic Educators Association) conference in a Chicago suburb in my late thirties, I noticed a group of noisy people as I stood in line in a fast food restaurant. Full of my usual self-preoccupations, it took a few loud laughs to draw my attention to the easy banter among them. Their joy radiated like heat from a fire. Their smiles were full and their laughter contagious. My spirit bounced like a buoy on dancing waters as I watched them from my place in line. I smiled in spite of myself. The envy periscope surfaced from my heart, wanting what they had. When I asked others in line who they were, some speculated the group came from a charismatic conference nearby. I'd never seen that kind of joy before. It tugged at me as a child begs for candy before dinner. Uneasy with that much happiness, however, I shook it out of my net.

A year after the contemplative community formed itself online, we began to speculate on the prospect of meeting each other. Mercedes asked us how serious we were. After confirming our desires to meet, she happily arranged a retreat at St. Benedict's Monastery in Snowmass, Colorado. She planned it for six days.

Yikes! I can never be away for that long, I thought. My children were thirteen and ten at the time. My husband worked at Edwards Hospital in Naperville, Illinois, and I was a leader with a million-dollar team. Despite the obstacles, I sensed the Holy Spirit pulling me into the deep waters of this retreat, this time alone with my Creator. God attracted me, and I wanted to please Him. I knew I had to find a way. The cost was not a factor. My income easily covered it. I valued time too much. I didn't want to give it up for all the many things I felt were oh-so-important for my various roles; I felt stingy about giving my time over to God.

After discussing it with Joe, we negotiated how to take care of the children until he got home from work. I committed to attending the retreat. Those in the online community who could not manage the time or cost began praying for those who could attend.

"It's not so much what we do in a retreat, but what we receive that is most important ..."[61] counseled Fr. Thomas Keating. The retreat was scheduled for four days, with two additional days for travel. The retreat coordinator at Snowmass, Bonnie Shimizu, and Mercedes planned for plenty of silence, liturgy, prayer, Liturgy of the Hours, and time for communal sharing.

I invited Joy Donahue from St. Luke's to share a room with me. We had served in several parish ministries together. A gentle soul and easy company, she was one of the eight women and four men in our group.

"St. Benedict is kind of magical," Mercedes told us in our online community. "The natural setting is nestled among the Rockies, with their snowcapped peaks even in the summer time; the deer often pass by gracefully in the night when we drive to the 3:00 a.m. Liturgy of the Hours, their eyes shining reflections of the car lights." I'd never been to a monastery before. Her description of its beauty, its silence, and lovely chapel stirred my heart and imagination. She prepared us for the sound of the monks' boots on the wooden floor as they walk down the hall to the chapel in the darkness of the early morning hours dressed in their Cistercian black and white robes, their arms lost in their long sleeves, their eyes filled with sleep.

"The chanting, oh, the chanting ..." she continued. "They begin with a loud cry from the heart: 'O God, come to my assistance; O Lord, make haste to help me' followed by the Gloria ... as they bend forward in a sign of submission and worship to God Whose name and mercy we all implore. You will see. As Chris would say, how can we keep from singing!"

Just as in Marriage Encounter weekends where individuals and whole parishes pray that each couple opens to the kneading God wants to do in their hearts, so too did the prayers from our online community support us during our time away to surrender ourselves to God's tender, tender, merciful love.

Jim, a sensitive soul in our online community who could not attend the retreat, gave us a warning. He wrote that he'd gotten a copy of our retreat schedule from Snowmass, and told us we'd better look at it:

3:30	Rise
3:45	Bracing dip in glacier pool
4:00	Vigils
5:00	Meditation with guided imagery: St. Simeon Stylites on his pillar in a blizzard
6:00	Lauds
	Eucharist
	Lectio: "One Hundred Years of Solitude"
9:00	Terce
10:30	Shovel the walk
11:15	Scavenge for lichen
11:30	Lunch
12:00	Private time: send e-mail distress messages
12:30	Sext
1:30	Recreation: Making "snow-saints"
4:00	None
5:00	Meditation with guided imagery: dinner
6:25	Vespers
7:00	Recreation: hatch escape plan
7:45	Compline
8:45	Bed check
9:00	Ice cream run
9:30	Caught by security monks outside 7-11
9:50	Explain it to Brother Abbott
10:00	Escorted back to cells

Jim ended his note. "Just kidding, gang! I know you'll all have a joyous time."

As each of us arrived, one of the brothers picked us up at the airport and drove us to the retreat house that sits half a mile above the monastery on the mountainside. My timid soul experienced awe ascending like the sunrise in this majestic setting in the Rocky Mountains. The design of the contemporary retreat house allowed light to pour into its ample space. Like sorting socks, long hugs followed greetings that paired faces with names that had appeared on our computer screens for more than a year. The souls who'd bared their hearts to one another now stood enfleshed in smiles. I introduced Joy to everyone. White haired, little Mercedes' face glowed as the last of our group arrived.

Abbot Joe Boyle and a few other monks barely contained their curiosity regarding how God helped us find one another in cyberspace. The monastery maintains a website that invites men seeking the monastic way of life to "Come and see." They seemed eager to hear how the Great Vocation Maker had called each of us to the contemplative life and the About Contemplation online community. They gobbled up our stories until 11 p.m.

The retreat followed the usual monastic day of prayer. Benedictine monks usually begin their day at 3 a.m. by singing the ancient psalms and reading from Scripture. The plaintive male voices rising in unaccompanied song prayer in the darkness of the chapel will quiet the heart and lift the soul and mind into a place without gravity or time, where the pureness of Peace kisses you like a soft, supple breeze on a warm summer night. Very pure. Full of longing. The single candle flickering in the dark made it difficult to look elsewhere.

Most of us attended this service at least once, walking back to retire to our rooms afterward. The monks continued in prayer or reading until breakfast. One or two sits of centering prayer preceded a morning prayer service in the chapel, followed by the day's Eucharistic liturgy. Work then began for the monks. Monasteries sustain themselves with products they make (e.g. baked goods or farm produce). We continued with conferences, sits, and free time to walk the mountains and commune with God through nature, reading, prayer, or journaling.

One retreatant, David, described driving up to the retreat center and happening upon a tall man decked out in a snowsuit and cross country skis. The man introduced himself as Father Joseph, the Abbott of the monastery, a well-spoken man with a kind, reassuring voice. He suggested attending vigils. "The energy for prayer is great at this time." I made a mental note of that.

I loved the story he told of getting up for vigils at 3:00 the first morning. The moon reflecting off the snow-capped mountains appeared surreal during the walk to the monastery. He and his roommate, Lefty, heard their steps echo through the dark cloistered halls of the monastery. His boots squeaked and startled the beautiful silence. Uh-oh. They became lost and found themselves in a dark room. A monk appeared out of the darkness—said nothing. He motioned to follow him and led them to the chapel.

During a sit of thirty minutes of centering prayer, one of the temptations is to open your eyes and check out what everyone else is doing. David confessed to doing so. "I opened my eyes and scanned the room. I saw Mary with her palms raised upward and that beautiful smile even in meditation. Her smile was the smile of a human being filled to the top of her head with the grace of God. What a beautiful sight."

We all agreed to observe silence in the main areas of the retreat house each day until dinner. Whether to keep the silence in our rooms and hermitages was left up to each person. Joy and I kept silence during the afternoon free time by reading or journaling. Silence was, of course, observed in the monastery. Speaking in the prayer room was permitted during a conference with Mercedes, Bonnie, or Fr. Theophane, and at dinner.

Here was the agenda for March 5, 1996:

5:45	Rise
6:15	Two 20 minute periods of CP with a monastic walk
7:30	Mass at Monastery
8:15	Breakfast
9:45	Two 20 minute periods of CP with walk
11:00	Fr. Thomas video tape
12:15	Lunch
1-3:30	Afternoon break
3:30	Two 20 minute periods of CP with walk
5:15	Supper and celebrations

7:00   Vespers
8:00   Closing

Fr. William Meninger, who presided at Sunday's Mass, quoted his book, *1012 Monastery Road: A Spiritual Journey.* "Something of the monk exists in every one of us." Photos in this book show some of the monastery and chapel where we prayed with the monks including Fr. Thomas Keating, who has written many books on centering prayer. After services, some monks met us in the adjoining bookstore. I had little to say as I stood in awe of men who dedicated their entire lives to God in silence, prayer, and work. They smiled easily.

Several dozen people from the local community attended Mass on Sunday, sitting in a separate area of the chapel reserved for the public. Afterward, Fr. Theophane seemed delighted to hold one of the infants despite his wails as his mother stood beside him.

The stillness and uninterrupted prayer time worked on me in ways I could not comprehend. It deepened a change I'd sensed. A feeling of uneasiness shimmered within me, which I'd shared with the online community months earlier. My strong career ambitions had subsided into a tide pool after God had filled me deeply during centering prayer times. I felt like I was under construction but I wasn't the general contractor. What was He building within me? For what was He preparing me? Would I have the strength to say yes to it as Mary did? I didn't dwell on these questions long. There were no immediate answers. I simply knew I was changing, and it was He Who was doing it within me. I could only pray the words of the Our Father: "Thy will be done."

As long as I can remember, I have always wanted to know for what purpose God created me. I used to think if I knew my purpose, I would be able to make better decisions at key times. Now, I began to understand how important it was that I not know. The unknowing led me to stop, look, and listen for His guidance. I wasn't used to giving up control, getting out of the way so God could do His work within me and through me.

Several kind souls had responded online before the retreat to my uneasiness caused by my changes. One suggested being drunk with the blood of Christ might be the source of my non-concern with world affairs. "Perhaps a sip has been offered you to help you maintain your concentration on your goal until such time as you reach it—here or hereafter.

"And, by the way, your post answered some questions I'd had. Parallel thoughts which you unknowingly answered for me. Thanks, God!" That made me feel good.

Another sweet young man was unsure of his place with us and his calling. He kept thinking about leaving us. Many of us shared our thoughts that God had brought him (and all of us) together in cyberspace for a reason. He, too, responded to my uncertainty.

"I am extremely rusty at centering prayer and the contemplative life," he wrote. "It would be easy for me to forget about it and give it up. Yet I keep trying and I keep coming back here. Why? Because I can see the glory of God here. How can I see this glory? It comes through in the words that you post. Every word you write fills me with the need to keep coming back, to continue centering, not to give up. God is truly working through you just as he is working through Mercedes. Yet you somehow feel in a state of uncertainty? Could it be the night of the sense, perhaps? I'm not sure. What I am sure of is that God is definitely preparing something for you, but you must be silent and patient. Please keep us informed on your journey, Chris. Be patient, be patient, something is coming and soon." He offered his peace and many prayers.

None of the kind replies lessened my uneasiness, although I could see how we were helping each other even in our struggles. Mercedes explained to the group that I was going through a normal process on the contemplative path. She explained God was consoling me intensely and rejoicing in me, although that sounded a bit over-the-top to me. I was all too aware of my failings and sins. She reminded us that Father Thomas Keating talked about the tension between the experience of God in prayer and in daily life, particularly in lay people, and the difficulties they experience when they are challenged and called by the ministry (service) of the daily routine and not-so-routine events. The body, the psyche, the person is not used to it, she wrote. "As you go along it will get easier because the faculties and the senses become more refined and then one can go from prayer to daily life more easily. However, when one experiences the intensity of God's love and presence in the midst of work, cooking, whatever, I don't think that it is ever easy. The Lord can be a bit distracting at times. When the love of God envelopes us, and we are in a conference or a meeting or doing written work, and it does happen, what can one do, but trust in the Lord? But it will never be easy. God's love kind of wipes us out, doesn't it?"

God's love, indeed, had a tendency to wipe me out at times, including a big one in Sister Pascaline's Forest of Peace.

CHAPTER 25

RE-ENTRY

*For contemplation cannot be taught. It cannot even be clearly
explained. It can only be hinted at, suggested, pointed to,
symbolized....*
—Thomas Merton, *New Seeds of Contemplation*

NEVER HAVING BEEN on a contemplative retreat before, I had no
idea that re-entry into the world left behind would be so challenging.
Sacred time flows in slow motion, and the rest of the world zips along
as usual. The contrast jarred my nervous system. For relief, I turned to
my online contemplative community. They understood.

Those of us fresh from the retreat shared with the rest of the group
a few impressions for which we could find words. We couldn't help
ourselves. The Holy Spirit poured out of us. Mercedes posted from John
Cassian: Conference Ten. "Still, He withdrew to the mountain so as to
pray there alone, and surely in this withdrawal, He set us an example so
that if we should have the wish to pray to God with a pure, clean heart,
then we, likewise, must withdraw from all worry and turbulence of the
crowd. While we still hang around in this body, we must reproduce some
image of that blessed eternal life promised for the future to the saints so
that among us it may be a case of 'God – all in all' (1 Corinthians 15:28)."

We had done that. Withdrawn to the mountaintop to pray and be together for a few days in a very special way. "Jesus' prayer to the Father was not in vain," she continued. "He said: 'So that the love you have for me may be in them, and they in us' (John 7:26). The love with which God 'first loved us' (1 John 4:10) came into our hearts. This summarizes for me our Snowmass experience."

Listening at a deep level was my biggest takeaway from the retreat. I listened with my ears and heard the soft rustle of monks' robes in the deep silence and early morning darkness of the chapel; a contemplative coyote howling his prayer with us one morning as we centered; coughs and sneezing as some persisted through colds and altitude sickness; the sound of the bell announcing the start of vespers; the wind in the mountains; the stomp of sheep's protective stances as author Jerilyn Dufresne and I approached lambs in the barn; the bleating of a newborn lamb out of his pen, forlorn at the separation from his mother.

I'll never forget the unadulterated song of deep male voices in prayer—the true song of souls that tugged at my own as they soared heavenward; the hoarse voice and pure love of Father Thomas as he pushed himself despite illness to share his big, generous grin for a few moments with us; and the sound of each person's voice, which until now had been silent words on a computer screen.

I listened with my eyes ... and saw mountains in the shape of two hands holding the monastery and retreat house in its snowy palms. I saw a single candle in the corner beneath the chapel's tabernacle, which seemed to be a fireplace burning with faith and love—oh, how I long to be back there! I saw a dozen white-robed monks bending low before the Lord in adoration while singing deep praise to the Father, Son, and Holy Spirit. I saw the choirmaster try three times to sing a responsorial psalm. With the melody temporarily lost to him, he sent a selfless look beckoning help from a brother monk. I saw the light of Christ in the eyes of all, and diamonds, millions of them, resting atop the snow-filled mountain fields lit by a blue-white moon. I saw people of God in all shapes and sizes fill the vaulted-ceiling prayer room whose windows cropped the mountains. I watched Father Theophane, looking like John the Baptist, limp into chapel, and Brother Jeff's eyes light up like two 100-watt light bulbs when we spoke of our computers and how we formed a prayer community in cyberspace. I saw Mercedes' joy at bringing her flock together and the loving looks Monti the cook (former monk) sent to his wife as they prepared our meals together.

I listened with my arms and felt bear hugs from six-foot-seven-inch tall Brother Raymond, and gentle hugs from Fathers Joseph and Thomas and many others.

"We have only to allow ourselves to be borne along the tide of divine action to achieve sublime holiness," writes Jean-Pierre de Caussade. It is easy to surrender oneself to such a tide in Snowmass.

I am physically home and answering a few business calls, but my mind and heart and spirit are still in Snowmass and the blissful arms and embrace of our loving God.

"How to get more love in our lives?" someone asked during the retreat. Who could forget Father Thomas' answer? "Love more."

Many of us struggled in our adjustment to return to "normal" life after we got back from the retreat. We needed a period of adjustment; that's for sure.

Faith goes up the stairs that love has made and looks out the windows which hope has opened.

—Charles Spurgeon

I didn't know what to do with myself for a while. Reality, children, meal preparation, business demands all chirped at me like hungry nestlings when the mother bird returns to the nest. The timelessness within the stillness and peace played like a low lullaby beneath all the noisy chirpings. How I longed to return to that peace; yet it was time for me to share it now with others. The chasm between the two worlds closed like a long exhalation.

Yes, it was an amazing experience. We walked a path of intimacy with God and for a few passing moments, experienced the earth as the Garden of Eden. God's compassionate love for us and our receptivity to that wondrous love helped us taste Father Thomas' teachings of the union with God. Mercedes pointed out the monks' prayers—how they held us in their hearts before their Lord for all the months we waited for our journey to begin.

"We will always remember this occasion as a core discipleship experience in our lives," she wrote, "when the Lord asked us to come apart with Him for a while in silence and give praise to His heavenly Father."

During the next ten years, I attended a half-dozen retreats with Mercedes and the online community. To borrow a phrase from Bishop Gregory L. Parkes, my bishop in the Pensacola-Tallahassee diocese of Florida's panhandle, I found myself "called to a vocation of discipleship which function[ed] parallel to [my] life's vocation." (*The Church Fully Alive* brochure).

I was hooked.

CHAPTER 26

LITTLE CHRIS

He who is plenteously provided for from within,
needs but little from without.
—Johann Wolfgang Von Goethe

IN THE ONLINE contemplative group, Laura, a Christian minister, asked me: "Why do you sign your emails, 'little chris?' You're taller than me!" I told her it was an interior label, not exterior. "Self-diminishment. The smaller I can become, the greater Jesus can become within me."

"Ah, yes," she replied. "'He must increase, and I must decrease.' I actually suspected it might be that, but didn't want to assume.

"Little both of us, yes? May God's will be done … and may we cooperate with it!"

I love the story that Fr. Keating tells of walking in the woods one day in Colorado. In fall, the aspen turn their iconic yellow. A perfect breeze accompanied his walk. If you've ever seen aspen trees, you know their leaves flutter quickly, almost nervously in the wind. It's as though they're shuddering in anticipation of winter. As he walked, Fr. Thomas became aware of the leaves waving at him.

Oh my, he thought, *how lovely that they're all waving at me.* "Hello!" he replied back, not quite sure if he spoke the greeting aloud. And then, very quietly, he realized they weren't waving to him at all.

They were waving to their Creator within him.

Pastor Don Piper, the author of *90 Minutes in Heaven,* experienced a similar insight when he survived a terrible car crash and endured a long, grueling recovery for thirteen months and thirty-four surgeries. When he finally got out of the hospital, he wanted to get back to church to worship with his congregation. Family and friends enjoyed building a ramp for his wheelchair and reconfiguring a van to transport him. They wheeled him into church to the front of the sanctuary, and the congregation became aware of his unannounced presence. As a microphone was placed in his hand, he began to realize he'd physically pushed himself too far. Exhaustion caved in from being out of bed so long. As the congregation's applause broke out, it embarrassed him, for he felt he had done nothing meritorious beyond surviving. Many times he wondered whether he could hold on, why God didn't let him stay in heaven during his near-death experience.

Every person stood to celebrate the moment. The applause continued for a long time. His emotions overpowered him. *If they only knew,* he thought. *If they only knew.* Then he heard a clear voice in his head.

"They're not applauding for you."

Our preoccupations with ourselves get in our way, or more accurately, God's way. Consumed by self-focus and self-love, we so easily allow distractions. We are our favorite book or TV show. The less we put forth our self to the world, and whatever personal advantage we seek, the more God within us, our True Self, can shine forth. Ah, it sounds so easy.

For most of my life, I have been full of my false self like a loaf of bread that has risen unhindered and needs to be punched down to become finer dough. The parable of the talents (see Matthew 25:14-30) tugged at me like a child at a parent's knee asking to be picked up. As long as I can remember a realization existed in me that much had been given to me and much was expected in return. My enthusiasm for my home-based business came from this awareness: All of the talents and gifts within me seemed tapped and put to good use for the first time in my life. I felt finally able to be a good steward of all I had received.

My wise and wonderful parents repeatedly told us we could do anything we set our minds to do. Being young and impressionable when I heard this, I believed it and found I easily learned most things. When I began leading my growing team, however, I ran into difficulties from assuming everyone had the same self-confidence and courage to try new things as I did. When I discovered that many on my team had low self-esteem, I scratched my head at how to correct it. Everything I suggested to them, they did, but when they did not experience positive results, I had proof that they lacked belief or confidence in themselves.

Denis Waitley's *Seeds of Greatness* helped me build their self-esteem. I followed the famous prayer of St. Francis to "seek first to understand rather than be understood …"[62] Tips from Waitley's book helped me create stepping stones of success for two team members who soon achieved the first level of management and increased commissions. Norman Vincent Peale's *The Power of Positive Thinking* added another staircase to help my team climb out of the basement of doubt and insecurity to new heights of confidence and internal power as they built their businesses.

After years of successful climbing, reaching more and more gorgeous views from the top of my business, I experienced a shock when I purchased a collection of tapes by Anthony de Mello, SJ during the Snowmass retreat. I'd never heard of him. The tapes contained a rare recording of one of his workshops where he laughed and laughed at the way I had viewed the world until then. For the first time, I heard the concept of big "I" and little "i" which deMello presented in a most entertaining fashion. The extraordinary depth of teaching he shared was enhanced by his marvelous sense of humor, which neutralized my usual argumentative disposition. His technique of laugh-jab-of-truth-laugh made for an active boxing match in my mind, effectively breaking down my resistance to the truth he taught.

It's a little hard to be aggravated at someone who blissfully tells you, "You're going to hate what I'm about to say, but it's true, so there you are!" In pure delight, he'd giggle, then tell another story that made me laugh, then zap! Out came another difficult-to-swallow truth like this: "Spirituality means no longer being at the mercy of any event or any person or any thing." What a challenging concept to acknowledge that 1) I was responsible for choosing my emotional responses to any given situation or person and 2) I could progress to a point that I could choose not to let that old tape play in any given situation. He'd call the internal dialogues we have with ourselves, either about ourselves or others, our "old tapes" that we replay interminably to rationalize or justify our emotional responses.

"Now this doesn't mean not to love people. You're just no longer at their mercy. No matter what happens, you're not going to upset yourself. 'But I'm not the one upsetting myself,' you want to protest, '*he* is! You have no idea how irritating he can be …'

"Stop! You're playing your old tape again!" he'd chide[63] in his lyrical British-Indian accent. I'd stop the recording after teachings like this. They gave me spiritual indigestion and took a while to absorb.

The concept of not being at the mercy of any event or person was a breakthrough shaped like a bell curve. We begin life knowing nothing but innate instincts and primary needs. We spend years depending upon our parents or caretakers, and then more years learning to be independent of them. Ideally, as adults we reach equilibrium with balanced interdependence: self-sufficient in some areas, and accepting of our connection with and need for one another in many others. As we age and experience the loss of some of our senses, memories, and physical abilities, we re-learn our dependence on others. Or not.

It's usually along the top of that bell curve that God starts asking us for more space in our lives. We must release some of our ego to give Him room. This is ridiculously easy to say, and one of the greatest challenges I ever faced. It is the biggest obstacle to becoming holy: our desire to protect what we've learned and who we've become. "I don't want to change," our ego says. "I'm doing fine just the way I am. I don't need any help, thank you very much." This is all big "I."

To reach little "i," we must admit we haven't done it all by ourselves. Try as we might, we're not going to grasp certain insights without God's help. The trick is letting Him show us.

*Impress in me such a deep sense of my poverty, O Lord, that I
may look to You for everything and attribute to You, to You alone,
all that is good.*[64]

—Father Gabriel of St. Mary Magdalen

Humility is the necessary condition for self-forgetfulness. Jesus insisted on this point in His teachings, guiding us to protect ourselves from pride and vainglory. "Unless you become as little children ..." Jesus challenged His apostles during their debate about who was the greatest. "He that will be first among you shall be your servant" (Matthew 18:3). One of His last acts showed His apostles the extent to which they should be humble: washing one another's feet (John 13:14). Before sending them into the world to "bear much fruit," He said: "Without Me you can do nothing" (John 15:5).

I started letting God in a little, usually for an hour or so on the Sabbath. But even that hour had its distractions: judgments about how others dressed; the quality of the homily; the quality of the music; the sound system; and the temperature of the church building. The agenda of the day popped into my thoughts. Either my children misbehaved or someone else's did. How much money I should tithe, how boring the service was, and how to improve it pierced my thoughts like mosquito bites in summer. Although I was physically present in the church, God didn't always get my full attention.

God seemed happy to make the most of whatever time He did get from me. He increased within me as I gave over more of myself to Him, in prayer, in praise, in thanksgiving. The more He transformed my heart, the more I seemed willing to do His will. A tiny surrender allowed me to get a little smaller, closer to the little "i." A tiny surrender allowed Him to increase.

*I have so great a desire to give Myself. If you only knew the effort
it was for Me – not to give to you, but to refrain from giving....
That is why your requests relieve Me. My heart is a fire that
suffers when its consuming flame is diminished. Fan it. Fan it.*

—Jesus to actress Gabrielle Bossis, *He and I*[65]

It never occurred to me that it would pain God in any way when I didn't spend much time with Him. Did anyone ever tell me this earlier in my life? Was I too obtuse to hear it at the time? Too full of myself to care about His pain at my lack of attention?

By the time I finished listening to Fr. de Mello with his lilting dialect and contagious laugh, I felt utterly committed to diminishing my big "I" as much as I could. Easily said! Right up there with *I should lose twenty pounds.*

It takes time, but gradually, like water rushing over rugged rocks, the way becomes smoother, the "I" grows smaller. Signing my online community emails in lower case as "little chris" reminded me of my intention to give God more space in my heart.

Becoming aware of my thoughts was the first awakening step in training myself to create a fertile interior foundation on which to build my business. After I'd studied the PMA (positive mental attitude) masters—Napoleon Hill, W. Clement Stone, Norman Vincent Peale[66]—and learned how powerfully negative thoughts could obliterate my goals and efforts, I systematically attacked them. New rules reigned in my brain. Negative thoughts were unwelcome. I stood in control, not them. No longer would I allow my mind to sabotage my desires and goal. I applied the same discipline in my spiritual life.

Negative thinking is not of God. It is blown in by the breath of the Evil One. We must learn to turn our backs to such winds, to close the doors and windows of our temple until they pass.

By increasing awareness of my thoughts, I pulled back on the reins and slowly brought to a halt the negativity I tolerated within myself and, unfortunately, often poured onto others. Most of us don't realize we're doing it. Negative self-talk is not a method of self-diminishment in the spiritual sense. It slams the door on all the potential God gave us. It's a form of self-pride that needs to be purified.

> *Ask Me often to take your hand, because you are always little.*
> *Don't ever think that you can do anything good without Me.*[67]
> —Jesus to Gabrielle Bossis, *He and I*

Pride has so many useful applications—in our work, heritage, family, and accomplishments—that I failed to see its dark side for many years. I saw it listed among the seven deadly sins once, but dismissed it from having any application to me.

I didn't go to confession often because, quite frankly, I couldn't think of any sins I'd committed that were serious enough to confess. When I finally confessed pride as one that had been keeping me from the sacrament, I received my first compliment during confession.

"Now that was a good confession," the priest said.

During my retreat with Sister Pascaline, I found myself drawing a busy bumble bee in my journal. I don't usually draw things. This new image appeared in my mind. "Too fast," I wrote in my notes. Too fast through my days, my career, my driving, and often my time with my family. I took pride in my multi-tasking efficiency, rationalized my type-A tendencies, and found satisfaction and fulfillment in all I had achieved. Rarely did I rest to appreciate and enjoy the accomplishments. The day-to-day energies to maintain such a pace did not allow much room or time for the deeper and holier living to which God called me.

> *God doesn't want our deeds;*
> *God wants the love that prompts them.*
>
> —St. Teresa of Avila

Like the bee, my "words sometimes sting when I speak to others," my journal reminded me. Even though I'd eliminated sarcasm from my speech, and swear words once our babies were born, I had a command of the language and a direct style of communicating that had a bite. It came from places in my heart I still protected childishly, where hurt and pain had not healed. Perhaps I was more like Martha of the Gospels than I knew. Even today, God's grace continues to make me aware of when I've spoken or acted thoughtlessly, thinking only of myself.

CHAPTER 27

CHASTISED INTO COMPUNCTION

The only cure for the false self is death.
—Thomas Keating [68]

FIVE YEARS AFTER the Snowmass retreat, twenty-eight members from the contemplative online group met at another Trappist monastery, this time at Our Lady of the Holy Spirit Monastery in Conyers, Georgia, in 2000. Author and Abba M. Basil Pennington O.C.S.O. was completing his assignment to help increase vocations there and agreed to direct us. His words and counsel were holy and wise. Our group had grown to more than one hundred, including members from Central and South America, U.K., Philippines, and Canada in the decade we'd formed ourselves in cyberspace.

Throughout the years we slowly read and discussed a variety of spiritual books online. Sister Mary Margaret (Meg) Funk joined us through Mercedes' invitation when we chose to discuss her books, *Thoughts Matter* and *Tools Matter*. We relished the rare privilege of asking the author for clarifications and further teachings as we read along. In 2004, Sister Meg completed the third in her series, *Humility Matters*, and offered to teach it in a retreat in her monastery. Our response was immediate and positive. Some of us found our feet doing a happy dance beneath our computers. Around forty of us met Sister Meg at Our Lady of Grace Monastery in Beech Grove, Indiana, in early August 2005.

The book had not been published when the retreat rolled around. We read from photocopies she provided us. Her teaching flowed fresh and fluid with a fruity tartness from her dry humor. As with any rich food, we took small bits at a time. Sister Meg wisely limited our portions. We sat in rapt attention as she doled out faith history from a well of knowledge dug with years of silent monastic study. Each day of the retreat she lifted new thoughts to our parched hearts.

She began each teaching session by playing a different musical instrument with an occasional "oops!" or raised eyebrow when she hit an errant note. Entering the classroom in a formless, ankle-length blue-gray jumper, she used the music as a prayer to gather and close her workshops reverently. Because she based much of her writing on John Cassian's recondite works, some of her teaching was difficult to grasp. I heard her lesson about compunction without fully understanding it. Unbeknownst to me, Holy Mystery had a second lesson planned for later.

Mercedes had asked me to bring my guitar to the retreat since I was driving. "It might be nice to have a little concert one night," she suggested. "Linda will be there. She has a lovely voice. You two can collaborate and come up with some songs for us. What do you think?" Mercedes possesses exceptional skills at facilitating. I had no desire to turn down anything she gently requested. With barely serviceable singing and playing skills, I rationalized that my enthusiasm would cover any flaws.

An unusual incident preceded our "concert," which was simply a gathering in the chapel for a few songs. As Linda and I were setting up our music stands and chairs in front of the altar, we noticed two ghostly figures huddled together behind us some ten feet back. Neither of us caught a full glimpse of them. When we turned around for a better look, they were gone. We glanced at each other and confirmed we both had seen the same thing. Not knowing what to make of the figures, we asked Sister Meg about them. She guessed they were probably two deceased nuns from the monastery. Music is a large part of the sisters' prayer life, she explained, with daily singing of hymns and psalms for the Liturgy of the Hours and daily Mass. More than likely, they were excited about the concert, she proffered.

It is mind-boggling to think that spirituality is dying into yourself.
But there is a death in it and people grieve. There is a grief that
occurs when who you thought you were starts to disappear.
—Ram Dass

Before leaving the retreat, I wrote the following in my journal.

August 13, 2005

I'm all packed and about to leave the stillness and silence of this retreat time, this deep resting with our Lord.

Dying to a part of myself on this retreat shouldn't have surprised me. For weeks, I had been praying the words of the Our Father "Thy kingdom come" with a different intent: the intent that His kingdom would come to me, would become alive within me, rather than intending the words to mean God's kingdom coming some day in the distant future.

God prepared me in advance. As I walked the monastery grounds early one morning, I came upon a baby rabbit lying dead on the sidewalk, eyes open, flies and insects eating away at its back. The fur was gone; the back lay black and exposed. The face of this bunny remained untouched and beautiful in death. I stepped around it with a feeling of foreboding. I knew it lay there as a message for me. I thought about moving it off the path with a stick but avoided doing so, partly because my mind had already begun to process the question, *What's about to die in me?* I didn't want to face the question. I pushed it out of my mind and walked away.

On returning from my walk, the rabbit still lay on the sidewalk. No one had removed it yet. The same feeling of foreboding quickened my stomach muscles. Again, I walked in a wide arc around the carcass. Our bichon frise used to do this around rabbits—live and statuary—in our backyard. My son called him a wimp, not worthy of being called a dog.

Later that day, while working at a picnic table nearby, someone cautioned a passerby to be careful not to step on the dead bunny. Working near the symbol of death but choosing to ignore it made me wonder: *How many other signs from God do we do this to in our everyday lives?* Since it had no meaning to the passerby, she picked up a little stick and pushed it off the sidewalk into the grass. How effortless that gesture looked when not filled with the emotional weight of dread of the future.

At Mass that evening, the Gospel held another symbol of death for me. The priest read the parable of the grain of wheat from John 12:24. After his homily, we sang "Unless a Grain of Wheat" which reinforced the symbol with its refrain:

> *Unless a grain of wheat should fall*
> *Upon the ground and die*
> *It remains but a single grain with no life.*

When I began my centering prayer the next afternoon, the day following Sister Meg's teaching on the afflictions of the soul (acedia, depression, and pride), the presence of God greeted me in an unmistakable manner I'd never experienced before. His large and luminous presence loomed directly before my mind's eye, blocking the way to my heart where I go to rest in Him. I apparently wasn't going there today. I tried but found no way around Him. None! I sent my attention to the left, then the right. He blocked the door to my heart.

"Don't you think you've been avoiding this pride thing long enough?" He seemed to ask me. "I certainly have been tolerating it long enough."

Oh, pierce my heart! My loving God chastised me. And He was right, of course. When is He ever not right? Tears welled up immediately. I knew I had allowed pride to creep into my heart. He then showed me places, incidents, and people I had hurt due to my prideful ways. He showed me how my difficulty with being early was connected to my pride, thinking my time had greater value than others when I chose to squeeze in one more activity than I had time for. I thought if I was late, others would either wait or start without me, which I had found acceptable. He showed me how I breezed by others in my rush to appointments or daily activities, often literally brushing against them with a quick "Oh! I'm sorry!" as I hurried past. I became aware of the peace I disturbed in those whom He loved when I did so. And He showed me how my rationale at not being able to get in my second centering prayer time at day's end had its source from feeling I was "advanced" enough not to need it, or at least to be able to get by without it.

Blood rushed to my face in shame as I saw my actions and heart through God's eyes. What a wound He gave my heart. I didn't want this disapproving "look" from Him. I only wanted to please Him, as any child does her parent. Tears continued to flow. My nose began to run. Without a tissue at hand, my prayer shawl began to dampen. Deep sighs, sobs had to be suppressed in order not to disturb the others at prayer. Between twenty-five and forty-five people prayed at these silent sessions lit by a single candle to remind us of Christ's reassuring presence. I spent the rest of the prayer time in total contrition, unable to stop the tears and aghast at pushing God's tolerance to the brink.

The next few hours were a blur. Thankfully, we maintained silence during this time. After evening Mass, I prostrated myself before God on the stone floor of the empty chapel and uttered only, "I am so sorry!" from the deepest part of my spirit.

The schedule included the sacrament of Reconciliation that evening. I'd decided earlier not to go. Pride reigned then. Now, I simply paced myself until I felt the line of penitents would be short. Confessions ran from 7:30-9:00 p.m. I arrived at 8:30, but three others waited ahead of me. A minute before 9:00 p.m., my turn came. I feared the priest would announce I'd have to come back tomorrow night. I wasn't sure I could endure a night with this on my heart. I entered the reconciliation space, and he didn't turn me away.

Tears flowed again as I spoke my sin of pride to the priest. I knew I'd expressed pure contrition before the Lord earlier that evening, but it needed to be spoken aloud. "To root out our regret, someone must feel our sorrow," teaches Sister Meg, "just as in wanting to love, someone must be there to love." I wanted the graces of the Sacrament of Reconciliation to ease the deep anguish I felt. He absolved me gently.

The beginning of compunction is the beginning of new life.

—George Eliot

The next day my spirit felt lighter. Deep sighs returned to me, which had been missing from my life for a while now. My centering prayer practice had become fragmented in this past year of shifting back and forth between my Florida and Chicago offices. After lunch, I felt washed out from the compunction the day before. I couldn't read. I felt an odd abdominal disturbance and tried to take a nap to sleep it off. Sleep wouldn't come. A tight whirling in my abdomen did not ease by effleurage, a movement similar to childbirth techniques taught to me by a healing practitioner in Canyon Ranch in Tucson. That provided only momentary relief; the whirling energy persisted. A similar energy had buzzed in my head one other time after long periods of contemplative prayer and breakthroughs when I first discovered the richness of centering prayer. I had responded gluttonously to it, drinking deeply for too long as when I snorkeled for the first time and breathed too deeply through the mouthpiece making myself light-headed. This whirling tightness in the abdominal chakra area responded to windmill-like arm movements and a long walk to move the energies. It dissipated by the end of the day.

My heart sings gratitude for the Sisters of St. Benedict at Our Lady of Grace monastery: for their stillness; their delicate voices in chanted prayer song; their loving prayers. The holy space they created in their retreat center and the support they offered Sister Meg to do her writing research helped bring essential teachings and books to spiritual seekers such as me who received release from an affliction.[69] Sister Meg is right: their monastery is one place among many where grace certainly abounds.

CHAPTER 28

MY RULE OF LIFE

*Contemplation is no pain-killer. What a holocaust takes place
in this steady burning to ashes of old worn-out words, clichés,
slogans, rationalizations!*
—Thomas Merton, *New Seeds of Contemplation*

AT THE NEXT retreat I attended in 2007, Fr. Keating gave a week-long
talk on Mary and Martha, two Scripture figures popular with Christian
contemplatives. When Jesus visited their home in Bethany where they
lived with Lazarus, Mary did all the listening and Martha did all the
meal preparation. Somewhere between the two of them lies the best part
of the Christian contemplative Tradition. Mercedes invited me to join
the retreat to hear his teaching.

I met her local group in a south Florida retreat center where the
daily structure flowed with less rigidity than monastic retreats. The
loveliness of a day bracketed by set prayer times continued to intrigue
and attract me. It would be wonderful if I could carry that over to my
life back home.

The inspired questions posed by the online group often produced
answers that deepened my insights and understanding of my spiritual
journey. Sometimes I learned new words, such as horarium, (Latin for
of or related to the hours), which refers to the daily schedule of those
living in a religious community. Each retreat followed the rhythm of

the monastery's horarium. The regular reminders throughout the day to join the community in prayer helped me pay closer attention to God and lean on Him for my understanding. Sister Meg explained there was a counterpart to the monastic horarium lived in monasteries. In lay life it is called a rule of life. Who knew?

She asked our group if anyone wanted to share his or her rule of life. I gave it a try. My rule of life had a resemblance to a monastic horarium only in its early hours, I replied. As a contemplative working in the world, one week does not always look like the next regarding scheduled activities or even physical location.

When my children were little, the only way I could guarantee getting in a twenty-to-thirty minute cocoon of contemplative prayer time was to give no indication of being awake in the morning. So my rule of life would begin between 5:30 or 6:00 a.m. (rising when my body awoke, except for days of travel or early business meetings). I would sit up straight in bed, rearrange the pillows for an upright, alert sitting position, and direct my very first conscious moments of awareness to God (if they weren't already).

When my children were old enough to leave them for short periods of time, I began going to daily Mass at 6:30 a.m. Lectio took place either before daily Mass, or after, but not every day except for the five to six years when I did an intensive Bible study course. Mercedes once slowed my reading of Merton's *The Sign of Jonah*.

"You're reading *way* too fast," she cautioned. I knew nothing about sacred reading at that time. She taught me that besides reading, lectio divina could involve lived experiences other than Scripture or holy works.

I had found lunch hours during the past twenty years not very conducive to prayer or lectio divina. There was just too much activity in a home with young children plus a business: phones ringing, high energy, staff and children coming in and out. Now when I work, I sometimes don't stop for lunch until 3-4 p.m. because the work often flows effortlessly.

Vespers is the same: an impossible time for a mother to "disappear." In a household with children, late afternoons resound of chaos and crankiness and "When are we going to eat?" After they went off to college, I occasionally succeeded at a vespers-like chanting of the psalms, but never felt a need for it to become praxis.

Much of my day is prayer now in many different forms. It all seems to flow continuously, not like St. Luke's baptismal font that gets turned on and off for services. All of nature speaks to me of God from light and dark to wind and sky, to water and growing things. Gardening is prayer. Responding to business phone calls often draws me in prayer to Jesus within the person on the other end of the line and the needs of his or her heart.

When I notice frustrations and anxieties, I return to prayer or sacred reading, recognizing the moment as an opportunity to trust our Lord and draw close to Him, again. A walk, a bike ride, a slow driver ahead of me when I'm late for the airport … all feed morsels of gratitude to my soul, helping me see God in all things, calling me always to trust and follow Him. Colloquy continues as an ongoing practice. My usual query begins: "What would You have me do now?" As Fr. Tony deMello referenced in his talks, I feel I'm finally "awake."

Just as I do Sudoku daily to sharpen my analytical thought processes, part of my rule is an immersion in the "through Him, with Him and in Him" Eucharistic prayer before the Great Amen at Mass, and the "as I am in You and You are in me" from John's Gospel. I know God is in me, as He is in all of us.

I have no regular evening practice, as that is often the only good time I have to connect with family. Sometimes I have to work in the evenings. At least once on weekends I'm out late with friends. I retire to my bed when I am spent, often having already fallen asleep on the couch. I can read no more than a few sentences at night before falling asleep. Most often, I simply lie down, whisper a prayer of gratitude for all I received and experienced that day, send a soft "I love You" to the Trinity and imagine falling asleep in the arms of God.

My "rule," as with my spiritual path, is ever evolving as I move through the transitions of my life and travels and offices. If I get too lax, the Holy Spirit makes no bones about getting me realigned. Lately, when I've been wayward and have shortchanged My Lord of His alone time with me, I sense an immediate wave of relief from God that I'm "back" (like the prodigal son's father experienced). My eyes well with tears at the realization of how much God missed me and how pleased we make Him when any of us return to His arms in prayer.

To me, my rule is a little like going to the refrigerator for food. I stand with the door open and sometimes look to see what I feel like eating. Other times, I know what I want before I open the door, often from a primal response that tells me what my body needs. Always, I find something there to sustain me. Always my Counselor guides me to the banquet or the still waters.

By answering Sister Meg's question with my actual rule of life, I realized that as long as my children were home with constantly fluctuating schedules, a day ordered by set prayer times was not realistic. The natural transitions my life provided had to be my guide. Sister Meg, on the other hand, found my "lack of rigidity but faithfulness to prayer" a delightful variation to the structure of her monastic schedule, "folding all life into a prayer but treasuring the life of work, family, travel."

Books by monastics such as Thomas Merton resonated with the details in my life. Being a lay person, however, caused me to experience some dissonance when I'd recognize elements of my spiritual journey being referenced as monastic life, as in Merton's quote below.

> *The thing that you must realize as you go along in the monastic life is that you know nothing about the spiritual life. It is this realization of our ignorance and our foolishness and of our inability to make a good job of it that makes us begin to live the monastic life. As long as we know what we are doing and where everything fits, we haven't begun. It is when it gets beyond us that it begins, because only then does our Lord come in and take over.*
>
> —Thomas Merton

It made me question how appropriate my experience could be, not being a vowed monastic. It did not cause me to question my actual prayer and mystical experiences, but I felt hesitant to admit any of it as if it shouldn't be happening to a lay person. Of course, it should I know now, but books I read didn't validate my lay experiences. I felt benched without a uniform and no chance of playing in the game. The dearth of spiritual stories from contemplative working moms similar to me fueled the writing of God's patient pursuit of my soul.

Sister Mary Luke Tobin, SL, was one of fifteen women—and the only American woman—invited as an official observer at the Second Vatican Council in Rome. She was president not only of her religious community, the Sisters of Loretto, but also the Leadership Conference of Women Religious, LCWR. At one time, she managed the Thomas Merton Center for Creative Exchange in Denver, Colorado. She gave me the above Merton quote when I met her at her motherhouse just outside Gethsemane, Kentucky. I was on a retreat there with Commonground, a non-denominational group of spiritual seekers from Bloomington, Indiana. We traveled daily to the monastery, the hermitage, and the University of Louisville, home of many of Merton's journals, paintings, and works.

One of the elderly nuns in the motherhouse had suggested I visit Sister Mary Luke in her room. I had no idea who the tiny, white-haired, firecracker was at the time. I thought I was performing a spiritual work of mercy visiting someone who may be lonely. Years later, when I heard her name mentioned in conversation, I was surprised to find it was the same person I'd met.

Sister Mary Luke took me under her wing the afternoon I knocked on her door and asked if I could visit. She was a gracious host and made room for me on the chair by her bed near her paper-filled desk. We enjoyed a lively conversation and talked for several hours.

She inspired me to learn more about Vatican Council II. Her eyes sparkled when she spoke of it. When I learned of Cardinal Suenens' Jesus-like interpretation of the Holy Spirit's charisms applying to everyone, and her involvement on some of the Council's committees—quite radical at the time in the mostly male enclave—I understood her excitement. She shared eight pages of typewritten notes excerpted from talks Merton gave to the sisters. They are undated. Here are a few of my favorites:

"#16. Compunction softens the heart. One of the reasons for coming to the monastic life is to find compunction: to cast off that which is hard, competitive, aggressive, and fruitless. Compunction makes a person overcome himself rather than project his problems on to another and be fighting all the time.

"#17. The only true joy on earth is to escape from the prison of our false self. The exterior I is the I of projects, of temporal finalities, the I that manipulates objects and persons and controls them. This "I" seeks recognition, applause, approval, and wants accomplishments, success." (This point echoed to me what I'd learned from Anthony deMello regarding the Big I and the little i.)

"#19. Freedom to enter into the true self is denied to those who are held back by dependence on self-gratification, sense satisfaction, pleasure seeking, anger, self-assertion, pride, vanity, love of comfort, and greed. The exterior "I" has a compulsive need to measure up to greatness, heroism, and infallibility.

"#25. The false self has got to come out. We can't get rid of it by ourselves; it has got to be got out for us. Usually, God Himself puts you in situations where you have to sweat it out. You have to get rid of this useless concept of yourself and this is a great liberation.

"#26. The false self doesn't exist; it isn't there; it is an illusion. When it gets torpedoed, don't defend it; let it go. Then you will have freedom.

"#30. The basic freedom that Scripture talks about is the freedom from idolatry and the real idol is me. Only the cross can free us from our idol, that self which is opposed to God. We have to die a death to the false self.

"#32. If we ask for the Holy Spirit, what we will get first is the cross to kill self and acquire humility and a spirit of charity toward others, not fighting others and trying to prove they are wrong.

"#34. Having a private self which refuses union with Christ prohibits prayer. We can get rid of this private self by loving our brothers and sisters. If I can get rid of the separation which I place between others and me, then I have gotten rid of the separation between Christ and me. If I am refusing love to others, then I am resisting Christ.

"#61. All we can really give God is our freedom to operate in us. And that is all He wants from us, freedom to work in us. He wants a free hand to communicate His goodness to us. What we should do with all our heart is to give Him a free hand to open the way so that He can communicate His life to us. That is all He wants to do—give goodness to us."

As almost always happens to me after reading Merton, my soul was stirred, then still and silent.

CHAPTER 29

HOW CAN THIS BE?

No grace comes to us from heaven except He looks upon our hearts. And what is more—He looks at us from within our own hearts, for we and He are one.[70]

—Thomas Merton

I KEEP BUTTER in the freezer. My daughter keeps hers on her kitchen counter so it's soft and easy to spread on bread and toasted English muffins. When I'm ready to bake, I take out a frozen butter stick and either let it soften on the counter or slice off what I need.

One of my favorite breakfast recipes is a puff pancake similar to a Dutch Baby Pancake I used to order at the Original House of Pancakes in Oak Park. I've been baking it for nearly thirty years. My daughter-in-law, Jaime, asks me to bake it often. I'm happy to do so because cooking for my family members is one of my favorite ways to share my love with them. All my feelings for them are poured into every action, slice, whisk, and spice I add to each dish I set before them.

The first step in making the puff pancake is preheating the oven to 400° and buttering the pan. A cast iron skillet may work just as well as the high-sided oven pan I use. Slicing off two tablespoons of butter, I grease the sides of the pan, then pull off the piece of wrapper around the frozen butter square, drop it in the pan, and place it in the oven to melt as I prepare the pancake.

The rest of the ingredients—flour, milk, eggs, honey, cream cheese, salt, and baking powder—go in a blender. After blending a minute, it's best to scrape down the sides of the blender container for any wayward flour and blend again.

There are two times to witness marvelous transformations in this recipe when the oven door is open. The most dramatic comes at the end of baking. The pancake reaches an amazing height as the heat puffs it into the shape of a deep bowl of deliciousness, its sides rising far above the two-inch sides of the baker. It is glorious to see and makes a dramatic presentation when it comes out of the oven. As it cools, the puffiness settles. My pleasure in eating a slice is enhanced by fresh-squeezed lemon juice drizzled on top and a dusting of powdered sugar.

The other transformation takes place when checking the butter in the baker after the ingredients have been blended. Is it melted yet? Sometimes, when a yellow lump is still sitting in the baker, I grab a potholder and tip the butter pat to slide it into a hot puddle of buttery happiness to finish its melting. Other times, sizzling bubbles and froth cover the bottom of the pan, waiting excitedly for the batter to be poured.

Perhaps that was what the Presence was waiting patiently for—my melting—as I sat on the bench in the Forest of Peace on a hot sunny day. He was ready for me. He'd been ready and waiting since the day He formed me. Since the day He formed all of us. He was waiting for my transformation, for the final piece of me to melt away in readiness for Him.

That pure, radiant energy from the Presence was still pulsing before me. My body was tensed for what? It didn't know. My breathing was shallow as tears ran down my face. I had been sitting with this silent, patient, waiting Presence for a long time and I was beginning to feel anxious. It seemed to be my move, somehow, though I had no idea what to do. If I opened my eyes to see the Presence, I knew I risked death. I simply didn't know what else to do. I had waited and waited. I'm not good at waiting. The Presence seemed to be waiting for me.

Willing to show courage when needed, I made my decision. Filled with trepidation, I knew this could be my last moment alive. I took in a quick breath to steady myself, held it, and then opened my eyes. What I saw shocked me.

There was nothing there. No body. No being. No Presence. My eyes squinted at the brightness and strained to see the lake gleaming in the distance. Untouchable sunlight shot like spears through trees. The powerful Presence I'd felt had disappeared. I wanted to scan my surroundings more, but my eyes resisted opening any further. The brightness hurt them.

I couldn't believe the Presence would just vanish silently after waiting, waiting, waiting for me to respond somehow. It didn't make sense. The lake in the distance didn't interest me now. I wanted to know where the Presence had gone. I shook my head in disbelief and growing sadness. I'd blown it.

Blinking at the brightness as if that would materialize something or beam me up to wherever the Presence had gone like a Star Trek transporter, I tried to breathe normally. *What just happened?*

"I'm here. I'm with you."

Everything stopped. This response came from within me. My mind became aware that the Presence, Who had stood before me moments ago, now was residing within me.

I didn't dare breathe.

How can this be? I heard myself suck in a sudden breath of air as my mind tumbled in the wave of this truth.

This is difficult to write, perhaps difficult to believe. It took me years to discern whether I should even share this. As simply as I can put it, my entire being filled to the brim with the presence of God. Deep, deep breaths recurred as my mind tried desperately to grasp this startling phenomenon as if it had lost its balance and needed to right itself in a wave. I felt unworthy. Tears streamed from my eyes uncontrollably. Long sighing breaths alternated with sudden gasps for air. My mind balked.

He was inside me! My mind reported this like a child with wide-open eyes who had just awakened in a strange place. I couldn't stop the gasping breaths. It was too much. Each time I tried to comprehend this shift—the vibrant energy and pure love that had been external was now coming from within—my mind stumbled as though knocked over by this repeating Truth. Tears ran freely down my cheeks and neck.

Deep calls to deep in the roar of your waterfalls;
All your waves and breakers have swept over me.

—Psalm 42:7

Wiping in vain at the tears, my chest kept rising with sighs, and my lungs kept trying to suck enough oxygen to deal with this powerful Presence. It felt solidly in place. Somehow I knew He'd just made a home inside me, which made me cry like a baby. It was too much to believe. Who could absorb this? By opening my eyes and choosing to see His face, I had somehow let God in.

I couldn't move. How do you move when God suddenly fills your entire being? He no longer resided only in my heart where I would descend with my mind's eye for intimate moments in prayer. It seemed He filled my entire being. My lungs felt pushed up to make room for Him like a full-term baby presses against its mother's organs. I had to keep taking deep breaths to keep enough air in me. Or perhaps, perhaps my heart ... was it enlarging? For what? For the great God of all creation—of galaxy upon galaxy—to fit into my little being? I shook my head in confusion and wonder. *What was going on?*

Tears continued to flow unceasingly. I blew my nose with the one tissue I had and swiped at the tears, knowing the effort was useless. I couldn't stop them. I was overflowing. *We* were overflowing. I struggled in vain to comprehend what had transpired, finally giving up. I kept shaking my head as more tears erupted from the knowledge of Who lived now inside me. He filled every molecule of me, and the awareness of this kept stopping my breath. I can't explain the purity of the love, the exquisite tenderness in which He bathed me. The vibrant energy made me feel super charged, triggering the gasps. My senses wanted to shut down from overload. I sighed and gasped and wept in shocked awe.

Time hung suspended about me. I had no idea how long I sat there, and it didn't matter. I couldn't move. The tears eventually subsided, but my nose continued to run. My lone tissue shrank into a useless mass. Slow sighs replaced the gasps after half an hour, an hour, or was it just a few minutes? Time prostrated itself on the ground. It could not raise its head. Everything had stopped. Heaviness descended upon me. My limbs felt like 100-pound anvils. My body refused all commands.

You should be getting back soon, I thought. Or did He say that? Everything blurred. Afternoon prayers started at 4:30. I wasn't sure I needed to pray anymore with God now fully inside me. I didn't know what to do. Nothing in any book had prepared me for this. Incredulity tumbled inside me at the fullness of my being, a fullness I felt unworthy of carrying, because of my shortcomings and the places in my heart that lacked selfless love.

> *Through knowing the love of Christ, which is beyond all*
> *knowledge, you are filled with the utter fullness of God.*
> —St. Paul

A fresh wave of tears cascaded as my mind again grappled with what had just taken place. *You really should head back now if you're going to make afternoon prayer time,* some part of me coaxed. Deep sighs returned. I still couldn't move.

What time was it? I had no idea. It felt like late afternoon from the quality of the light in the forest. I slowly looked at my watch. Even that action seemed wrong, too worldly, but my survival instincts started to kick in. It was a little after four. Oh, gosh! I had a fifteen- to twenty-minute walk back to the monastery. I knew I had to go back there, but I could not find the strength to do so.

"You're doing great," the Voice said. "I'm right here with you. We'll take it one step at a time."

With an enormous effort of will, I forced myself to stand up from the bench. I nearly fell at the sensation that God stood in my feet. I staggered, my balance unstable, and slumped back on the bench. Whatever was happening had depleted my physical strength. I rested. Trying again to gather myself, I leaned forward to stand again. It felt peculiar to sense God's presence flowing down my legs as the muscles adjusted to bear my standing weight. I wanted to sit back down. It felt too odd.

"You're doing great. Let's try just one step now."

I knew I had to move. Could I do so yet? I felt rooted to the earth as if a magnet held me in place. I didn't know if I had the strength. Surely I could do one step, though.

With considerable effort, I moved my right leg. It was heavy. My knee almost buckled at the sensation that God was taking that step inside me. My body weight shifted as I planted my right foot on the ground. If my leg had a flexible tube into which warm fluid poured in slow motion, that is what it felt like as the Presence rolled like gelled liquid filling my leg.

Another deep sigh escaped my overwhelmed body. The knowledge that God was walking with me, inside me, rocked my reality. St. Joan of Arc had difficulty explaining her spiritual experiences and the voices she heard. St. Catherine of Genoa lost consciousness and fell into a kind of ecstasy when a ray of Divine light pierced her soul. At least I was still conscious while my mind struggled to grasp what was happening to me. I wiped my runny nose with the shreds of the tissue balled in my hand.

"You're doing fine. That's it. Now the next foot."

He coaxed me the way one would encourage a baby. How aptly that described me at that moment. Birth had occurred. I didn't understand it at the time. It dawned on me years later what had taken place that afternoon in the woods. I only knew that everything felt unfamiliar and overwhelming. My breathing drew a new kind of air with a changed consciousness. Something made me gasp with almost every breath. A new union with God had taken place. His first step with me felt like taking the first step in a new pair of shoes. The second step didn't feel much better. My legs still felt as heavy as anvils. To move them required a concerted effort of will. I felt wiped out.

"That's my girl!"

I sighed. After a pause, He encouraged me again.

"Now one more step. You can do it."

I marveled at His encouragement. How did He know I needed such elementary instruction? I knew how to walk; I just didn't know how to do so with God, quite literally. I clung to each spoken instruction with an intense focus and trust. I concentrated on willing the right leg to move forward again. So heavy. Then the left.

"Good! I'm right here. You're doing fine...."

It didn't feel fine. It felt near impossible. There was something quite odd about feeling the Presence of God taking each step with me. At this rate, I wouldn't make it out of the forest before dark. I could do nothing more to move any faster. Like pouring honey from a jar, my pace crawled in a supreme effort that seemed perfectly acceptable to Him-Who-was-within. We had no hurry to get to chapel for afternoon prayers. A part of me knew that was unnecessary under the circumstances, but the sun would set soon. A conscious act of will impelled another step forward. Waves of tears continued to crest and subside, crest and subside.

"Just one more step ..."

On and on He encouraged me. My head felt like a medicine ball. A fallen tree lay across the path. I sat on it because I could find no strength within me to climb over it. With snaillike movements, we lifted one and then the other leg over the wide log and even more slowly pushed off to stand back up. We had a long way to go.

"I'm here. I'll always be here with you. We're together now. Just one more step."

My steps were not my own anymore. I took them with God, and this awareness made itself known with each placement of a foot on the ground and every flex of my knees. I shook my head amazed, weary, and overwhelmed.

More than half an hour later, we reached the monastery's back door. My pace barely had increased, step by slow, heavy step. When we got inside, the chapel doors were closed. Too late. Afternoon prayer had begun.

Weary, I dropped onto the corner of the stone fireplace, relieved to rest from the exhausting effort of the long walk back. The tears and sighs had slowed. Gratitude fell like a veil over us. The emptiness of the room settled around us like gelatin for the half hour before the chapel doors opened. I moved to a chair by the window and tried again to understand what had transpired.

If anyone loves me, he will obey my teaching. My Father will love him, and we will come to him and make our home with him.

—John 14:23

After a while meal preparations began silently after the sisters slipped into their shoes outside the chapel. Like a sloth, I moved to fill my plate, eating out of habit more than desire, unable to speak and unsure of what I would say if I did. If conversation took place at dinner that night, I have no recall of it. I felt relieved by the general silence. If someone had asked me anything that night, I would have been unable to reply. I had no words. I offered minimal assistance at clearing the table and cleaning the kitchen afterward.

Somehow I made it to my little house that night. I may have slept in my clothes; I can't remember. I slept deeply, saying goodnight to God within me.

In love, all things are shared and so if you love Jesus, everything of his is yours.[71]
—anonymous writer of *The Cloud of Unknowing*

CHAPTER 30

TRANSFORMATION

*Let me not pray to be sheltered from dangers but to be
fearless in facing them. Let me not beg for the stilling of
my pain, but for the heart to conquer it.*
—Rabindranath Tagore

OUTWARD APPEARANCES GAVE no clue I was no longer the same person. It felt like what Blessed Mary, the Mother of God, must have felt marveling at the new Presence of the Son of God mysteriously now inside her, at once unsure, yet trusting in God's plan for the future. His Presence settled quietly within me and became more comfortable day after day. My human weaknesses lived on (darn it!), but my heart grew tender, more open, more loving of others, surprising me sometimes with its kindness to others.

The symbolism of the mingling of the water and wine during the Eucharist had a fresh, new meaning for me. "By the mystery of this water and wine may we come to share in the divinity of Christ, who humbled himself to share in our humanity" (Eucharistic prayer of the Mass).

Upon returning home after my week in the Forest of Peace, I caught up on snail mail (delivered by the U.S. Postal Service), email, and exchanges from the online contemplative community. Someone posted a message of encouragement for Tess, a member of our community whose husband, Rufo, fought against a disease. He wished to share his favorite scripture, Isaiah 43:1-5, with her. Sister Pascaline had given me this same psalm to meditate on before leaving, an example of the confirmations God bestowed on the community regularly.

> *The Lord who created you says,*
> *"Do not be afraid—I will save you.*
> *I have called you by name—you are mine.*
> *When you pass through deep waters, I will be with you;*
> *your troubles will not overwhelm you.*
> *When you pass through fire, you will not be burned;*
> *the hard trials that come will not hurt you.*
> *For I am the Lord your God,*
> *the holy God of Israel, who saves you.*
> *I will give up Egypt to set you free;*
> *I will give up Ethiopia and Seba.*
> *I will give up whole nations to save your life,*
> *because you are precious to my eyes*
> *and because I love you and give you honor.*
> *Do not be afraid—I am with you!"*

None of us have any idea at the time we write something how apropos our words or cited Scripture passages are to someone else. God uses each of us to reassure one another of His love and care. As the online contemplative community wrote to one another, we became aware of this; we could see the visual evidence on our computer screens, apparent even for those who hadn't the inner knowledge yet to confirm it.

God wanted me to get this message. That I knew. He seemed to be reassuring me that He had claimed me as His own, that He was with me (gosh, I had no doubts about that anymore), that there were trials and fire ahead for me, and I'd not be burned by them, but set free. I didn't want to think about trials at the time, no matter how distant. I'd already been through a purifying fire or two. I knew His protection during trials. I clung to the words of consolation from Isaiah and learned for the umpteenth time that God's eternal Word is alive and life-giving in Scripture as well as other spiritual works.

I reflected on one of my favorite quotes that came to mind from Marianne Williamson's *Return to Love*. Many know it from Nelson Mandela's inaugural speech.

"Our deepest fear is not that we are inadequate. Our deepest fear is that we are powerful beyond measure. It is our light, not our darkness that most frightens us. We ask ourselves, Who am I to be brilliant, gorgeous, talented, fabulous? Actually, who are you not to be? You are a child of God. Your playing small doesn't serve the world. There's nothing enlightened about shrinking so that other people won't feel insecure around you. We are all meant to shine, as children do. We were born to make manifest the glory of God that is within us. It's not just in some of us; it's in everyone. And as we let our own light shine, we unconsciously give other people permission to do the same. As we're liberated from our own fear, our presence automatically liberates others."[72]

What should I do next, I wondered, with the new light within me? Holy ones I read about went off by themselves to their cell, ashram, or desert to ponder and process such an experience. I had a family with clothes to wash, dinner to make, and groceries to buy. My business rolled like a peaking wave, cresting during the holiday season with multiple shows per week, Christmas gifts to be mailed to 120 personal, first-line team members, and preparations for the upcoming Leadership Conference to be completed.

My return to performing my various roles made everyone happy. I wasn't the same, however, and a hushed silence within me felt like mornings when I'd discover a deep covering of newly fallen snow upon waking. For the first time, I appreciated the wide-open awe teenage Mary, the Mother of God, must have experienced walking around with the new knowledge of Who grew within her that no one else—save Joseph and eventually Elizabeth and Zechariah—knew. Was Jesus wanting me to draw closer to His mother? She kept coming to mind.

Do you not know that you are the temple of God,
and that the Spirit of God dwells in you?

—1 Corinthians 3:16

What do you do with this awareness of God's presence within you? Did anyone else walk around with it? How do you find that out? Did any of the clergy feel this—my parish priests, deacons, nuns? When I'd try to talk with close friends or parishioners about it, I'd see a blank look in their eyes and uncertain smiles. I wanted to share the gift I'd received, but their reactions discouraged me. Each day God's presence felt like the excitement of Christmas mornings as a child. That buzzy feeling reminded me of Who dwelt within me. What was I supposed to do next?

Bright morning light pierces a room when you first draw back the curtains. My heart blinked and strained to open its eyes in the presence of Divine Mystery. I felt like the foal I'd seen in a stable by the National Stud Museum in Naas, outside of Dublin, Ireland. County Kildare had been a horse breeding area for two millennia. We discovered the stable on our walk around the grounds. A newborn foal struggled to get his legs under him. The mare's ears perked immediately upon our approach; she protectively positioned her body between us and her foal.

Such beauty newborns have. The foal put one skinny leg, and then the other in front of himself. He thrust his body upward. His back legs were too close together. He immediately collapsed. He repeated the attempt: one front leg, then the other; another push upward; and another collapse. The foal rested. The mare eyed me warily. I stayed until the foal's efforts reminded me of my own fatigue.

Like the foal, I stood none too sure on my new spiritual legs, nor did I know how to use them. It would be years later that I'd read Martin Laird establish a "foundational assumption" in his book *Into the Silent Land,* stating, "Union with God is not something we are trying to acquire; God is already the ground of our being. It is a question of realizing this in our lives."[73]

I began to grasp that revealing this inner light would give others permission to do the same. The writing I'd reluctantly started evolved into one of the ways God's light could shine through me. I felt a new purpose emerge and, at the same time, a new fear. How could I write about this? I had no theological or seminary degree for credibility. My mind spun a long string of discrediting facts to trip up my efforts to stand on new legs.

A faint voice spoke to that doubt, pointing to fishermen, stammerers, adulterers, deceitful tax collectors, murderers, crazy ones, and pagans, all of whom God used throughout history to increase belief in the One Who Matters. It soothed enough of my concerns to encourage me to keep testing my legs and moving forward, trusting the inner knowledge and redeeming grace opening within me.

When God called Abram, He didn't tell him where the new land lay. He asked Abram to start walking "to a land that I will show you" (Gen 12:1). I moved forward awkwardly with many stumbles, trusting my spiritual muscles would eventually increase.

How beautiful a horse looks when it's swimming across a river. It appears stationary above the water while its legs paddle below the surface, though they no longer touch the bottom. The water supports this large animal easily and carries it along its current. Keating references the depths of communion with God in centering prayer with similar imagery, above the river where our thoughts can be seen and dealt with, and below the river where we let go of our thoughts and allow the waters of Life to suspend us. Without looking any different on the surface, Grace moved mysteriously below in my heart, beyond my control.

My heart sighed in fatigue. Like an inverse of birth, instead of pushing a baby out and walking tenderly while the body heals from the trauma of birth, God had entered my heart and made His abode with me. Fresh love pulsed within me like a new way of breathing. Its exquisite tenderness regularly brought me to tears, just like a baby. Slowly, I learned Love's rhythm and how to pace myself with it. I certainly still had all my weaknesses and pride, but let's say if I was a loaf of bread, my hard crust had softened. I sensed the interconnectedness of all of life. Even spiders received sympathetic responses from me. I found myself coaxing them onto a piece of paper and releasing them outside instead of smashing them without another thought. Calls to and from my team sounded subtly different. Who was this person letting teammates take up the first part of the monthly leader call so they could celebrate their own successes before starting her training portion? I always used to put my training segment first.

Had I lived in a monastic community, I may have been able to absorb the shock of this theophany more holistically. I wanted to take long walks to process Who resided within me, to sit in prayerful silence and let God's grace slosh around me like a washing machine cycle, loosening what stubborn resistance and willfulness stuck to my insides. Instead, laundry, groceries, meal preparation, bills, email, and demonstrations demanded my attention. I leaned into my daily activities, not knowing what else to do.

Mothers remind children to put on clean underwear before a doctor's appointment. In a similar fashion, I kept reminding myself Who resided in my heart when a gnarly attitude raised its head, when I felt like being mean back to rude or unkind behaviors, or when traffic moved too slowly for my liking and I wanted to choose anger for a response. My boat no longer wished to be attached to the pier of judgment and power, but I kept finding myself cleat-hitched to its dock. Transformation is a work in progress.

CHAPTER 31

COMMUNION

*If I could give you information of my life it would be to show
how a woman of very ordinary ability has been led by God in
strange and unaccustomed paths to do in His service what He has
done in her. And if I could tell you all, you would see how God
has done all, and I nothing. I have worked hard, very hard, that
is all; and I have never refused God anything.*

—Florence Nightingale

IN MOMENTS WHEN I find myself saying such things as "I'm at
the end of my rope," "I'm spent," or "I've got nothin' left to give," I
remember the poor widow at Zarephath (see 1 Kings 17:7-16) reduced
to her last bit of flour and all but a few drops of oil. She had planned to
make one last little cake of flatbread to share with her son and then die.
God sent Elijah to visit her, not one of the rich or great men of Sidon,
and he asked of her the one thing she had left to give. I've tried to put
myself in her shoes to wonder how I would have responded. I imagine
whittling down my meager supplies day by day, using smaller and smaller
portions, and hoping against hope that someone would share a little
something with me. And instead, I am given the gift of an opportunity
to give away the last that I have.

I might have been inclined to deny the request and send Elijah away, determined to have my last meal with my son in peace and self-pity. I might have been so thrilled with a visitor that I invited him in. I might have been too weak from hunger to think very clearly.

Just as I wanted the personal friendship with Jesus that Ron of Young Life referenced in my youth, I'm sure that divine light emanated from the eyes of Elijah with such intensity, the poor woman had no choice but to do as he instructed. It would have been life changing to see those eyes.

That is what good bread does. It calls to you in a way that is hard to resist.

In the Bible and our everyday lives, we experience critical moments when we're asked to give from our essence. We don't want to. We're attached to our possessions, our money, and our security. We resist. We pretend to be too busy. Stories sustain our courage. They help us reply "Yes," as Mary did, as the widow did. God continually replenished the widow's flour and sustained her supply of oil. The five loaves and two fishes fed more than 10,000 people (*including* women and children). The poor woman who gave her two meager coins to the poor earned eternal acclaim.

The Bread of Life never stops giving or calling you and me to partake. It's up to us to recognize new manna. Or not. Jesus is making "an everlasting gift" of us to His Father when we are ready to be transformed. He is the Way to the peace and love our souls long for, thirst for, hunger for. "Eat this bread, drink this cup, come to me and never be hungry ..." are more than words from a communion song. They are an everlasting invitation to a never-ending feast.

> *... the One who began a good work in you*
> *will go on completing it....*
>
> —Philippians 1:6

There is no life without God. "Bidden or unbidden, God is present," a Gaelic saying reminds me daily as it hangs in our lanai, a gift from our son, Bryan, and daughter-in-law, Jaime.

Prayer opens the heart to love that softens into mercy and compassion that pours into our neighbor, the same as pouring into God. And around we go again.

Say yes when a chair or space beckons you. Have a sit and close your eyes. The door to God is always open. Make your heart likewise. Take a tiny step into love. No matter how much you accomplish in life, no matter how many riches or homes or cars or shoes or awards or friends you accumulate, nothing is more important or worthy of your effort. God does the work from there. Just take that first step. Pay attention to Him after that. Nothing else matters. Nothing. *Nada.*

A change in human consciousness is happening. We need to transform the way we see each other and the world. Thomas Keating reminds us, "The spiritual journey can never be a privatized set of practices, because whenever you start the spiritual journey, the whole of humanity, and perhaps creation, goes along and shares the journey with you."[74]

We can be like the Pharisees and choose not to see the holy before our eyes, or allow the grace of God to relax our need for control, power, and affection in order to understand how we are all one Bread, one Body.

May the circle of those with whom we break bread be as wide as the earth. May we allow God to bless and break our hearts open so others can find new life in Christ. We have only our daily bread with which to work. That and God's grace are enough. Who is He giving to you for nourishment? To whom is He sending you?

On a warm August day in Beech Grove, Indiana, in a prayer room on the top floor, our retreat group had begun one of our last sits. The candle in the center of the room stood as a sentry for the group of forty to fifty of us encircling the walls in chairs, on pillows or meditation benches. Peace held us in the quiet afternoon as we turned our attention to our Lord. In that silent prayer time, as I sat with my eyes closed resting in Him, the "stranger" from my dream in the Forest of Peace reappeared in my mind's eye. He offered me His back again, for another piggy back ride. I climbed on and wrapped my arms around His neck to hold on. I smiled for I knew He was reminding me not to get too intense, to have a light heart. He wanted me to be happy and have a playful spirit.

He walked me to the edge of the woods and set me down, as gently as one would a baby, crinkling the dry leaves on the forest floor as He did so. He looked into my eyes and my heart melted like butter on warm bread. I knew without a doubt that He loved me. My dream had come true. We were alone. Together. Friends.

CHAPTER 32

WE NEED TO TALK

*It was not you who chose Me, but I who chose you
and appointed you to go and bear fruit that will remain.*
—John 15:16

ENCOUNTERING GOD GAVE me a mission. Indeed, it gives one to us all. I spent the first part of my life not wanting to offend anyone with my faith. I choose to spend the second half of my human life not worrying about that. Jesus offended quite a few people with talk of His Father, His flesh, and His Spirit. I'm willing to follow in His footsteps.

What do you do with mystical experiences other than share them as I have done here? Well, some keep them to themselves, feeling they are too private or not knowing how to speak of such intimate experiences. That didn't serve me well as I walked the path before me. If we are all to work together as One Body, it helps the other parts of the body to know what's going on elsewhere. It gives the Body signals of what to expect. It helps the Body prepare and respond appropriately and without fear of the unknown. It helps the many parts of the Body work in harmony together.

None of us can explain how or why different gifts are given to one and not another. Why some receive many blessings and others experience many setbacks. We *can* talk about it, however, and make one another aware of what is happening, how we're dealing with the various pains, sufferings, and spiritual experiences in our lives. We *need* to talk about them. When we don't, the Body tries to walk on a foot that's not feeling anything and something breaks, as my foot broke at a workshop when it fell asleep and I didn't realize it.

When our children heard Joe or me say "We need to have a little talk," they knew the routine. We wanted them to walk with us to the front room of the house, which we used for serious conversations. My daughter recalls an uncomfortable pink floral chair on which she had to sit for such talks. Fear rumbled in their stomachs because they knew the little walk to talk usually meant they'd done something wrong. Sometimes they had. Other times, we wanted to understand the details of an event we'd heard about and didn't want to jump to any conclusions or make judgments before knowing all the facts.

I've been asked what is the purpose of this book. It is not to invite or encourage you, my reader, to become a million dollar sales team leader. If that is your goal, I wish you every success along your journey. Pray and listen deeply to God along the way. There are other books for that purpose.

It is not to show you how I learned to gently evangelize through my direct selling business whenever the opportunity presented itself. That was a byproduct of my awakening faith journey. Nor is its purpose to show how people of faith can evangelize by sharing the God they have come to know and trust. I do not know how to do that. It's taken me almost twenty years to figure out how to say this much and I still haven't done it very well. It's the best I can do for now and that's all we can ask of ourselves at any moment.

The purpose of this book is not to showcase how God chose to endow me with talents and energy and an invitation into mystical prayer. If that's what you get out of this book, then I failed. The point isn't that I had a lot of talents and worked hard and therefore was one of the lucky ones that God made successful and rich. My mother had a lot of talents and worked hard. She had a life of intense pain, physical limitations, and crippling disease. We all know plenty of good people, hard-working people, faith-filled people who have more than their share of troubles, losses, and failures.

It's not what happens to us, it's how we choose to respond, according to many wise ones before me. Part of the gift of knowledge that opened within me was the knowing that I was to share the mystical experiences with others. I'd have preferred not to do so. I don't know about you, but obedience is rarely easy for willful me. Recording my experiences was a task given to me. And now that I've completed it, I must say the next difficult thing. We all are asked to talk about this. "Go and teach all nations," Jesus said. Tell them your story, what you know, how you came to believe, what you struggle to believe. In whatever way you can do so according to the talents and gifts God has given you, you are to be salt, and light, and whatever part of the Body of Christ you were made to be. You need to tell us what's going on with you so the rest of the Body (of which you are a part) can work together with you.

We need to know that He still acts in strange, mysterious ways, reaching out to us in ordinary moments when we give Him a few ticks of our time and our hearts. I am sure experiences such as mine happen all throughout the world to people of different faiths, nations, and races. Experiences completely opposite mine enliven the discussion as well, such as Jennifer Fulwiler on the Catholic Channel on Sirius Radio (just to name one of thousands), who lived a mostly atheist life before too many God-incidences caused her transformation. We need to share these intimate, holy moments so that one part of the Body knows and understands what is happening to the other. God is reaching out to us in ways we can receive, perceive, and weave into the lives of others.

His nature surprises us not because of its totality of love but because we can only consider Him from the limitations of our mind and experiences of human love, which are as blemished and self-serving in understanding as those of an adolescent who thinks he knows everything.

"Come and see," said Philip to Nathaniel with childlike excitement as he described his discovery of Jesus (John 1:43-51). The Samaritan woman at Jacob's well with whom Jesus spoke showed similar enthusiasm. In John's fourth chapter she says, "Come, see a man who told me all that I ever did!"

I still fluctuate between the excitement of Nathaniel and the Samaritan woman on the one hand, and the silly, rational doubts humans harbor on the other. The best decisions and actions I ever took involved giving up my precious time in order to pray and then following, however tepidly, what I sensed in my heart or heard God ask of me. When I didn't know what to do, I stepped forward in the raging water of indecision like the Levites carrying the Ark of the Covenant across the floodwaters of the River Jordan to Jericho. Stepping out in faith is all Jesus wants before He parts the waters of our life so we can move forward. Surrendering my ways to follow God's will was the price of my peace.

I strive for a slower pace now as God's grace works within me. I retired from direct sales at the end of 2013 in order to focus on my writing and complete this book.

My spirit calls for more stillness within and prefers steady walks instead of the roadrunner approach to things. It's a work in progress. A new rhythm and balance continue to evolve to this day. I still sometimes rush unnecessarily. Like balance and faith, time management is a work in progress.

There is no separation between God and us. I see that now. After we recognize where we refuse Him—"No thanks, maybe later ..."—we have the freedom to open to Him or not, at will—a will He gave us from pure love. He is always here with His fathomless mercy and love. It's hard to trust that sometimes, just like it's hard to try some strange new food sitting on a plate. He waits for us to choose Him. He easily forgets about how long we've made Him wait. His patience and mercy are eternal. Just as in delaying an act of forgiveness, we hurt ourselves in the delay. The only thing that matters is our actions, the intentions of our heart which He reads and knows. He invites us daily, hourly. Listen for it. Look for it. Taste it.

The everyday sacred graces God gives us are meant to encourage me and you. Perhaps the crumbs from God's pursuing me will guide you to find Him along your path. He "... *sent Christ to make peace between Himself and us, and He has given us the work of making peace between Himself and others*" 2 Corinthians 5:18 CEV.

"Let us begin heaven," God said to Gabrielle Bossis in *He and I.* Do I hear an Amen?

GRATITUDE

Plans fail for lack of counsel,
but with many advisers they succeed.

—Proverbs 15:22

TO THE AMAZING development editor Suzanne Kingsbury: Thanks for liberating some chapters and your wise guidance.

To my editor Dennis E. Hensley and my publisher, Athena Dean Holtz, and the Redemption team: Thank you for your talent, integrity, prayers, and patience.

This book would probably not have been written without Dr. Mercedes Scopetta: Thank you for befriending my awakening soul. My heart holds tenderly the wisdom, compassion, and love you share.

Thank you to those in her online communities. Your presence and questions improved my understanding and realization of God's work within me.

To my sisters and brothers in the direct selling industry: Thank you for showing me in word and action how you walk daily with our Lord.

To my friends and family: I have withdrawn at times to till the soil of my soul and to write. Your love, understanding, and support have sustained me as God pruned and graced my heart. Special thanks to Lyn

Collelo for being my biggest cheerleader; to Chris Keuer for introducing me to BSF, homiletics, and prayer journaling; to my oldest friend, Sarah Fishburn, for keeping our love nurtured for fifty years and for publishing my poetry; to Susan Kiley for doubting I'd ever finish. That spurred me on more than you'll ever know.

To the leaders with whom I worked in the direct selling industry: Thank you for sharing the rarified air of leadership with passion, humor, and kindness.

To my recruiter: Thanks for asking, for leading the way, for Christ-centered friendship, and one heck of a journey together.

To my team: Thank you for the memories; for changing lives including my own; for building your businesses well; and prioritizing God and family, friends and food.

To Mary Margaret Funk, OSB: Thank you for hand-carrying the manuscript to New York, for your books, and your beautiful teaching.

To my Beta readers: James Bratager, Jean Barousse, Fr. Tom Collins, Fr. Kevin Johnson, Nancy Parker, Lyn Collelo, Jo Ann Mann, Katherine Fitzsimmons, Tess Manion, Jaime Manion: Thank you for your insights, suggestions, and precious time. You helped make this book better and encouraged me.

To my St. Rita daily Mass roundtable buddies: Paul, Francisco and Tommy, Mary Rita, Mary Pat, Patsy, Billie, Ross, Zeke, Jim, Liz, Kevin and Donna, Ron and Paula, Linda, Joe and Kathy, Ed, Travis, Michele, Felita, Katherine and Brady, Lyn and Joe. Thank you for your encouragement, prayers, laughs, camaraderie, and keeping the body of Christ strong.

To my Word Weaver and local critique groups who encouraged me and kept me accountable: Sheryl Hartwell, Suzanne Spurvis, Lauri Corkum, Jessica Borsi, Susan Card, Pierre Gilson, Ann Kief, Marilyn Turk, Susan Neal, Ken Marquardt, Kati Trawick, Craig Gleerup, and Jenny Bowman.

To Brian Bird for your example of courage and sacrifice in Christian writing and producing.

To Jim Marion for your description of the Christian path, the levels of human consciousness, and your writings of Christ consciousness that helped me understand my own journey in the kingdom of God.

To Blaine Searcy for introducing me to Hafiz, the Great Sufi Master.

To my five siblings and their spouses: Michael and Debbie Sauter; Jean-Marie and Bob Seidl; Dave and Dolly Sauter; Rich and Martha Sauter; Kevin and Sonya Sauter. Thank you for standing strong as family with love and laughter.

To my extended family members, especially Paul and Marianna Manion; Jeff and Janice Spain for being mirrors and models of faith and love.

To Bryan, Tess, and Joe: Thank you for all the love and space to write, think, and find my way as a leader and a writer.

END NOTES

⟨ornament⟩

1   A term used by Monsignor Romano Guardini in his book, *The Lord*. Washington, D.C.: Regnery Publishing, Inc., 1954, p. 529.

2   Guardini, Romano, *op cit.,* p. 171. As a young Jesuit seminarian in the 1950s, Pope Francis kept a copy of Guardini's book *The Lord* on his shelf. Guardini eventually became a major inspiration to many of the fathers of the Second Vatican Council, including St. Pope John Paul II and Pope Benedict XVI.

3   From the Penguin publication: *The Gift, Poems by Hafiz*. © 1999, Daniel Ladinsky. Used with his permission.

4   O'Donohue, John, *Longing and Belonging: The Complete John O'Donohue Audio Collection*.

5   Sarah Fishburn is a talented artist in Fort Collins, Colorado. www.sarahfishburn.com.

6   Merton, Thomas, *The Sign of Jonas*. New York: Harcourt Brace & Company, 1981, p. 273.

7   Bossis, Gabrielle, *He and I*. Sherbrooke, QC, Canada: Èditions Paulines, 1969, p. 79.

8   Author of *The Magic Monastery*.

9   Csordas, Thomas J., *The Sacred Self: A Cultural Phenomenology of Charismatic Healing*. Berkeley: University of California Press, 1997, p. 247.

10 More choices exist now. Among them: Bishop Robert Barron's study series www.wordonfire.org/study-programs include "Word On Fire; Priest, Prophet, King"; and "Catholicism: A Journey to the Heart of the Faith"; *The Great Adventure Catholic Bible Study* by Jeff Cavins; Little Rock series; and Dr. Scott Hahn's Bible study written with Mark Shea www.CatholicExchange.com website.

11. Lectio Divina is one of the great treasures of the Christian tradition of prayer. It means Divine Reading, which is reading the book we believe to be divinely inspired. This tradition of prayer flows out of a Hebrew method of studying the Scriptures which was called haggadah. Haggadah was an interactive interpretation of the Scriptures by means of the free use of the text to explore its inner meaning. It was part of the devotional practice of the Jews in the days of Jesus. (http://www.contemplativeoutreach.org/sites/default/files/documents/lectio_divina.pdf).

This is the essence of the prayer form:

1. ASK the Lord for the grace to hear His Word in your heart. READ the Scripture passage. Listen with the "ear of your heart." What phrase, sentence, or word stands out to you?

2. REFLECT, relish the words. Let them resound in your heart. Be attentive to what speaks to your heart.

3. RESPOND spontaneously. A prayer of praise, thanksgiving, or petition may arise.

4. REST in God. Simply "be with" God's presence as you open yourself to a deeper hearing of the Word of God. If you feel drawn back to the Scriptures, follow the lead of the Spirit.

12 Catholic Answers magazine offers additional explanation on the topic of sola scriptura. A former Southern Baptist wrote this article. http://www.catholic.com/magazine/articles/according-to-scripture.

13 Bossis, Gabrielle, *op cit.,* p. 83.

14 Ibid., p. 258.

15 Fr. Gabriel of St. Mary Magdalen, *Divine Intimacy*. London: Baronius Press, 2008, p. 24-25.

16 For more on colloquy, see *Tools Matter for Practicing the Spiritual Life* by Mary Margaret Funk, New York: Continuum, 2001, p. 113-116.

17 Funk, Mary Margaret, *op cit.,* p. 114.

18 Anonymous, *The Cloud of Unknowing*, trans. William Johnston. Doubleday: New York, 1973. New York: Continuum, 2001, p. 136.

19 In monastic circles, lectio is usually pronounced LEK-see-oh.

20 An active word is a spiritual tool. In lectio divina, or sacred reading, the reader listens internally for a word or phrase that stands out or snags the heart. Attentiveness to snagged word or phrase allows one to notice it, ponder it, and carry it in one's heart for a while as Mary carried "all these things" in her heart Luke 2:19.

21 Words of Jesus to His new disciples who asked where do You live? John 1:35-39.

22 Bossis, Gabrielle, *op cit.,* p. 110.

23 Their website describes their vision further: "The contemplative dimension of the Gospel manifests itself in an ever-deepening union with the living Christ and the practical caring for others that flows from that relationship. We identify with the Christian Contemplative Heritage. While we are formed by our respective denominations, we are united in our common search for God and the experience of the living Christ through Centering Prayer. We affirm our solidarity with the contemplative dimension of other religions and sacred traditions, with the needs and rights of the whole human family, and with all creation." www.contemplativeoutreach.org.

24 St. John of the Cross, *The Collected Works of St. John of the Cross,* translated by Kieran Kavanaugh O.C.D., and Otilio Rodriguez, O.C.D., Washington, D.C., ICS Publications, Institute of Carmelite Studies, The Ascent of Mt. Carmel 2, 14, 4, 11.

25 Anonymous, *The Book of Privy Counseling,* edited by William Johnston, New York: Doubleday, 1973, p. 170.

26 Bossis, Gabrielle, *op cit.,* p. 251.

27 Coff, Pascaline, O.S.B., "Existential Breakthrough" article in *The Other Half of my Soul* compiled by Beatrice Bruteau. Wheaton, Illinois: Quest Books,1996, p. 101-103.

28 Laird, O.S.A, Martin, *Into the Silent Land: A Guide to the Christian Practice of Contemplation.* New York: Oxford University Press, 2006, p. 53-54.

29 de Hueck Doherty, Catherine, *Poustinia,* p. 24.

30 Ibid., p. 24-25.

31 Bossis, Gabrielle, *op cit.*, p. 217.

32 Matthew 28:16-20; Mark 16:12-18; Luke 24: 44-53; and Luke's Acts of the Apostles 1:12.

33 Roland Romuald Roper, cbl, OSB quoting Bede Griffiths, an English Benedictine monk and one of the outstanding spiritual leaders and mystics of the 20th century. *Swami Bede Dayananda Testimonies & Tributes.* Saccidananda Ashram: South India, Shanti Venam Publications, 1994, p. 78.

34 Cardinal José Saraiva Martins, "One with Christ, One with Sinners."

35 www.alessandra.com.

36 See the Toltec path of Don Miguel Ruiz.

37 Steindl-Rast, David, *Gratefulness, The Heart of Prayer.* New Jersey: Paulist Press, 1984, p. 22.

38 See Teilhard de Chardin, *The Divine Milieu, Part 2.*

39 Savary, Louis M., *Teilhard de Chardin – The Divine Milieu Explained.* Mahwah, NJ: Paulist Press, 2007, p. 95.

40 Keating, Thomas, *Intimacy with God.*

41 The seven gifts of the Holy Spirit were enumerated in Isaiah 11:2-3. They are present in their fullness in Jesus Christ but are found in all Christians who are in a state of grace. We receive them when we are infused with sanctifying grace, the life of God within us—as, for example, when we receive a sacrament worthily. As the current Catechism of the Catholic Church notes, "They complete and perfect the virtues of those who receive them." Infused with His gifts, we respond to the promptings of the Holy Spirit as if by instinct, the way Christ Himself would. http://catholicism.about.com/od/beliefsteachings/tp/Gifts_of_the_Holy_Spirit.htm.

42 Anonymous, *The Cloud of Unknowing.* Introduction by William Johnston. New York: Doubleday, 1973, p. 26.

43 Gerald May, *Will and Spirit.* San Francisco: Harper,1982, p. 1.

44 Hilkert, Mary Catherine, *Speaking with Authority.* Mahwah, New Jersey: Paulist Press, 2001, p. 42.

45 Leon Joseph Cardinal Suenens, *A New Pentecost?* Trans. Francis Martin. New York: The Seabury Press, 1975, p. xii.

46 Hilkert, Mary Catherine, *op cit.,* p.43-44.

47 Fr. Gabriel of St. Mary Magdalen, op cit., p. xxiii.

48 In its current form, the symbol first appeared in the West during the 17th and 18th centuries, but representations of an all-seeing eye trace back to Egyptian mythology and the Eye of Horus. However, Buddhism first associated the eye with a triplicity. Buddha is also regularly referred to as the "Eye of the World" throughout Buddhist scriptures (e.g. Mahaparinibbana Sutta) and represents a trinity in the shape of a triangle known as the Tiratna or Triple Gem. Later, the enclosed triangle was seen as a more explicit Christian trinitarian symbol in Christian iconography.

49 Lutz, Tom, *Crying: The Natural & Cultural History of Tears*. New York: W. W. Norton & Company, 2001.

50 Chittister, Joan, *God's Tender Mercy: Reflections on Forgiveness*. Fenton, MO: Twenty-Third Publications, 2010.

51 Paula Huston "The Dilemma of Demons," *Give Us This Day, Daily Prayer for Today's Catholic*. Collegeville, Minnesota: Liturgical Press, 2015, reflection October 9, 2015.

52 John Richards, *Tears – Gift of the Holy Spirit?* 2001. http://www.HelpForChristians.co.uk/articles/a28.asp. (c) John Richards/Renewal Servicing. www.HelpForChristians.co.uk. Used with permission.

53 Jim Marion, *Putting on the Mind of Christ: The Inner Work of Christian Spirituality*. Newburyport, Massachusetts: Hampton Roads Publishing, 2011, p. 3.

54 *Humility Matters*, Sr. Mary Margaret Funk, OSB. Collegeville, Minnesota: Liturgical Press, 2013, p. 101.

55 Catherine Dougherty, article titled "Entering the Sea of Forgiveness" Restoration, Feb. 1998 issue, http://www.madonnahouse.org/restoration/1998/02/february_1998.html.

56 Frederic and Mary Ann Brussat, "Tears are for the Soul" (www.beliefnet.com/story/174/story_17455_1.html).

57 John Richards, *Tears – Gift of the Holy Spirit?* 2001. http://www.helpforchristians.co.uk/articles/a28.asp. Copyright (c) John Richards/Renewal Servicing. www.HelpForChristians.co.uk. Used with permission.

58 John Richards, *ibid.*

59 Thomas Keating, *Open Mind, Open Heart*. New York: Continuum, 2006, p. 104.

60 John Richards, *op cit.*

61 Keating, Thomas, from a retreat he gave in Miami in November 1998 to the Lux Divina online community participants.

62 *Prayer of St. Francis.*
Lord, make me an instrument of your peace.
Where there is hatred, let me sow love.
Where there is injury, pardon.
Where there is doubt, faith.
Where there is despair, hope.
Where there is darkness, light.
Where there is sadness, joy.
O Divine Master,
grant that I may not so much seek to be consoled, as to console;
to be understood, as to understand;
to be loved, as to love.
For it is in giving that we receive.
It is in pardoning that we are pardoned,
and it is in dying that we are born to Eternal Life.
Amen.

63 deMello, Anthony, SJ "Rediscovery of Life" tape 2, conference talk given to Fordham University students.

64 Fr. Gabriel of St. Mary Magdalen, *op cit.,* p. 974.

65 Bossis, Gabrielle. *op cit.,* p. 104.

66 Other authors in the human potential genre I found helpful were Og Mandino, Samuel Cypert, Jack Canfield, John Maxwell, and Jim Rohn.

67 Bossis, Gabrielle. *op cit.,* p. 81.

68 Keating, Thomas, *The Better Part*. New York: Continuum, 2000, p. 109.

69 Sister Meg teaches: The antidote for pride is to return to the four methods of responding to any thought or feeling that rises:
    1. Enter into direct dialogue with the thought and refuse the invitation, using teachings from the tradition of Scripture or previous experience.

2. Replace the thought with another, either with a short affirmation prayer or with ceaseless prayer. John Cassian recommends the call to prayer (Psalm 70:1). "O God, come to my assistance. O Lord, make haste to help me" is the form we use at Our Lady of Grace Monastery. The Jesus Prayer is the most substantive mantra that has come from the experience of the desert tradition.
3. Anticipate thoughts that become afflictions through vigilance, watching, and guarding the heart. This mode of awareness dismantles the thoughts, and soon the eye of the heart detects their first risings before they get strong enough to offer a temptation. Notice the moment of consent and get ahead of it.
4. Do selfless service with a total focus on the present moment. Being in the Presence takes all of our attention, and we experience the stillness of being.

If we use these four practices as well as manual labor, the cell, prayer, common life, and apostolic service, the afflictions will be purified. Pride will be rooted out and replaced by humility. Thinking, acting, and inner ascetical work often contributes to pride. When we unthink, undo, unwork in total surrender, we receive the Spirit of Jesus. Our right effort is to refrain from consenting and going up the chain of thought. From *Humility Matters*, "Second Renunciation: Thoughts of Former Way of Life," p. 78-79.

70 Merton, Thomas, *The Sign of Jonas*. Harcourt Brace and Company: New York: 1981, p. 272.
71 Anonymous, *The Cloud of Unknowing*, ed. William Johnston, Doubleday: New York, 1973, p. 51.
72 Williamson, Marianne, *A Return to Love*, Harper Collins: New York, 1992, p. 165.
73 Laird, Martin, *op cit.*, p. 4.
74 www.spiritualityandpractice.com/ecourse Forgiveness—Growth in Love.

ABOUT THE AUTHOR

CHRIS MANION, a powerhouse leader in the direct selling industry, has been writing and reflecting on the spiritual side of life for over twenty years. Chris is an honors graduate of the University of Dayton. Known for being an inspirational speaker, she was the former host of the talk show HealthBeat (Triton College, River Grove, Illinois) and an award-winning catechist from the Archdiocese of Chicago. Chris lives with her husband in Destin, Florida where she kayaks, plays the cello, and photographs the beauty of the Emerald Coast.

Visit ChrisManion.com to receive several free gifts when you join her email list, including a deleted chapter.

CONTACT INFORMATION

To order additional copies of this book, please visit
www.redemption-press.com.
Also available on Amazon.com and BarnesandNoble.com
Or by calling toll free 1-844-2REDEEM.